About the Author

Professor Emeritus of Stanford University and current member of the faculty of St. Patrick's Seminary in Menlo Park, California, Kurt F. Reinhardt is the author of numerous studies in history and philosophy. Among his publications are *Germany: 2000 Years, A Realistic Philosophy,* a study of *St. John of the Cross,* and *The Existentialist Revolt.* A native of Munich, he took his doctorate in the University of Freiburg, where he studied under Edmund Husserl and Martin Heidegger.

The Theological Novel of Modern Europe

AN ANALYSIS OF MASTERPIECES BY EIGHT AUTHORS

The Theological Novel

of Modern Europe

An Analysis of Masterpieces

by Eight Authors

Kurt F. Reinhardt

Frederick Ungar Publishing Co.

NEW YORK

TO

Russel van Arsdale Lee, M.D.
great physician and friend

Preface

THIS BOOK contains the greater part of material used and tested in a lecture course which I taught at Stanford University for several years prior to my retirement. I was induced to present this thoroughly revised version upon the urgent request of students and colleagues. In its present form the book provides the basis of a seminar which I taught for the Deacons of St. Patrick's Seminary in Menlo Park, California, as a member of the faculty, in the autumn and winter of 1967–1968. The response on the part of the seminarians was as encouraging as had been the response of the Stanford students, and I have been asked again to offer seminars dealing with theological novels during the current academic year.

It has also come to my attention that a growing number of colleges and universities in this country have added courses on "Theology in Literature" or similar titles to their curricula, especially in the humanities. The response of their students has proved equally gratifying, notwithstanding the vast scope of the subject matter and the need to confine the presentation to either segments or cross-sections of the field. The extensive bibliography, however, should make it possible for teachers and students as well as for the general reader to explore the main themes in greater depth.

It remains for me to acknowledge gratefully that an extensive study and presentation of "Theological Novels" as a literary category was first suggested to me in discussions with Professor F. W. Strothmann, my colleague and friend at Stanford since 1930. I am also greatly indebted to Mrs. Florence Brokmeyer, Secretary of the Stanford Department of Modern European Languages, for transcribing and typing the taped material of a substantial part of the book in her spare time. And last but by no means least my thanks are due to Mr. Frederick Ungar, my publisher, for his continuing interest in and encouragement of my writing.

KURT F. REINHARDT

Palo Alto, California
October 1968

Contents

INTRODUCTION

The Religious Mind

Every state of mind expresses or reflects a specific relation to reality as a whole; it may stress, however, one specific aspect of reality in particular. States of mind color to a certain extent all human perceptions, thoughts, feelings and sentiments. Things are seen differently, depending on whether the one who sees is in a sad or happy mood, whether he is young or old, cynical or idealistic, despairing or hopeful. Reality thus often looks like a true mirror of states of mind. It is also possible that a state of mind completely distorts man's view of reality, as happens in neurotic and psychotic states, especially in schizophrenia. Emotions and passions such as hatred, resentment, hostility, love, and so on are often transferred or projected willfully or involuntarily to the external world; or, as is the case in the person who loves, his love or his loving disposition idealizes and transfigures the external world. Likewise, states of fear or anguish may completely transform the external world and turn it into a world of terror. This is perhaps best exemplified in the novels of Franz Kafka. Every theoretical and practical activity, therefore, reflects in varying degrees corresponding mental dispositions. Prayer reflects the attitude of devotion and reverence that is prevalent in the mind of the one who prays. The person who fights is said to be in a "fighting mood." To be able to fulfill the exacting tasks imposed by contemporary working conditions, the worker's mental disposition must be dynamic rather than one of static repose.

With respect to poetry and painting, it has been said that "a landscape is a state of the human soul" and the "discovery of the landscape" in post-Renaissance painting is usually associated with the awakening of "nature feeling." The sight of the open sea may reflect or project a disposition of the soul, as is illustrated in Wordsworth's saying, "This sea in anger and that dismal shore": here the poet describes the sea which has become angry and swallowed a man in shipwreck, and the shore presents a dismal view. In poems by Verlaine and by Rilke titled "Autumn Day," the autumnal sadness of nature rises simultaneously in nature and in the soul of the poet.

We may ask then: What mental disposition is prevalent in the person who is in search of truth? The answer of Greek philosophy was that what is primarily felt is admiration, astonishment, wonder (*thaumazein*). What is required, furthermore, is an ability to listen and, on the part of the listener, a certain leisure (*otium*), trust, serenity, love. If this attitude is present, reality will begin to speak. If, however, it is correct to say that the ability to listen is found only in the person who finds himself in a corresponding mood, it can be easily seen that it is this person who can best appreciate the identical mood expressed in a poem or in any work of literature. On the other hand, it is equally true that a good poem, a work of classical music, a good novel are each in turn capable of arousing corresponding moods in the sensitive reader or listener, such moods as love, nostalgia, despair or serenity. Here we speak of a sympathetic or empathetic participation, or we may call it a spiritual manner of communication which in turn may lead to a deeper understanding of life and a better way of communication among human beings.

It has been convincingly stated that there exist two different kinds of thinking, each of them legitimate and equally valid in its particular sphere: the one is technical, calculating, ultimately deriving from the will to manipulate and dominate external nature or, as Nietzsche would say, deriving from the will-to-power (*Wille zur Macht*); a second kind of thinking is meditative, philosophical and essentially receptive. For example, for a genuine understanding of Plato a degree of idealistic thinking is required, that is, an intrinsic faith in the reality of such ideas as the good, the true, the beautiful, freedom, justice, peace. Similarly, authors who advance a religious or theological thesis, whether expressed in a theoretical treatise or in a work of literature, can be appreciated only by readers who live and think sympathetically and empathetically within a similar frame of reference. Our own mental attitudes and capacities as well as our own receptivity determine to a large extent the range and depth of our understanding. The force of logical or purely syllogistic arguments remains often purely external, abstract and unconvincing because these arguments do not affect man's innermost being. They do not engage man existentially. Cicero, speaking about Stoic philosophy, says that even those who assent to a thesis affirmatively have rarely experienced in themselves a corresponding mental state, "and they go away unchanged in their mental disposition. Far from inspiring and arousing those who listen, Stoic logic even extinguishes the flame in those who have come to learn." The German philosopher Fichte, with some exaggeration, compared philosophic convictions with poetic convictions, asserting that adherence to truth depends entirely on the attitude of the human mind and the human heart. This means that every philosopher, according to Fichte, chooses almost of necessity that philosophy which corresponds to his own temperament or mentality. In the same extreme form this view is defended by some existentialist thinkers when they describe philosophy as the art which knows how to generate "fear and trembling," anguish and despair (for example, Kierkegaard, Sartre).

Life and reality as such comprise sadness and joy, faith and skeptical doubt, hatred and love, anguish and trust, despair and hope, restlessness and peace of mind. He who wants to know reality must learn to see all of its aspects, all of its nuances, light and darkness, grandeur and misery. Human knowledge, therefore, rests and feeds not on *one* state of mind only but on a large scale or spectrum of such states, and at the apex of this ascending scale are placed hope, trust, faith, peace of mind.

The ultimate source of human thinking and doing and therefore of all mental dispositions and attitudes is always either in the positive or in the negative sense colored by *religious* convictions. Religion understood in this broadest sense determines either positively or negatively the idea which man forms of life and reality. In affirmation or denial, man's convictions concerning the meaning of existence as such are radically transformed. The person, for example, who sets his belief in a wrathful, arbitrary and terrifying Deity is intimidated, downhearted, frightened or despairing. The one who places his trust in a benignant and loving God, on the other hand, becomes either joyful and serene, or he may comfortably lapse into complacency and pharisaical self-righteousness, feeling himself safe and already saved as one of the elect.

If what is generally assumed is true, namely that most human beings feel inclined to accept and profess that kind of faith which best corresponds to their own physical and emotional mode of being, this attitude or this kind of faith represents the radical opposite of what occurs in genuine "revelation," when man is addressed by a suprahuman power, totally regardless of his personal likes and dislikes. Yet even those who persist loyally in the kind of religion they have inherited usually try to make it conform more or less to their personal mode of living and being. However, no matter whether it is religion that transforms the human being, or whether it is the human being who chooses freely the religion of his preference, trying to adapt it to his own measure, the result is the same: the religious climate in which men live and breathe forms them as individuals and also their living in social groups.

It was Tertullian (c. 160–230) who coined the phrase, *anima naturaliter christiana*. This means not only that in the innermost depth of every human being there is alive a sort of *natural religion* with its standards of true and false, good and evil, but also that a definite religious attitude persists even in those of different denominations who have turned against the tenets of their creeds or who have pronounced themselves agnostics or atheists. One may even speak of a typical Roman Catholic, Protestant, Jewish form of atheism. Auguste Comte and Voltaire were and remained typical Roman Catholics without a Catholic faith; Jean Jacques Rousseau, André Gide and Ludwig Feuerbach were and remained typical Protestants without a Protestant faith. And the teachings of Karl Marx no doubt represent a secularized form of Judaic messianism.

In view of the major themes that will be encountered in the novels to be analyzed in the later sections of this treatise, it would seem appropriate to ask: What is the main difference in the religious mentality of Roman Catholics and Protestants? And to what extent do they share the identical religious ideas, ideals and attitudes? These of course are, strictly speaking, problems of dogmatic theology, and any answer that can be given in this context must of necessity appear preliminary and to some extent unsatisfactory.

There is no doubt that Catholics and Protestants would agree, for example, that man is separated from God by an infinite qualitative difference, by an unbridgeable distance or by an abyss; that man is as nothing in comparison with God, his Creator; and they would paradoxically quote the conviction they hold in common that this nothingness which is man was aboriginally made in the image and likeness of God and represents thus a mysterious synthesis of opposites. But while in orthodox or Old-Protestantism there is this irreconciled and irreconcilable cleavage between the Creator and the creature, in Roman Catholicism, both medieval and modern, God is not only the "totally Other" but simultaneously intimately present in the creature and in creation as an indispensable, sustaining, life-giving power, so much so that all Catholic mystics speak of the desirability and possibility of a mystical union with God. Orthodox Protestantism, on the other hand, traditionally looks upon mysticism with suspicion: it sees in mysticism and in the mystical aspiration a kind of sacrilegious presumptuousness on the part of the finite creature. In Protestantism, therefore, mysticism, having been ostracized by Protestant orthodoxy, has traditionally sought and found shelter only in separatistic sects and conventicles.

Christianity as such presents a synthesis of two ancient conceptions of the Deity: the Jewish-Hebrew belief that there actually is an infinite distance between Creator and creature, and the post-Platonist Greek conviction that the gods are projections of man, that, in Protagoras' phrase, man is the measure of all things.

Roman Catholic as well as Protestant dogmatic theology teaches this paradoxical synthesis of opposites: a synthesis of divine love and divine justice, of divine causality and human freedom, of sin and grace, of the mysterious cooperation of grace and free will. Orthodox Protestantism, however, traditionally inclines strongly toward a religion of the "either-or": the infinite majesty of God is here much more radically opposed to the sinfulness of fallen man; the absolute freedom of the divine will is radically opposed to the fragility of the human condition in which freedom is almost totally lacking and the ultimate human destiny appears fixed once and for all by divine decree.

The Protestant "either-or" was experienced and expressed most uncompromisingly by Martin Luther and Kierkegaard. Here God is experienced as the "totally Other," separated from man by an unbridgeable gulf. The narrow way of faith passes of necessity, as was the case in Luther's "Theology of the Cross," through anxiety, dread (*Angst*) and existential despair. It is in anguish that faith is said to be born. Thus anguish expresses, as it were, the very nature of man. As Kierkegaard stated, "if man were a brute or an angel, he would not be the prey of anguish." However, dread means isolation, radical aloneness in the world, constant close proximity to death, and only by a miraculous "leap" can man gain access to this paradoxical faith. But faith does not do away with the dread of anguish and the proximity of the naught. Anguish and faith coexist. Anguished dread is one of the constituent elements of faith. And the weight of man's sinfulness is said to be so great that only the unmerited and unmeritable gift of grace can alleviate this heavy burden. Thus sinfulness is experienced as man's very essence, the being of a fallen and corrupted nature.

The Protestant Reformation in Germany was largely the work of Martin Luther (1483–1546), a man who by nature and temperament was radically opposed to the spirit of the Renaissance. The Reformation in Romanic countries, on the other hand, was to a large extent the work of John Calvin (1509–1564), whose mind had been formed by a humanistic education, and the aim which Calvin pursued with his reform of the Church consequently represents within Protestantism an effort which has much in common with the Catholic Counter-Reformation, namely, a reconciliation of Renaissance, humanism, and Christian faith.

From the outset the spiritual characters of these two reformers differed radically. Luther was the revolutionary who started his revolt almost single-handedly and opposed his individualism to the Church of Rome and its traditionalist doctrines and dogmas. Calvin was backed by the teachings of some precursors, whose doctrines he adopted and modified (Wyclif, John Hus). In addition, Calvin carefully preserved and cultivated those classical and humanistic values which his education had implanted in him. Calvin was a jurist, that is, a member of a profession which Luther despised more than any other. In his youth Calvin had published a learned commentary on the Stoic philosopher Seneca's *De Clementia* in which he expressed his admiration of this pagan thinker. His major work, *The Institutes of the Christian Religion (Institutio christianae religionis)*, is the first systematic elaboration of a Protestant dogmatic theology. It was first written in Latin and subsequently in French, but the French version, too, has a strong Latin flavor. Calvin's favorite words are "moderation" and "sobriety," and he constantly admonishes his readers to "inquire soberly," to "restrain their souls," because the life of a Christian must "be tempered with sobriety." He inveighs against temerity, intemperance, frenzy, audacity, and the "folly of irrationality." Soberly and rationally he expounds his terrifying doctrine of the total corruption of human nature and absolute double predestination. Bossuet, the illustrious court theologian of Louis XIV, was the first to point out the fundamental contrast between Luther and Calvin: Luther's mentality Bossuet describes as choleric, impetuous and insolent, whereas he says of Calvin that he was correct when he said of himself: "All France knows my integrity, my patience, my vigilance, my moderation." He might have mentioned Calvin's frugality, his austerity, his keen reasoning power and his frigidity. What Calvin lacked of Luther's dynamic genius, he made up for by his genius of scholarship, his mental discipline, his hard and systematic working capacity.

Luther's theology grew out of a unique personal experience of anxiety and existential despair. Calvin was a man of tremendous zeal, of many preoccupations and cares, but anxiety and despair were experiences totally alien to him. "The saints," he says (and this means the "elect"), "have never any reason to despair because they rest in the divine promise." A similar difference in temperament is noticeable concerning the problem of chastity. While Luther constantly refers to his sufferings caused by temptations of the flesh, Calvin disposes of this matter with a few sober words. Man, he says in effect, has not been created for a solitary life. The need for companionship with the other sex remained with man after the Fall, and he finds a remedy and a fulfillment of this need in matrimony, which is a good and wholesome divine dispensation though by no means a sacrament. Some, however, have received a special gift of continence.

The real paradox in Calvin's mentality lies in the fact that here we see side by side the terrifying doctrine of absolute double predestination, of heaven or hell—much more radically formulated than is Luther's teaching or the dogma of the Roman Catholic Church on the same subject—and a mental disposition of great calm and serenity. Completely absent in Calvin's teaching is also the other extreme of Luther's theology: the "leap" from a "Theology of the Cross" to a "theology of consolation" (*Trosttheologie*), from "fear and trembling" in view of possible damnation to the joy of "salvation by faith alone" (*sola fide*, fiducial faith). Calvin and with him all genuine Calvinists are and remain rather grave, austere, and somewhat sad individuals, hostile toward natural joys, dry and unimaginative. They are strangers to those scruples, obsessions, and terrors which plagued Luther's or Kierkegaard's soul. On the other hand, Calvin was a man who could never be truly relaxed. He was at all times obsessed by a cold zeal which made him impose upon his followers, especially in the theocratically ruled city of Geneva, an almost inhuman gravity, austerity and iron discipline.

Calvin was, as might be expected, averse to mysticism in any form: he was and remained a stranger to the life of contemplation or the life of leisure. These states of mind he terms "labyrinths," "frivolous and puerile subtleties" which interest only the "theological sophists of the Roman Church." Calvin was in fact more of a political and social propagandist than a preacher and minister. In all matters of an intellectual nature he confined himself to a systematic exposition of dogma, trying to adapt it to the spirit of the Romanic peoples and nations.

As far as the interrelationship or the dialectic of reason and faith is concerned, Calvin attributes much greater value to *reason* than did Luther, who had no use for rational philosophical arguments and who called reason a "harlot." Calvin seriously discusses philosophic rational doctrines, in particular those of Aristotle, whom Luther called a "rancid" philospher. He says of the wisdom of the great philosophers that it is like the lightning which illumines the dark night: not quite sufficient as a guide, but nonetheless very helpful and very real. All in all, the Calvinistic religion is not irrational, like the Lutheran teaching, but rationalistic. Calvin tried to expound rationally the mystery of divine predestination and human freedom, using an almost absurd logical consistency and ending by teaching a positive reprobation or a predestination for damnation and hell. Why, then, can Calvin assert that his "prudent" doctrine saves man from despair? Because he knows with absolute certitude that he is one of the "elect," and he addresses the "elect," that is, he speaks to individuals who are equally certain of their eternal salvation. Therefore let the *massa damnata* worry and despair. The "elect" have no reason whatever to despair.

Luther and Calvin also differ completely and essentially in their views on ecclesiastical or canon law. Luther's antijuridical sentiment calls for a "religion of faith." Calvin's juridical mind, informed by the legalistic principles of the Old Testament, calls for a "religion of law." For Luther, "law" is to be administered by the State and thus lies outside the province of the Church. For Calvin, contrariwise, the Church is the sole authentic administrator of the Law, and he therefore established in Geneva a strict and thoroughgoing theocracy.

In his emphasis on the "abyss" which separates man from God, Calvin goes even farther than Luther. Indeed the essential characteristic of Calvinism, from Calvin to Kierkegaard and the early Karl Barth, is the absolute emphasis on divine transcendence and on the omnipotent majesty of God. It is from this concept of absolute and totally arbitrary divine omnipotence that the doctrine of double predestination ultimately derives.

Although Calvin follows Luther in the denial of the merit of "good works," he does not teach "justification by faith alone": "We profess," he says, "with St. Paul that only a faith that is joined with love is a faith which justifies." Calvin's faith is thus not, like that of Luther, a "faith of trust" but a faith of absolute and unconditional obedience. In this respect Calvin is in essential agreement with the views of his great contemporary and antagonist, St. Ignatius of Loyola, the main exponent of the spirit of the Counter-Reformation. Yet the center of Calvin's theology is not "justification" but "predestination," or the idea of God's omnipotence and omnicausality, which excludes the efficacy of any secondary (human) causes. "For these two things," Calvin asserts, "mutually exclude each other: that the faithful owe their sanctity to divine election, and that they were elected because of their sanctity." The only alternative Calvin sees is either Pelagianism or absolute double predestination.*

Luther felt himself justified by faith and by faith alone, but simultaneously he continued to worry about the possibility of damnation. Calvin, as we have seen, had no such worries because he added to the Lutheran dogma of the certitude of justification by faith alone the certainty of predestination. This means that whatever happens, the "elect" are saved. Grace, once received, can never be lost. For those, on the other hand, who, prior to being born, are damned, it would be better indeed if they had never been born. There is then no alternative in Calvinist orthodox thinking but either the indescribable terror of the damned or the calm self-assurance which accompanies the certitude of divine election. Thus Calvin propounded what amounts to a sort of spiritual "race theory," similar to the Old Testament doctrine of the "chosen people of God."

Once again the "classical" temper of Calvinism asserts itself. The anticlassical Lutheran is condemned to live in insecurity and anxiety, while classical man stands on firm ground, a ground which sustains him and allows him to rest in self-assurance and certitude.

The ground on which the Catholic Orthodoxy of the East and the Roman Catholic teaching of the West rest is the Church, regarded as the living mystical Body of Christ. A Calvinist must find his firm ground elsewhere. And he does find it in the certainty of his election. The individual is called upon to incorporate in himself all those means which the Roman Catholic Church had placed at the disposal of the faithful to aid them in their justification and sanctification, such as the sacraments and the intercession of the Saints. Even more than in Lutheranism, religion appears spiritualized in Calvinism: it is characterized by a total absence of all imaginative, artistic and poetic forms of liturgical worship. Even music, for which

*Pelagius was a monk from Brittany or Ireland who lived in the fifth century. The gist of his teaching was the denial of original sin and thus of the need of grace in order to avoid sinful action and to practice virtue. Grace, Pelagius contended, coincides with a gift of nature and the doctrine and example of Christ.

Luther had made allowances and of which he was exceedingly fond, was excluded from the services of the Calvinists. The sacraments of baptism and Holy Communion were regarded by Calvin as mere external signs by means of which God manifests to man His benevolence and His promises. They are useful because they augment faith and impart the strength to profess it. Strictly speaking, however, these sacraments are not necessary. Calvin referred to the Catholic Mass as a "pestilential error," and he was on the whole much more radically opposed to all liturgical rites and ceremonies than was Luther. On the other hand, he strongly affirmed the Church as the communion of the saints and, though the Church is conceived as invisible, it was for Calvin actually a much more substantial reality than for Luther.

The neo-Calvinism of the later Karl Barth takes a critical view of both the orthodox Lutheran and the original Calvinist theologies. Barth calls the Lutheran dogmatic theology dangerous in some respects, especially in its denial of free will. And with respect to Calvin's dogma of double predestination Barth is taking an independent stand. He agrees with Calvin when he asserts that it is impossible to draw a hard and fast dividing line between theology and philosophy. In the many volumes of his *Church Dogmatics*, Barth shows an increasing esteem of the theology and philosophy of the Middle Ages and of Thomas Aquinas in particular; he frequently quotes from Aquinas' works and he generally moves into closer proximity to certain positions of Roman Catholic theology, especially when he admits that there is a certain continuity on the way from man to God, from nature to super-nature. This in turn makes it possible for the later Karl Barth to admit the possibility of a sort of "natural theology" or theodicy.

The fourth volume of Barth's *Church Dogmatics* is of special interest because it shows the changing and changed theological position of Karl Barth most strikingly. Here God is described as essentially Love: as Father, Son, and Holy Spirit, God is in and by Himself Love, and in this superabundance, in the overflowing of His love

He loves His creatures. God loves from all eternity, but as Creator He loves His creatures also in time. Love, however, is always an elective act, an act of divine preference as well as of divine judgment. God says "yes," and in His "yes-saying" He says "no" to everything He does not affirm. Even God's wrath and judgment are genuine expressions of His love. Barth's doctrine of predestination—considered from the point of view of the history of this dogma—is, as Hans Urs von Balthasar states, of an almost dazzling luminosity. Barth avers that he himself was almost blinded, as it were, by the light of his discovery or rediscovery of the meaning of predestination. He regards this doctrine as the key of the core of his entire theology. Already in his famous early work on Paul's Epistle to the Romans, Barth had deviated sharply from the Calvinistic teaching on predestination. But now, in the fourth volume of his *Church Dogmatics*, he devotes his entire eloquence to elaborating this dogma in a totally novel manner. He writes an almost dithyrambic hymn covering over six hundred pages. Every recourse to the "abstract" God of the philosophers appears to him as disastrous for theology. The doctrine of divine election Barth describes as "the sum total of the gospel, the real key that unlocks the understanding of divine revelation in God's creation, atonement, and redemption." The doctrine of election is "a testimony that all the ways and all the works of God have their origin in divine grace." Every created nature has its being, its essence and its existence by virtue of grace. And even the enemies of God are God's servants and thus servants of His grace. Thus God is always "full of grace."

The principle and origin of all divine election are seen in Christ Jesus, in whom God chooses Himself in the form of the creature, even prior to the foundation of the world. In Christ He elects His chosen people and in His chosen people He elects the individual human beings in their private, personal relationship to God.

Barth sees the main fault of the earlier interpretations of the dogma of predestination in a neglect of the Christological basis of divine election, its misinterpretation as a purely individual relationship between a human being and an abstract and therefore terrifying divine Absolute. Actually, the Son of God is elected from all eternity to lead all of creation home to the Father. Christ atones for all who have fallen into sin, and Christ Himself becomes in this sense the object also of divine reprobation. In God everything is luminosity, love and grace. In Him there is no darkness. And this is why the Gospel is indeed wholly and throughout an evangel, that is, glad tidings.

In God's eternal choice, prior to the foundation of the universe and the world, there was the foreknowledge of everything that world and creature could be and could become. Thus in Christ Himself election is a "double predestination," and "in the election of Christ Jesus, which is the eternal will of God, the Creator has chosen for man blessedness and light, and for Himself (that is, for the Son of God) reprobation, damnation, and death." God will have to judge sinners, and He will have to elect and draw to Himself the Son of God, Who alone is without sin. But He will do this in such a way that the Son of God, taking upon Himself all sin, will "taste damnation, death, and hell" (*Church Dogmatics*, IV, pp. 177 and 179) in such a way that he will liberate all for the sake of the Son, "in order to have mercy on all" (Rom. 11:32). This is the exchange which took place on Golgotha, where God chose the criminal's cross as His throne, where the Son of God did suffer what the Son of Man had deserved to suffer. And this is the real reason why there is *nothing damnable*—nothing at all—in those who abide in Christ Jesus (Rom. 8:1 [*Church Dogmatics*, IV, p. 182]). Therefore no one who believes in Christ can at the same time believe in his own reprobation or damnation. For once a person has learned to know God's infinite mercy and justice, it follows that he is no longer permitted to be in fear of reprobation (*Church Dogmatics*, IV, pp. 183–184). God is the head of both the elect and the damned: "If the believer testifies with his testimony of truth to the will of God, the unbeliever testifies with his lying testimony to what is not God's will." In this way they both serve as witnesses to the revelation of the divine will. However, with all their godlessness the unbelievers are no longer able to bring back that perversion for whose destruction Christ gave His mortal life. They are unable to rekindle the fires of the divine wrath because in His sacrificial self-giving Christ Himself has taken upon Himself these fires of wrath and has been consumed in their flames. Thus Christ is in a very aboriginal sense both the elect and the condemned. The will of God (I Tim. 2:4) is intentionally directed toward the salvation of *all*, and His will is also mighty enough to save *all*.

There is, however, according to Barth, never any experience of one's own election and thus no absolute subjective certitude of salvation. In this respect the reformed teachings must be "totally revised" (IV, p. 373). There is no other certitude except the one which is objectively founded in faith in the Redeemer and in the personal testimony for Christ. The one thing that is *definitive*, however, is the reality of grace, whereas reprobation and the judgment of damnation are only provisional.

The evolution of Karl Barth's theology is characterized by a steady broadening and deepening of an essentially Christocentric perspective: from a strictly neo-Calvinist and antiliberal stance through an intermediate phase of "dialectical theology" and an integral supranaturalism to an ecumenically oriented universalism and an eventual reaffirmation of the position of Origen and other early Greek Church Fathers, an *apokatastasis panton*, that is, a final redemptive restoration of all creation and all creatures to the aboriginal state of total integrity.

Confronted with the monumental edifice of his theology, friend and foe tend to agree that, with Schleiermacher, Kierkegaard and John Henry Newman, Karl Barth must be counted among the truly great theologians of modern times.

Jansenism and Pascal

The spirit of Protestantism was carried into Roman Catholicism by Jansenism.* Thus it is only by understanding the nature of Jansenism that it will be possible to understand Pascal and the mentality of those who are his kin. Miguel de Unamuno sees in Pascal the spiritual brother of Luther and Kierkegaard.

Jansenism represents a milder version of Calvinism. It is closest to Calvinism in its doctrine on grace, and it differs most from Calvinism in its teaching on the sacraments; in this latter respect it is essentially Roman Catholic. But while Jansenism theoretically continues the Roman Catholic teachings, in its practice it deprives the faithful of the consolations of the sacramental life by making the assurance of absolution or the forgiveness of sin more and more difficult. It asserts that the individual Christian is unworthy of receiving the sacraments—especially the sacrament of Holy Communion—except on very special exceptional occasions and after a most rigorous preparation and examination of conscience.

What Augustine describes as the *delectatio* (spiritual joy) of the faithful, Jansenius interprets as *voluptas* (sensual pleasure). Thus Jansenius was actually a sophisticated and subtle hedonist: he teaches in effect that the will is always moved—toward good as well as toward evil—by a craving for pleasure. However, this pleasure may be either supranatural or purely natural and worldly. If the latter, it is sinful pleasure; if the former, it is induced by divine grace. The effects of infused grace are thus described as a sort of celestial voluptuousness. But it must be asked whether such a hedonistic concept of grace is not incompatible with the Jansenist idea of the

*Cornelius Jansenius (1585–1638) was the theologian from whom Jansenism received its name. His controversial work on St. Augustine was published posthumously in 1640. One of Jansenius' precursors was Michael Baius (1513–1589), Professor of Philosophy at the University of Louvain, Chancellor of the University and the Royal Inquisitor of the Netherlands. Baius taught that the original grace of Paradise was part of the nature of man and thus not supernatural; consequently human nature appeared totally corrupted by the consequences of original sin and thus totally unfree.

terrifying majesty of God and likewise with the cold austerity of a type of religious devotion which strips the altars of every adornment and impoverishes the liturgy and the sacramental life of the Church. The Jansenist approaches the altar in fear and trembling. There persists in Jansenism the Christian severity of the Calvinist mentality. According to the French nineteenth-century rationalist Sainte-Beuve (1804–1869), what Port-Royal (the former Benedictine monastery located in the vicinity of Versailles) and, generally speaking, the French type of religiosity lack is "the lightness and joy of the saints and the children of God." In France, says Sainte-Beuve, we have "just men, honest men" (*hommes honnêtes*), in Italy they have "saints."

The Jansenist religion was dry and cold; it was both anti-Jesuit and anti-Franciscan. The believer suffers from extreme scrupulosity. He rejects all the popular traditional forms of devotion, such as in particular the veneration of the Virgin Mary, the veneration of the Sacred Heart of Christ, the prayers for the intercession of the saints.

As Henri Bremond points out in his *Histoire du sentiment religieux en France*, Pascal (1623–1662) was intellectually and spiritually formed by this "sinister" Jansenist piety. Nonetheless, like Kierkegaard, he passed through an "aesthetic stage" and retained in his religious mentality the humanizing elements of the *bel esprit* and therewith an appreciation of aesthetic, literary and artistic values. Thus in Pascal's religious experience the Calvinist, Jansenist and Roman Catholic ingredients appear interlinked. This explains in part Pascal's appeal to modern thinkers and the influence which he still exerts on some of the best Protestant and Catholic minds.

Pascal was looking for the living God (*le Dieu vivant*), the foundation or ground of religion, not in nature or in the external world but rather in the interiority of the individual soul. He wanted to construct a religious metaphysics of the human person. And the anguish of Pascal's soul could not be satisfied with a Calvinist self-assurance of divine "election": "As I do not know whence I have come, I neither know whither I go. All I know is that when I depart from this world I shall fall either into nothingness or into the hands of a zealous god." However, from the contents of Pascal's famous *Mémorial* we know that he, too, like the Jansenists, had received an unmistakable "sign" of his personal salvation. In the most memorable pages of his *Pensées,* Pascal writes not so much of the state of his own mind and soul as of the misery, the insecurity and the gnawing doubts of man and the human condition as such. And he writes chiefly for those who have not received an inner testimony of their eternal destiny. In speaking of Pascal, William Barrett says: "Reading this, we are no longer in the world of a Tertullian or a St. Augustine, not in the Romanesque world of St. Bernard, nor in the world in which Duns Scotus debated the positions taken by St. Thomas and in which Christian faith was so strong that it could make a miraculous marriage with the philosophy of Aristotle. No; it is our world, the modern world, that Pascal depicts, and reading him we enter that world as our home just because we are as homeless there as he was" (*Irrational Man,* p. 104).

The main themes of Pascal's *Pensées* are in fact identical with those enunciated in Luther's Theology of the Cross: the profound sentiment of the constitutional insecurity and the precarious nature of human existence; the anguish caused by a sense of guilt and sin; the contempt for nature and for the world; the idea of a fragile existence stretched out between the abyss of nothingness and the abyss of infinity; the "tremendous mystery" (*mysterium tremendum*) of an inscrutable and incomprehensible divine dispensation.

Pascal had lost all confidence in the conventional religion of his day and age. He accused the Jesuits in particular of practicing moral casuistry and of thus debasing and corrupting the Roman Catholic religion, and yet he remained convinced that it was necessary to continue in this Roman Catholic tradition. Pascal was one of those prophets in whom the traumatic conflicts of an entire civilization are experienced as a personal crisis, as was the case with Kierkegaard, Nietzsche, and Unamuno, conflicts of which the majority of their contemporaries remain totally unaware.

Man has a "need for security" (*un besoin de sécurité*), a security which nothing and no one can give him: neither nature nor history, nor philosophy, nor science, nor even faith, because even divine revelation remains forever ambiguous, and God remains a *Deus absconditus* (a hidden God). Doubt tortures the soul even where it had hoped to find absolute certitude. It is extremely difficult to know whether God does or does not exist: "Reason is here incapable of arriving at any definitive conclusion." Thus it all amounts to a tremendous gamble with the highest stakes, and there persists the constant risk that one may lose all. However, it is necessary to face the alternative: either total affirmation or total denial, either faith or atheism. Religious indifference, free thought, skeptical doubt are vain attempts to delay the great decision, to delay the acceptance of the risk of this great wager. You may say, however, "I was made in such a way that I cannot believe. What am I to do?" Pascal answers: "Act as if you had faith": sacrifice your reason, and you will end up as a believer. And thus, despite his violent attacks on the Pope, Pascal, who in many respects tried to be "more papal than the Pope," could write: "We know that all the virtues, martyrdom, austerities, all good works are useless outside the Church and outside our communion with its head, the Pope. I shall never separate myself from that communion. At least I ask God that He may grant me this grace, without which I know I shall be lost forever."

Pascal speaks of the constant presence of an "abyss," and he defines man as an "instant of being," suspended between the infinite and the naught. And, as in the case of Luther, Kierkegaard and Unamuno, man is carried to the height of redemption only after having passed through the depth of despair.

In his antimetaphysical polemic, Pascal anticipates the *aporias**

---

*The term *aporia* occurs first in the writings of Plato and Aristotle. The Greek rootword *poros* denotes passage as well as exit, a transition as well as an open road, a slow progression through shallow and muddy waters as well as the ways and means leading toward a definite goal. *Aporia* thus has come to mean some logically irreconcilable theses or statements which appear equally tenable or equally incomprehensible.

of Kant. He wrote: "It is incomprehensible that God exists, and it is incomprehensible that He does not exist; it is incomprehensible that the soul forms a union with the body, and it is incomprehensible that the body exists without a soul; it is incomprehensible that man was created by God, and it is incomprehensible that man was not created by God."

"Pascal's philosophic dialectic," says the French neo-Kantian Léon Brunschvicg, "leads to a negative conclusion: pessimism is for him the necessary ultimate dictum of philosophy." Pascal not only denies the conclusiveness of metaphysico-rational arguments in theology but even the possibility of a natural pre-Christian or non-Christian morality and thus an *anima naturaliter christiana*. Even if God, as St. Paul asserts, did originally inscribe His law in the heart of man, this inscription was blotted out by original sin. The religion of Pascal is thus, like that of the Jansenists, Christian in the most rigoristic and restrictive sense of the term: it is a religion that is centered exclusively in Christ, that is, in the Son, not in the Father. God the Father is for Pascal's Christian what He was for the Gnostics, namely, a demiurge, a god of wrath, a god of terror. And it is pride and presumption on the part of man to approach God the Father; it is impossible, useless and dangerous to know Him. Equally useless and presumptuous therefore are the metaphysical rational proofs of the existence of God. Pascal contends that extremely intelligent minds find the proofs for the existence of God entirely convincing, but equally intelligent minds find them totally inconclusive. This means simply that the proofs convince those who want to be convinced but fail to convince those who do not want to be convinced: "Therefore, not the God of the philosophers, but the God of Abraham, Isaac, and Jacob."

With some contemporary existentialists, Pascal militates against the multiple "diversions" and "distractions" of life. In order not to be forced to think and to reflect about his personal destiny, modern man hankers for diversions and distractions of all kinds; he seeks, in the words of T. S. Eliot, "distraction from distraction by distraction." Man tries to keep himself busy at all times and at any cost; leisure, rest, quietude, solitude, contemplation he fears and shuns like death. This explains why games, gossip, wars and revolutions, and any sort of noisy agitation but, above all, perpetual motion are so much in vogue and are so eagerly sought. They keep men externally occupied, giving them an outward appearance of gaiety and fulfillment. "All the unhappiness of man has its cause in his inability to remain in quiet repose," for man was not created for diversion and distraction but for thought and contemplation; therein consist his dignity and his merit. "The Stoics tell us: Enter into your own selves; there you will find repose. This, however, is not the entire truth. Others tell us: Go out of yourselves; seek happiness in diversion. This also is not true. Happiness is not to be found either within or outside of ourselves: it is found in God, that is, outside and within ourselves."

A comparison between this passage in Pascal's *Pensées* and a similar one in the *Spiritual Canticle* of St. John of the Cross (1542–1591) shows the difference between orthodox Catholic mysticism and Pascal's existentialist preoccupation with sin and death. The Spanish mystic is as much concerned with the ultimate mysteries of human existence as Pascal. He, too, demands that man realize himself by probing into the depth of his human destiny, that he take into account the fact that

life is short; the path of eternal life is narrow; the just man finds it barely possible to save himself; the things of this world are vain and full of deceit; temporal life is insecure, and perdition is easy, salvation difficult. And since it is already late and we live perhaps in the twilight of our day, we do well to renounce all things, with sighs and with anguish, and without delaying for a day or an hour, the soul should begin to call for its Beloved.

Like Pascal, St. John of the Cross points out that the human soul has a natural tendency to flee from the ultimate problems of existence, to dissipate and distract itself rather than to think of its beginning and end, a tendency to shun serious thought rather than to think of God. It is necessary therefore to halt the flux of this superficial manner of living, to take stock, to avoid dispersion, to give thought to the idea of eternity. Thus both authors advise that man detach himself from all his earthly cares, but whereas for the Spanish mystic this demand has the meaning that the soul may then be able to devote all its efforts and activities to the love of God and the neighbor, Pascal wants the soul to become free for its preoccupation with sins and with death. He compares the human condition with that of prisoners in a chain gang: all are condemned to death, and each one looks at the other with hopeless sorrow, each one wondering when it will be his turn to die (see *Pensées*, No. 199).

In Pascal's as in Kiekegaard's view, man is a fragile, temporal existence, a finite being suspended between two infinities, the bad infinity of nothingness and the good infinity of God. To escape both, man hands himself over to distraction and diversion. To the "abyss" of Pascal corresponds the "leap" of Kierkegaard; to the "wager" of Pascal corresponds the "risk" of a paradoxical faith in Kierkegaard. Man, in anguish facing nothingness, and in despair before God, risks the "leap" into the paradox of faith. But even in faith the risk continues, the abyss still calls and threatens. Pascal's and Kierkegaard's scrupulosity permits them no resting place in the salvific freedom of the children of God, in the consciousness that God's mercy and love take into account and pardon human frailty and imperfection.

Contemporary Roman Catholicism

The general insecurity of contemporary life is reflected also in contemporary Roman Catholicism. The contemporary Roman Catholic had until recently lived essentially in the religious and cultural climate created by the Counter-Reformation and the Council of Trent. He had come to regard himself in a fixed relationship to God and to the world and had come to see in the supernatural order a guarantee of his security in the world, in his family and in himself. He no longer seems to enjoy this feeling of security. He rather feels a certain justification in the accusations leveled at him by André Gide: "That which I perhaps regard as a heritage of Protestantism in my being," wrote Gide, "is my horror of any comfortable existence." He reproaches Roman Catholicism for being more of a sedative than a stimulant, and he says that Roman Catholics evade the drama of existence in order to install themselves in a comfortable spiritual situation. Perhaps what the present age needs most of all is not conformists but the witness of sanctity, the witness of saints, who are the greatest nonconformists. The authentic Catholic has, of course, no other security and support than that promised and provided by Christ and His Mystical Body, the Church.

In the course of the post-Tridentine centuries the lines marked by denominational separation had hardened to such an extent that communication had become almost impossible. That ecumenial zeal which had animated the minds of past "Christian humanists," from Nicholas of Cusa, Erasmus, St. Thomas More to Leibniz, was forgotten. In their firmly entrenched positions Protestants and Catholics alike had developed "closed" systems of dogmatic theology, essentially defensive and thus without that overtness which is indispensable for any mutual understanding or dialogue. What Friedrich Heer calls the "Third Power," that is, the force of the centuries-old Christian humanism of the West, seemed practically extinct.

Contemporary Roman Catholicism had enclosed itself in a self-created ghetto and had developed a corresponding ghetto mentality. The bigoted Roman Catholic and Protestant became targets of Unamuno's scornful attacks on "ghetto Christians," whose fear of facing the challenges of the modern world caused them to seek shelter behind the protective cortex of a merely conventional and therefore existentially meaningless religious stance. The result was an atrophied religious faith with distinctly puritanical and at times even neo-Manichaean features. The post-Reformation Catholic in particular came to regard his relationship to God, to his neighbor and to the world as inflexibly fixed, looking at the supernatural as a kind of life-insurance policy that permitted him to live securely in a world, in a society and in a Church in which all problems were shoved aside because all meaningful questions were already neatly answered in apologetics and catechetics.

Risk and uncertainty have become the rule rather than an exception in the life of contemporary Christians. Protestant and Catholic alike no longer enjoy the pseudo-security of former centuries, and man, as Unamuno had demanded, seems to have been plunged again into the ocean of life, deprived of every anchorage, so that he might learn once more what it means to exist as a human being.

The contemporary Christian thus begins to realize more fully that religious faith is dynamic rather than static, that it has to be tried and tested and conquered and reconquered from day to day. He therefore feels inclined to exclaim with that father in the Gospel: "I do believe; Lord, help my unbelief!" (Mark 9:23). "Conscious or not," wrote the late Jesuit paleontologist, Pierre Teilhard de Chardin (1881–1955), "a fundamental anguish of being strikes in the depths of all our hearts and is the undertone of all our conversations. There is nothing new under the sun, say the despairing. But what about you, oh thinking man? Oh man of the Twentieth Century, how does it happen that you are waking up to horizons and are susceptible to fears which your forefathers never knew?" (*The Phenomenon of Man*, pp. 226 ff.).

Some of the French writers of the *renouveau catholique*, whose work will be discussed in the main body of this treatise, have made a significant distinction between the "protected" and the "exposed" Christian. And Karl Barth endorses the position of the "exposed" Christian when he writes: "I do not like to hear it said, 'we the believers, and you, the unbelievers.' Who are these unbelievers? I do know one of them: his name is Karl Barth. I know him and I am engaged in a constant debate with him. And when someone tells me: You are a believer, I answer, yes, yes; I do have faith, but perhaps precisely for this reason I understand better than you those who do not have the gift of faith."

Thus the living faith of the "exposed" Christian, a faith that finds itself challenged again and again, has a deeper understanding of the nonbeliever than the smug and self-assured "Christian," whose "faith" can hardly be distinguished from indifference. The identical thought was given a most forceful expression by Dostoevsky in that memorable conversation of Stavrogin (the protagonist of the novel *The Possessed*) with the Russian Orthodox Bishop Tihon, where the Bishop tells his strange visitor that atheism stands on the penultimate step of the ladder that leads to faith, whereas indifference is farthest removed from faith.

It appears, then, that in our time the life of the Roman Catholic has the same tragic undertones as the life of the Protestant. But what about the attitude of contemporary Roman Catholicism regarding the mental state of despair? As we have seen, for Luther, Kierkegaard and the early Karl Barth, despair seemed the original motivating force which generates faith, and even after the "leap" into faith, despair remained as an open possibility and a constant threat. There is no doubt that in the present situation of the world, despair, dread, anguish are constant temptations and often stark existential realities. On the other hand, Thomas Aquinas defined despair as a "vice" and a "sin" (*motus desperationis est vitiosus et peccatum,* [*Summa Theologica,* IIa IIae, XX, 1]). Thomas even calls despair "the greatest and most dangerous sin," subjectively speaking (whereas objectively or in the absolute sense he regards infidelity and hate as greater sins). However, in this as in many other respects the spiritual atmosphere of our time is much more akin to the minds of St. Augustine and of Pascal than to that of St. Thomas. Thus William Barrett is correct when he states that the creature discussed by such classical thinkers as Aristotle and Aquinas in their treatises on man may resemble man but does not resemble us: "In what Pascal says about the human condition, however, we recognize ourselves all too painfully. As a psychologist, he is a contemporary" (*op. cit.,* p. 99). There are many testimonies to the fact that spiritual or religious despair can lead to religious faith. On the other hand, despair

(Kierkegaard's "sickness unto death" which may be healed by faith) may also lead to the loss of faith and thus to spiritual death. However, no Roman Catholic would ever assert with Luther or Kierkegaard that despair is an almost necessary condition of faith. At the most he might say with Gabriel Marcel (see *Etre et Avoir*, p. 55) that Christian hope has its starting point in that situation of "threat" and "danger" in which man finds himself constitutionally and radically placed. This is likewise affirmed by Kierkegaard and Heidegger and every existentialist thinker in between. Despair, says Marcel, remains always a possibility (*ibid.*, p. 150), and "the foundation of hope is laid in the consciousness of a situation which invites despair (for example, sickness, suffering, guilt, strife, death)" (*ibid.*, p. 108). Expressed in the language of Kant, "the conditions of the possibility of the birth of hope strictly coincide with those of despair." In other words, man is a being capable of despairing but capable also of rising from despair to faith and to hope. But faith and hope do not require despair as a precondition.

André Gide's indictment of the state of mind of certain Roman Catholics seems to have a limited justification in that many Roman Catholics tend to regard their religion as a "traditional doctrine" which they have "received" or inherited from their forebears, a doctrine which firmly and *once and for all* establishes a certain number of commandments, rituals and prescriptions, the acceptance and fulfillment of which assure almost magically their salvation. They tend to assume that by virtue of Christ's sacrificial death—an event which occurred in the remote past—they are already firmly implanted in the order of salvation, provided they do not refuse outright to cooperate formally with the grace offered them. Such an attitude, however, can hardly be said to penetrate to the actual depth of genuine religious experience. Kierkegaard was thus justified in demanding that the individual Christian "repeat" the religious experience from its very beginning in his personal existence, and in his contention that "Christian parents do not ipso facto beget Christian children." In other words, the individual Christian must, as it were, personally retrace every step of the life and the passion of Christ; he must inwardly "repeat" the movement of the entire religious history of the human race, from its pre-Christian phase to the advent of Christianity, from the state of forlornness and despair to the state of promise, hope, trust, faith, and love. He must, in short, become "contemporaneous" with Christ.

According to Arnold Toynbee, "Catholicism is unquestionably the Western form of Christianity which shows the most vigorous signs of life." It is an indubitable fact, on the other hand, that contemporary Catholicism has made room for certain modes of human existence which formerly used to be associated with non-Catholic patterns of life. Was Montesquieu perhaps right when he asserted in his *Cahiers* that "the Catholic religion is going to destroy the Protestant religion, and thereafter Roman Catholics will turn into Protestants"? Or is it perhaps more true to say that Roman Catholicism, after having recovered from the blow it was dealt by the Protestant Reformation, is gradually regaining its ancient equilibrium, its openness and its creative freedom? If so, it might be in a position to relinquish completely and definitively its ghetto-like negative and purely defensive attitudes and adopt all those positive values and truths embodied in Protestantism and also in non-Christian forms of religious devotion and existence.

Among the most original thinkers of the second half of the nineteenth century were Kierkegaard, Nietzsche and Cardinal John Henry Newman. Among these three it was Kierkegaard who not only made possible a rebirth of the original impetus of Protestantism (bearing fruit in the works of such contemporary theologians as Karl Barth, Emil Brunner, Reinhold Niebuhr, Rudolf Bultmann) but also injected new problems and challenges into modern and contemporary Roman Catholicism, opening up entirely new perspectives and dimensions in Christian theology as such. Kierkegaard deeply influenced several branches of contemporary philosophy (Heidegger, Jaspers, Sartre, Marcel)—especially existentialism and personalism—and his impact was almost equally strong on at

least two of the most prominent literary figures of modern Europe—
Henrik Ibsen (especially *Brand, Peer Gynt, Emperor and Galilaean*)
and Rainer Maria Rilke. In the Roman Catholic milieu only
Newman exerted and is more and more exerting a comparable
influence.*

For Kierkegaard, Christianity was much more an existential
message than a doctrinal system. It was in the truest sense existence-
communication. The meaning of Kierkegaard's message is basically
a call for an imitation and following of Christ, an assimilation to
Christ to be brought about by a reliving of the "brutal facts"
(E. Brunner) of the Incarnation, the Passion, the death, and the
Resurrection of Christ. Under the influence of this new theological
impulse, Roman Catholic theology is gradually passing beyond
the *doctrinaire* tendencies of the Counter-Reformation, especially
by placing a much greater emphasis on the ancient Pauline idea
of the *Mystical Body of Christ*, that is, on the existential participation
and incorporation of every Christian in the life of this *Corpus
Mysticum* of the People of God.

Both Protestant and Catholic theology today regard "being" or
"living in" the Truth as much more important than merely intellectually knowing the Truth. The practical efficacy of the "testimony" of the "witness" is much more important than any demonstration of rational preconditions or preambles of faith. Of course,
this need not mean a rejection of the significant and even indispensable spadework of *reason* but rather a stronger accentuation
of the suprarational and supranatural nature of *faith*.

It was Kierkegaard also who pointed out the great qualitative
difference between *religion* and *morality*, a distinction which seems
especially significant today when more often than not morality
is mistaken for religion.

It was this difference which Kierkegaard had in mind when he
elaborated (in *Either/Or* and *Stages on Life's Way*) on the three stages

*See especially the study by A. J. Boekraad, *The Personal Conquest of Truth Accord-
ing to J. H. Newman* (Louvain, Belgium: Nauwelaerts, 1955).

of existence (the aesthetic, the ethico-moral and the religious) and when, later on, he distinguished sharply between an "apostle" and a "genius" (*Two Minor Ethico-Religious Treatises*, 1849).

This distinction plays again a significant role in the novels of Graham Greene. In these novels reappears Pascal's and Kierkegaard's idea of the "wager" and the "risk" and the idea further elaborated by Karl Jaspers that God is encountered in the "limit-situations" of human existence (sin, guilt, strife, suffering, death): Greene's major characters find themselves as well as God precisely in such "limit-situations," that is, in situations in which the individual risks all because he knows that in this ultimate either/or he stands to lose or win all.

God in the Life of Contemporary Man

The diagnosis of such thinkers as Nietzsche, Heidegger and Jaspers suggests that we are today passing through a very "dark night": in this present age God is experienced largely negatively— by his *absence* and by the effects of this absence.* It is, of course, a highly paradoxical truth that God can be near in His absence, and that He can be absent in His presence. In other words, the absence of God can be experienced as a void that must be filled if life is to regain its meaning, and the presence of God may not be experienced at all because it is being taken too much for granted and thus fails to arouse either love or hate: the "believers" of this so-called Christian civilization have grown too complacent or too indifferent.†

It is commonly assumed and admitted that the external sign of a religious commitment is, on the one hand, the fulfillment of certain ritual acts, such as prayer, sacrificial offerings, the reception of certain sacraments and sacramentals, individual and communal

---

*See especially Anna Hellersberg-Wendriner's profound study on the novels of Thomas Mann, *Mystik der Gottesferne* (*The Mysticism of the Absence of God*) (Bern and Munich: Francke, 1960).

†See especially Raymond J. Nogar, O.P., *The Lord of the Absurd* (New York: Herder and Herder, 1966).

worship and, on the other hand, a fairly balanced "moral" life, the behavior of Pascal's *honnête homme*, that is, of a Christian "gentleman." It can readily be seen, however, how easy it is for such typical forms of conventional religion to degenerate into mere formalism. What is scornfully referred to by such authors as Kierkegaard, Karl Marx or Nietzsche as the religion of the bourgeois shows definite signs of decadence and degeneration: the bourgeois still pays lip service to his inherited religious values, but he looks upon them as guarantees of the pleasures of eternal life, to be achieved if the Christian wants to secure a safe road to "the golden streets of heaven," to use one of the Rev. Billy Graham's favorite clichés. Religion in this bourgeois milieu has lost most of its aspects of mystery: it is soothing rather than exciting, an "opiate" (Karl Marx) rather than an incentive. To think of death is especially inconvenient, for such thoughts may cause sleepless nights. It seems therefore preferable to forget all such disturbing reflections, and this one does efficaciously by indulging in multiple diversions and distractions. This is one aspect of the degenerate religion of the bourgeois; the other is an empty ceremonialism, as St. John of the Cross called it, a legalistic pharisaism which clings to external forms from which the vital content has long been drained. In *The Ascent of Mount Carmel* (Chapter XLIV), St. John of the Cross writes:

Devout persons should realize that the more they rely on these [external] things and ceremonies, the less confidence they have in God. There are people who multiply their petitions in order to obtain a certain thing, when it would be much better to pray for things of greater importance for them, such as a true cleansing of their consciences and a deeper understanding of matters concerning their salvation. In this way they would obtain what is most important for them and, in addition, all other things which are good for them (although they might not have prayed for them). For this is precisely what Our Lord promised when he said, "Make it your first and principal care to find the Kingdom of God and His approval, and all these other things shall be yours without the asking"(Matt. 6: 33).

And, as far as various ceremonies connected with prayer and devotion are concerned, we should not set our will upon other ceremonies and forms of prayer than those which Christ and His Church have taught us. And all He taught [his disciples] was the seven petitions of the *Pater Noster*, wherein are included all our spiritual and temporal needs; and He did not teach them any other kinds of verbal prayer and ceremonial. On the contrary, He told them that when they pray they should not desire to use many words since our heavenly Father knows well what our needs are (cf. Luke 11:1–2; Matt. 6: 7–8). He exhorted them only—but this most earnestly—to persevere in prayer; and on another occasion He told them that they ought to pray continually and never weaken in their prayer (cf. Luke 18:1). And the ceremonies He taught us to use in our prayers are only two in number: we should pray either in the secrecy of our chamber, where, without being disturbed by noise and without being distracted by anyone, we can pray with a pure heart and with our whole mind (cf. Matt. 6:6); or else, we should follow His example and go to a solitary and deserted place, preferably in the great stillness of the night. And thus there is no reason why we should set any limit of time, or confine our prayers to any special days or hours; nor is there any reason to use other forms in our words and prayers than those which the Church uses and which all can be reduced to those which we have described as being implied in the petitions of the *Pater Noster*.*

The mental attitude of the bourgeois as described above amounts actually to a mere *do ut des:* the promise of salvation is handled like a business transaction: I must be reasonably "good" if I want to get by and avoid this nasty business of damnation. It is the religious attitude of a healthy bourgeois mediocrity, and it is this very attitude which is common with the majority of bourgeois "Christians." If they play the game according to the rules, they cannot miss. This *petit bourgeois*, as Jean-Paul Sartre describes him, is an *honnête homme* who follows almost automatically and in a computer-like fashion the routines of his daily life: he dresses neatly, he attends dutifully to his business, he does God the tremendous honor of going to church for one hour on Sundays, and he generally lives the life of "the common man" and the "upright citizen." In the monotony of such a superficial existence of limited aspirations there yet lurks a relative happiness and a sordid kind of peace of mind.

*See St. John of the Cross, *The Dark Night of the Soul*. Trans. and edited by Kurt F. Reinhardt (New York: Frederick Ungar Publishing Co., 1957); pp. 154 ff.

An entirely different type of religious existence is revealed, for example, in the life of Simone Weil. This remarkable woman was born in 1909 of Jewish parents. She became a brilliant student of philosophy, and she could have had a distinguished academic career if her ardent love for the poor and humble and downtrodden ("the humiliated and the offended" of Dostoevsky) had not interfered with her normal aspirations. In 1934 she began—despite her very frail constitution—to share the life of the proletarian masses in strenuous work in a factory. She was motivated not by curiosity but by compassion—the great "passion" of her life. She desired to become as nothing, to disappear in the mass of workers, in the anonymity of a proletarian existence. A few years later she began to devote all her remaining strength to the Loyalist cause in the Spanish Civil War, fighting relentlessly for what she considered the cause of social justice.

In a letter addressed to Georges Bernanos she described the reasons which made her join the Loyalist forces, and she expressed the terrible disappointment she experienced when she witnessed the most atrocious crimes committed in both camps of this civil strife and the intoxication of the masses with the thirst for the blood of their fellow countrymen.*

After the outbreak of World War II, and after Paris had been declared an open city, Simone Weil went to Marseilles in the French South. The anti-Semitic laws of the Vichy government made it impossible for her to obtain a teaching position. This in her case was all the more pathetic because in her books (all published posthumously) this Jewess revealed her own often violently anti-Semitic sentiments. During her stay in Marseilles she came ever closer to Roman Catholicism, but she was never baptized, never received into the Church.

From Marseilles, Simone Weil went first to Oran and Casablanca

*Cf. the trilogy of novels dealing with the Spanish Civil War by José Maria Gironella, in particular the first volume, titled in English *The Cypresses Believe in God* (New York: Alfred Knopf).

and thereafter to the United States. However, because she wanted
to be closer to the actual theater of the war—to share more fully
in the common danger as well as to contribute her own services
more substantially—she soon returned to England. Despite her
severely impaired health she refused to consume more food than was
allotted to her starving compatriots in France. She contracted
pulmonary tuberculosis and literally starved herself to death. The
four books she had written were edited and prefaced by a befriended
Dominican priest, Père Perrin, and by Gustave Thibon.*

In Simone Weil we meet with a religious experience which is
paradoxically characterized by an apparent "absence" of God.
"He Whom we are called to love is absent," she wrote. For her,
Christ's outcry on the Cross—"My God, my God, why have you
forsaken me?"—expresses the true human condition.

This religious sentiment of total abandonment is, however, by
no means peculiar to Simonē Weil; it is rather a familiar theme in
contemporary literature. It is, for example, one of the main themes
in Franz Kafka's novels, especially in *The Castle*. The main theme
in this latter novel is the impossibility of establishing communication
with the mysterious and invisible Lord of the castle. Communication of a sort can be established only by the totally impersonal,
mechanical device of a telephone. But the telephone lines to the
castle are usually disconnected, and if perchance an answer does
come through, one never knows exactly who is on the other end of
the line. Contact of a sort can be established only by the roundabout
way of doubtful and ambiguous messages and by secretarial inter-
mediaries, and genuine communication is always thwarted by an
imprenetrable net of red tape. In a very similar vein, the French
aviator Antoine de Saint-Exupéry (1900–1944, missing in action)
wrote, "Lord, I have never been able as yet to penetrate to your
Majesty. But a God Who allows Himself to be reached and moved

*Cf. especially *La Pesanteur et la Grâce* (*Gravity and Grace*), 1948; *L'Enracinement*
(*The Need for Roots*), 1949; *Attente de Dieu* (*Waiting for God*), 1950; *La Condition
ouvrière*, 1951; and *Cahiers*, 1951–1956.

by man, is no longer God. For the first time I have discovered that
the greatness of prayer consists precisely in the fact that one does
not obtain an answer." A similar thought was expressed much
earlier by St. Teresa of Avila, the classical Spanish mystic, when
she wrote: "More tears have been shed over prayers that were
answered than over those which remained unanswered." Kierkegaard too was of the conviction that the best prayer consists in
listening rather than in speaking. "In proportion," he wrote," as
he [S.K.] became more and more earnest in prayer, he had less
and less to say, and in the end he became quite silent."

The note of total abandonment is made the most conspicuous
element even in the life and death of Christ and the saints. "Christ,"
wrote Simone Weil, "did not die a martyr. He died—infinitely
more humbly—a common criminal." At the hour of death Christ
was abandoned by all the disciples, and only after His Resurrection,
after they had gained the unshakable conviction of His power, did
they muster the courage to suffer all kinds of tribulations and
tortures. To suffer persecution and death for a cause that is strong
and victorious is infinitely easier than to die for a lost cause and
in total abandonment. Similarly, the protagonist in Graham
Greene's novel *The Power and the Glory* is not an idealized martyr
but a poor, vacillating and sinful priest, whose strength is revealed
in his weakness. In Kierkegaard's words, "The stronger a man is,
the weaker is God in him; and the weaker a man is, the stronger is
God in him."

"The truth is, " writes Graham Greene, "that the devil and God
are making use of simple folk, of the wounded and the crippled, to
attain their ends. If God has thus used them, we speak of nobility;
if the devil has used them, we condemn them as wicked. But in
either case the human material was pitifully weak." As seen from
this point af view, a religion of merely external obligations and
observances must be radically rejected. For the publican and the
sinner are to be preferred to the lukewarm and the Pharisees.

Equally dubious appears a religion which rests safely and complacently in the assurance of "eternal life." Thus the protagonist in Graham Greene's novel *The Heart of the Matter* is anything but a noble exemplar of the human species. Scobie receives Holy Communion sacrilegiously, and he commits suicide in the end. Since he is a "believer," he thus takes upon himself deliberately the terrible prospect of eternal damnation. And Scobie is impelled to do this by a strange yet overpowering feeling of pity and compassion and by an exaggerated sensibility for his being responsible for all those persons whose lives depend on him. We are led to surmise that Scobie truly loves God but that he cannot bear the thought that this love of God might nourish itself at the expense of the love he owes to any of God's creatures. The "heart of the matter" lies for the author in the fact that in freely accepting his own damnation, the sinning individual proves himself—despite everything—to be of good will and thus worthy of God's mercy and forgiveness. Characteristically, Graham Greene chose as the motto for *The Heart of the Matter* the saying of Charles Péguy, "The sinner is in the very heart of Christianity. . . . No one is as competent as the sinner in the matter of Christianity, no one unless it be the Saint."

To understand religion as a mere system of justice and order appears to both Graham Greene and Simone Weil as a view that is seriously out of focus because it demands both too little and too much. It demands too much of those who have nothing to offer but their own weakness and indigence.

Simone Weil speaks of two distinct planes of life: the first is the ordinary, normal human life, and the second represents her own intense and highly personal religious pattern of existence. As far as the first way is concerned, she says, no human being should be deprived of the relative goods of a home, a fatherland, a family, a tradition; these are the roots or the anchorage of man's temporal existence. Simone Weil defends these goods from the attacks directed against them by the forces of the uprooted civilization of the present age. She calls these values "mixed goods"; that is, they have their positive and their negative aspects: they contain good and evil, and they are like bridges which man crosses on the way to the higher and the highest goods. Nonetheless, they are necessary for a normal human existence unless this existence be that of a saint.

But after having thus outlined the pattern of a "normal" human life, Simone Weil describes her own *extra-ordinary* existence. She says in effect that for her it is necessary to remain forever without a home, alone, a stranger, in exile, without a family, even without friends. "It is true, one must love one's neighbor, but in the example given by Christ to illustrate this commandment [the example, of course, of the Good Samaritan], the neighbor is naked and bleeding, exposed and abandoned on the wayside . . . . It is a completely anonymous and therefore a universal love."

But it is Graham Greene who turns most vehemently against a Christian life that exhausts itself in a mild and well-mannered "everydayness." The protagonists of all his novels are haunted and persecuted creatures, people who find themselves in "limit-situations," naked and deserted, face to face with danger, guilt, despair, death—and face to face with God. And it is the same rarefied and breathtaking atmosphere—an atmosphere of suspense and excitement that has many characteristics in common with the suspense of a detective story—which we encounter in the majority of contemporary novels with theological overtones, in contrast to the well-tempered climate of the typical novel of only a generation ago. According to Sartre, what Dostoevsky, Camus, Koestler, Malraux and others create in their novels is a literature of such extreme limit-situations. Their characters are either at the apex of power or in the depths of dereliction; on the eve of death, torture or murder; in the midst of war, revolution, bombings and killings. On every page, in every line it is always man in his total existence who is called in question.

Thus, in this present age religion is no longer felt as a sure guarantor of a sheltered life, of security, providence and moderate happiness. According to Simone Weil, God has literally abandoned us in our temporal existence, and He visits disgrace and misfortune indiscriminately and almost absurdly upon the good and the bad, upon the innocent and the guilty. If man wants to save himself, he must accept this abandonment without any palliatives. For the way *of* God and the way *to* God pass through all sorts of doubts, temptations, shipwrecks, frustrations and total and fatal dereliction. But once man has come to the point where he can no longer suppress the outcry "My God, my God, why have you forsaken me?" and yet remains in this limit-situation without ceasing in his love, he shall find beatitude, even in the midst of abandonment and disgrace.

These introductory remarks are perhaps most aptly concluded with a reference to some of the sayings and some of the prayers of the "nightclub priest" of the Episcopal Church in the United States, Father Malcolm Boyd. "If St. Peter and Paul were alive today they would come here (that is, to this nightclub) too—if they could get out of jail long enough to do it." Or, "I am not against religious people; I am against people who worship religion instead of worshipping God." Or again, "I wonder at people who take the anthropomorphic view of God. A man once told me, 'When my wife and I engage in sex, God turns His back.' I told him: 'What a terrible thing to say about your wife, about your sex, and about God!' " What is Hell? "Hell," Father Boyd says, "is a condition in which you are all tied up in your own egotism, manipulating other people, living for your own aggrandizement. Heaven is when you permit yourself to be broken up."

Father Boyd has published seven books, including a volume of his own prayers entitled *Are You Running with Me, Jesus?** He wrote these prayers because, as he says, "One day I realised that I was a phoney. I couldn't pray any longer to 'thee' and 'thou.' " And finally: "It is morning, Jesus. It is morning, and here is that light and that sound all over again. I've got to move fast . . . and run

*Avon Books (New York, 1967).

some more. But I just don't feel like it, Lord . . . . Are you running with me, Jesus?" One value of Father Boyd's books, commented Bishop James Pike, is that they help other people who are lost to realize that they are praying, too.

CHAPTER ONE

Dostoevsky

THE POSSESSED

FYODOR DOSTOEVSKY lived from 1821 to 1881. The main themes of his works were man, history, morality and religion.

With his elder brother Dostoevsky entered the Military Academy of Engineering at St. Petersburg (Leningrad). His father, an army physician in Moscow, died a violent death at the hands of some of the peasant servants of his native village. When Dostoevsky heard of his father's death, he suffered his first attack of epilepsy.

Dostoevsky left the military academy in 1843 to accept a position as an army engineer, but he soon resigned. In 1845 he published his first novel, titled *Poor People*. The young author's alignment with the radical political groups in Russia led to his banishment for four years to a Siberian slave labor camp. This event proved decisive for the author's future as a writer. The second period of his works opens with the *Notes from the House of the Dead*. It shows a newly acquired sense of the tragic aspects of human existence. Even prior to this Dostoevsky had absorbed the ideas of "utopian socialism" from some of his favorite French writers, such as Saint-Simon, Fourier, Proudhon, all opposed to what they referred to as "scientific" socialism.

The basic creed of the utopian socialists included a profound faith in the basic and natural goodness of man, the firm belief that true and perfect happiness could be brought about by purely "natural" means and the rejection of the idea of radical evil, of original sin and its supposed consequences, and of the Christian ideas concerning the need for a "redemption" and individual "salvation." What Dostoevsky believed in at that time was thus a sort of "natural" religion, that is, a Christianity without Golgotha, a Christianity that was not concerned with the sacrificial death of Christ but was anchored in the affirmation of the nobility and innate goodness and holiness of the human soul.

"In 1846," Dostoevsky wrote in his *Journal* (1873), "I was initiated [through Belinsky] into all the 'truth' of a future reborn world and into the saintliness of the future communistic society. . . . This doctrine I accepted passionately." Dostoevsky never entirely relinquished this kind of Christian naturalism, this faith in the hidden but nonetheless authentic perfection, or rather perfectibility, of human nature.

Before being shipped to Siberia, Dostoevsky had been told that he was condemned to death and, with a group of fellow political prisoners, he had been led to the place of execution in Semenevsky Square in St. Petersburg. The condemned men learned only at the very last moment that they had been pardoned by order of the Czar and that the death penalty had been changed to a condemnation to forced labor in Siberia.

After his release, Dostoevsky stayed in Siberia for several more years. He married and he resumed his writing. In 1859 he received permission to return to St. Petersburg. In 1861 Dostoevsky, jointly with his brother, began to edit the review *Time* (*Vremja*), in the pages of which they preached the new ideas of "blood and soil" (*potchvennipchestvo*), trying to reconcile the Western and Slavophile ideologies: "We envisage that . . . the Russian idea will bring about a symbiotic synthesis of all ideas that have been developed in European history."

Dostoevsky's literary production after his Siberian exile includes among other works *Notes from the Underground* (1864), *Crime and Punishment* (1866), *The Idiot* (1868), *The Possessed* (1871), *The Diary of an Author* (1873–1877, 3 vols.), *The Brothers Karamazov* (1879–1880). A speech which Dostoevsky delivered in 1880 on the occasion of the unveiling of a monument to the first of the great Russian writers, Alexander Pushkin, made such a powerful impression that in the general enthusiasm all the differences among the Russian intellectuals seemed to be momentarily forgotten. All were captured by Dostoevsky's proclamation of the brotherhood of a "universal mankind."

Dostoevsky died in 1881, mourned by Russians of all strata of society. His funeral was attended by students, writers, scholars, even by large numbers of children.

The basis of all the thinking and writing of Dostoevsky was his religious search. Like Kirillov in *The Possessed,* he was "tormented" all his life by the idea of God. While he never doubted the existence of God, he always asked himself these two questions: First, what are the consequences of the existence of God for the world, for man and for human action in history? Second, how can the evil in man and in history, how can human suffering be explained and made acceptable from a theological point of view? These are indeed the basic questions in any attempted theodicy or natural theology. Dostoevsky gave different answers to these two questions at different times but, like Unamuno, at all times he struggled and wrestled with God and with the idea of God.

Dostoevsky was firmly convinced that somehow and in some way Christianity and civilization must be harmonized. He rejected the secularization of culture and was opposed to the separation of civilization from the Church. He was equally opposed to radical individualism and to modern atheism and materialism. His socialistic ideas had deep roots in his religious thought.

There always remained, however, a basic dichotomy or ambivalence in Dostoevsky's thinking. The "natural" freedom which he desired and proclaimed was fatefully destined to end in tragic failure and frustration because he was or became convinced that the double-edged sword of freedom was almost bound to lead man into sinful pride and depravity. Dostoevsky never found a real synthesis between his belief in "Christian naturalism," on the one hand, and his distrust of anything that was *merely* "natural," on the other. He passionately advocated the sacredness of the human person, on the one hand, and proclaimed on the other hand that "beauty will save the world," while almost simultaneously he, like Leo Tolstoy, bitterly meditated on the fact that "beauty is a terribly dangerous thing."

Dostoevsky's entire *Weltanschauung* consists essentially of variations on the one theme of human existence. Nothing is to him more worthy of consideration, nothing more precious, nothing more terrible than man. Man thus is the prime enigma. Yet with all his inherent contradictions, man—even in the most insignificant representative of the species—possesses an absolute value. If it is true that Dostoevsky was tormented by the idea of God he, like Pascal before him, was surely no less tormented by the idea of man, by man's misery and depravity as much as by man's grandeur. In his anthropological views Dostoevsky shows himself particularly intrigued by the "subterranean" region in man, that region which Freud, Jung and William James were later to refer to as the unconscious or subconscious.

In portraying and analyzing human characters, Dostoevsky depicts not only sin, vice, egotism and, generally speaking, the realm of the "demonic" in man, but just as powerfully and convincingly the justice and goodness or what he called the "angelic principle" in the human soul. Both his psychological and ontological descriptions are permeated by the element of the moral or the ethical, the struggle between good and evil. The true essence of man he saw in human freedom and in it alone. Human dignity is founded on self-affirmation and on the consciousness of human independence as against the supposed iron necessity which rules in nature. Man is authentically a self only by virtue of his moral life. In this respect he is unique and incomparable. The great enigma that man is consists precisely in the fact that he is a moral being and that as such "he is concerned with his own being" (Heidegger): man finds himself inescapably confronted with the dilemma of choosing between good and evil, and he who does not follow without deviation the path of goodness finds himself sooner or later fatefully caught in the web of evil.

The "subterranean man" gives the lie to the fiction that man is a reasonable and sensible being. This fiction does not take account of the fact that human nature includes in its possibilities all conscious and subconscious life. Desire may coincide with rational judgment, but very often and even most of the time desire contradicts rational judgment completely and obstinately. Judgment or understanding satisfies only the intellectual faculties of man, whereas desire is the manifestation of human life in its totality. Thus, in order to learn to understand man, we must go beyond and beneath reason and consciousness: we must descend to that "underground" where man is truly himself. In this subterranean region where man, that is, the "natural" man, is freed from all traditions and conventions, there is stench, chaos, evil; there are primitive drives, criminal designs; there is shamelessness uninhibited. There man is tempted to say with Raskolnikov (and with Nietzsche) that "everything is permitted," and nothing prohibits man to consent to any crime. In this abysmal depth, morality is deprived of every foundation, and liberty turns into a chaotic amoralism.

Raskolnikov, Stavrogin, Ivan Karamazov and most of the other Dostoevskyan "heroes" suffer because they have stifled in themselves the sentiment of the good (that is, the sentiment of God): *they are left alone with themselves.* And whenever man is left alone with himself, he becomes a slave of his own passions. Man has been created a moral being, and he cannot cease at will being a moral being. Crime thus testifies negatively to the fact that by divorcing himself from the good, man loses something very precious without which he cannot live a human life. It is their freedom that causes Dostoevsky's heroes to deviate from traditional morality, thus pushing them into their crimes and thereby implanting in them the seed of death. Man then enters the realm of demonic possession. But man cannot radically renounce the good and continue to live a life on the human level.

And yet freedom for Dostoevsky is not man's ultimate truth or value. The ultimate truth is determined by the root principle of morality, by that power which enables man to use or abuse his freedom. And this is the reason why freedom may bear within itself an element of self-destruction. It may, if used rightly, elevate man to the heights of a spiritual transfiguration. When used rightly, freedom makes man free to develop the "angelic principle" in his nature. But if freedom is abused or misused, it leaves man free to follow the course of demonic possession.

Frequently if is only by suffering and through crime and sin that man becomes capable of freeing himself from the temptations of evil and of turning again toward the good and toward God, that is, toward Christ, the God-Man. He, on the other hand, who rejects the God-Man will of necessity in the end worship the "man-god"; that is, he will arrive at the deification or idolization of man.

Man's authentic and creative attitude toward life has its measure or standard in a love which surpasses reason and understanding. Love becomes suprarational by being elevated to that "Franciscan love" which entertains an inner relationship with the entire world, animate and inanimate, the world of creatures and the world of things. "Love all things, and you will perceive the mystery of God in all things." This universalism of love, however, rests entirely on the experience of the living God. "It is not beauty which will save the world; it is the beauty in the world that must be saved," says Dmitry Karamazov. And the elder Verkhovensky in *The Possessed:* "The nations and peoples of the world are moved by a force whose origin is unknown and inexplicable. . . . The philosophers call it the esthetic principle; the peoples call it the moral principle; *I* call it simply the *search for God*."

In 1880, one year before his death, when Dostoevsky delivered that euolgy to honor the memory of Pushkin, Vladimir Solovyov referred to it as Dostoevsky's "last word and testament." In this speech Dostoevsky said: "To be a true Russian means to attempt a reconciliation in his own self of the European contradictions . . . and thus perhaps to speak the final word on the great universal harmony, the brotherly concord of all nations, in accordance with the evangelical law of Christ. . . . I am convinced that the *Russian* people above all others is called and destined to bring about such a brotherly union."

Because Dostoevsky himself gained most of his insights and his knowledge from suffering, he saw in the Russian people's capacity for suffering its predestination for becoming the "God-bearing" people, that is, a people that bears within itself the possibility of bringing about a transformation and eventual transfiguration of the world. This transformation was to grow out of the inwardness of man purified by suffering. To make this transformation of the world a reality, man must join his own forces with those powers which are not of this world. It is for this reason that Solovyov regarded Dostoevsky as the precursor of a "new religious art." For "art which has divorced itself from religion must freely enter into a new union with religion."

For Dostoevsky the standard of measurement for his judgment was his faith, a faith which elevated him above the currents of the zeitgeist and saved him from ever becoming submerged in them. His faith was truly a *fides quaerens intellectum* (Anselm of Canterbury).

Dostoevsky firmly believed in the coming of the Kingdom of God, and he realized that it was necessary therefore for man to work and sacrifice for this future realm. And he was convinced that it was his right as well as his duty to call for such work and such sacrifice because he himself had in his youth strayed far from the goal by following the wrong path. He knew from bitter personal experience what he was talking about. Thus his attitude became that of a man who felt his own heavy share in the guilt of all others, a man who felt the deepest compassion with his erring contemporaries. Dostoevsky's message cannot be understood logically or rationally, but only by a sharing of his will and desire for rebirth and resurrection. The fact that he experienced evil and iniquity more strongly than most of his contemporaries enabled him to descend into the subterranean regions of the "underground man" and to unmask the evils of the age long before their consequences became visible and tangible for all.

In the pages of the review *The Epoch* (*Epokha*), which Dostoevsky founded in 1860, he fought uncompromisingly against the materialism, the liberal enlightenment, and the atheism of the age. With the elder Verkhovensky he regarded the Liberals as the precursors of the atheists. And he expressed the conviction that all these negative tendencies had their roots in the modern scientific (or rather scientistic) concepts of the world and of human existence. "Think of it, young man," says Staretz Zosima in *The Brothers Karamazov*, "that secular science, which has become such a great force, has especially in the last century torn down all those divine things which were handed down to us in the books of the saints." And in the same novel it is stated that socialism is not merely a labor problem or a problem of the proletariat but primarily the problem of atheism, the problem of the contemporary incarnation of atheism and, more specially, the problem of the Tower of Babel, a tower which is being built without God, not for the purpose of reaching heaven from the earth but rather for the purpose of pulling heaven down to the worldy level.

Socialism, atheism, materialism and scientific positivism Dostoevsky regarded as the effects of one basic attitude which he calls Nihilism. By Nihilism he did not mean a totally negative passive pessimism but rather an empty, meaningless destructive activism, a superficial optimistic self-assurance, an attitude which Turgenev, the most "Western" of the great Russian writers, had portrayed in the nihilist Basarov in the novel *Fathers and Sons*, published in 1862. Basarov offers such pearls of the wisdom of "progressive enlightenment" as: "I prefer a piece of cheese to all the works of Pushkin"; or, "Any shoemaker is more important for mankind than either Goethe or Shakespeare"; or again, "An experienced chemist is twenty times more valuable than the best poet." Dostoevsky claimed that this kind of Nihilism was hiding its inner emptiness and barbarism behind the glittering facade of an unprincipled and ultimately aimless belief in progress.

The main characters of Dostoevsky's novels are illustrations of the horrible errors which Nihilism brings of necessity in its wake. One of these errors is the assertion that the city of man can be built without morality on the foundations of pure reason and scientific empiricism. This is the Nihilism of Shigalev (in the novel *The Possessed*) and his proposed system of "shigalevism."

Dostoevsky sees in this kind of a system the threatening emergence of the "herd" of the Antichrist. In this system only that is regarded as evil which disturbs the listless egalitarianism of the members of the herd. And as the Christian community rests on its communion with the blood of Christ, so the community of the Antichrist rests on the community of the blood of its victims: its "possessed" members are joined and chained together by their crimes.

For Dostoevsky, as for Sartre, freedom is the ultimate criterion of man's humanity. And freedom is lost whenever the superman or the man-god takes the place of God and the God-Man. Since only the Truth can make man free, the *hybris* of mere rebellious self-assertion is bound to lead ultimately to enslavement and to the internal and external destruction and extinction of man.

To this kind of Nihilism Dostoevsky opposes what he regards as Christianity in its pure, unadulterated form, which for him is embodied in that Russian Orthodox Church which he so loved and to which he belonged. The Christianity which Dostoevsky endorses must combine freedom and universal love, so that out of shared suffering the new community may arise. Thus the ideal order of life is not the *civitas terrena* but the *Civitas Coelestis*, that is, the moral world order, sanctioned by Christ and His Church. However, by presenting the Russian people as a new manifestation of Christ, destined to overcome Western Nihilism, the danger of a nationalistically narrowed Pan-Slavism and of a deification or idolization of the Russian people became almost inevitable. And Dostoevsky partially succumbed to this temptation. He never succeeded in attaining a genuine understanding of the truths embodied in other nations and peoples. Thus he occasionally indulges in ridiculous generalizations, in calling, for example, the French a nation of "vain dandies," the Germans a nation of "sausagemakers," the British a nation of "sophistic shopkeepers." Nonetheless, the abiding idea dearest to Dostoevsky's heart and mind was the reconciliation of the East and West, of Rome and Byzantium, both united in freedom and in eternal divine Truth.

Speaking about his vocation as an author, Dostoevsky wrote: "They call me a psychologist, but this is not true: I am a *realist* in the highest sense of the term; that is to say, I show the reality of the depth of the human soul." It is not the novel as such which is important to Dostoevsky, but rather the "idea" that underlies the novel. The real plot of his novels is always a spiritual adventure. In all our Western literature, commented André Gide, the novel, with few exceptions, deals only with the relations between man and man, relations of the passions or the intellect, family relations, social or class relations, but it never troubles itself about the relations of the individual with himself or with God—relationships which in Dostoevsky take absolute priority: most of his novels are reflections on the immortality of the soul and the existence of God. What torments his heroes is not illness or fear of the tomorrow: it is always God.

Some critics have seen in *The Possessed* a prophetic vision of the Bolshevik revolution. But Dostoevsky was a prophet in a much broader and deeper sense: he not only revealed to man the depths that are within him, but he opened up a new dimension in humanity as a whole. Raskolnikov, Stavrogin, Ivan Karamazov, and even the Grand Inquisitor strive for a region which Nietzsche termed "beyond good and evil," a region in which the human soul is revealed in its essential and unique quality. "I declare," said Dostoevsky of himself, "that love of mankind is something completely inconceivable, incomprehensible and even impossible without faith in the immortality of the individual human soul."

Dostoevsky the prophet was acutely aware of the crisis in the situation of modern man. Like Nietzsche, he lived this crisis. He too was personally present at the "death of God." He too foresaw the coming "religion of atheism" and the reign of the "superman." However, after having envisioned and lived the crisis, he tried with all his might to overcome it.

In *The Possessed*, Kirillov, the atheist, confesses: "God has tormented me all my life." The chief problem, said Dostoevsky, in pondering the main theme of a series of novels he intended to write, will be the one "that has consciously and unconsciously tortured me all my life: the problem of the existence of God." What tortured him and his heroes in particular was the mysteries of evil and suffering and the problem of how they could be reconciled with the *reality* of God.

With Ivan Karamazov, Dostoevsky rejected the world as it is at present, and with Ivan he rebelled "against all optimistic theology, shorn of its tragic elements." Nicholas Berdyaev avers that Dostoevsky's theodicy, that is, his justification of God, is at the same time a justification of man.

The argument everlastingly used against God is the existence of evil in the world, and the whole of Dostoevsky's work is an answer to that argument. I would sum it up, in a paradoxical form, thus: *The existence of evil is a proof of the existence of God. If the world consisted wholly and uniquely of goodness and righteousness there would be no need for God, for the world itself would be god. God is, because evil is. And that means that God is because freedom is.*

Thus does Dostoevsky arrive at the existence of God through a consideration of the freedom of the human spirit: those of his characters who deny this freedom deny God, and inversely. A world in which goodness and righteousness reign by compulsion, whose harmony is insured by undeniable necessity, is a godless world, a rationalized mechanism, and to reject God and human liberty is to push the world in that direction. The problem of evil and of wrongdoing is thus part and parcel of the problem of freedom.

"Wherever there is freedom there is evil: if there were no freedom then God alone would be responsible for evil."*

According to Dostoevsky, "Freedom degenerates into arbitrary selfwill, this leads to evil, and evil leads to criminal wrongdoing." Crime has thus a very important place in Dostoevsky's work; he was indeed, in his own way, a criminologist as well as an anthropologist. Berdyaev writes:

> Humanitarianism denies evil because it denies personality, and Dostoevsky combatted humanitarianism in the name of mankind. . . . The Staretz Zosima and Alyosha have known evil and have come through it to a higher state. Alyosha is by no means free from the troubles that arise from being a Karamazov: he is the man who has emerged victorious from the test of freedom. . . . To speak of wrongdoing raises the question of what is allowable. Everything? This is a question that always troubled Dostoevsky. . . . It is behind *Crime and Punishment* and, to a considerable extent, behind *The Possessed* and *The Brothers Karamazov*. . . . Are there moral norms and limits in my nature or may I venture to do anything? When freedom has degenerated into self-will it recognizes nothing as sacred or forbidden, for if there be no god but man then everything is allowable. . . .

Man then "lets himself get obsessed by some fixed idea, and under its tyranny freedom soon begins to disappear." Berdyaev responds to his own question:

> All things are *not* allowable because . . . human nature is created in the image of God and every man has an absolute value in himself and as such. The spiritual nature of man forbids the arbitrary killing of even the least and most harmful of men . . . it is a crime that no "idea" or "higher end" can justify. Our neighbor is more precious than an abstract notion, and human life and person is worth more here and now than some future bettering of society. That is the Christian conception, and it is Dostoevsky's.†

Dostoevsky himself "discovers that he is no superman but a weak, abject and unreliable creature. His experiment with his freedom—as did Raskolnikov's experiment—had a disastrous result." And as

*Nicholas Berdyaev, *Dostoevsky*. Trans. by Donald Attwater (New York: Living Age Books, 1959), pp. 87 ff.
†Berdyaev, *op. cit.*, pp. 91–97 (passim).

in the case of Raskolnikov, "the powerlessness of man and his pre-
tension to almightiness are revealed in sorrow and anguish; the
tortured conscience of Raskolnikov is a witness not only to his
transgression but also to his weakness."* It is Berdyaev's judgment
that the case of Raskolnikov illustrates the crisis of every man-
centered humanism: it leads of necessity to the suicide of man by
virtue of his absolute self-affirmation. The man-god always kills
true manhood and the "death of God" has as its necessary sequel
the demise of man.

In the novel *The Possessed*, Dostoevsky shows the fatal effects of
the twisted conscience that is brought about by collectivism as much
as by exaggerated rugged individualism, because in either case God
is excluded. Thus we see in the example of Peter Verkhovensky
how man can lose all human likeness. "Every criterion of good and
evil is then thrown aside, and life is lived in an atmosphere heavy
with violence and blood. The murder of Shatov, for instance, has
a horrifying effect: there is something everlasting and prophetic in
this entire passage of *The Possessed*. . . . Peter Verkhovensky, one of
Dostoevsky's most monstrous types, . . . has become unable to
repent. He is one of those who . . . have no future in human destiny
but . . . fall into nothingness."†

On the plane of pure reason Dostoevsky finds no answer to all
these problems. However, he insists that Christ did not come to
explain suffering rationally or to solve neatly the problem of evil:
He took evil upon Himself to deliver man from it.

In Raskolnikov, Kirillov and Stavrogin, it is their diabolical
pride which prevents them from accepting the reality of God. With
Feuerbach, Stirner and Nietzsche, they think that man will be able
to accomplish much greater things as soon as the spectre of the deity
has been removed from the human horizon.

Dostoevsky himself had thoroughly explored the possibilities of

*Berdyaev, *ibid.*, p. 98.
†Nicholas Berdyaev, *Dostoevsky* (New York: Living Age Books, 1957), pp. 89–102
(*passim*).

man without God. He had pondered the possibility that the ideas of good and evil might be nothing but prejudices on the part of the weak. Whenever he passed judgment on the immoralist, he did so on the basis of a profound understanding of both sides of the argument. In the person who denies God he discerned not only the horror and misery of betrayal but also the greatness of the drive for absolute self-assertion. This is forcefully brought out in the conversation between Stavrogin and Bishop Tihon: Stavrogin has decided to confess all his crimes to the Bishop. He goes to the monastery where Tihon lives in seclusion, and he finds an old monk who shows a deep understanding for Stavrogin's plight. Stavrogin makes it clear from the outset of the conversation that he is not moved by any feeling of repentance, that in fact he is an incorrigible, unredeemable and unrepentant atheist:

"Perfect atheism," replies Tihon, "is worth more than worldly indifference. . . . Perfect atheism stands high up the ladder, on the rung below that which leads to perfect faith . . . while indifference has no trace of faith."

"Have you read the Apocalypse?" asks Stavrogin. "I know the passage. I remember it," replies Tihon. "Do you know it by heart?" inquires Stavrogin. "Then say it." And Bishop Tihon begins reciting: " 'And unto the Angel of the Church of the Laodiceans write: These things says the Amen, the faithful and true witness, the beginning of God's creation: I know your works, I know that you are neither cold nor hot. I wish you were cold or hot, but because you are lukewarm and neither cold nor hot, I will spit you out of my mouth.' "

But is the "believer" certain of his faith? Is he not also human— all too human, like everyone else? Can the believer fail to see that "strength of the earth," that "violent and brutal force" which impels Stavrogin to oppose God? Ivan, the skeptic, also has some glimmerings of faith, and Alyosha, the monk, has occasionally feelings of doubt and skepticism. This is in all probability the reason why Gorbatchev, one of the Soviet editors of Dostoevsky's *Letters*, could say in his preface that Dostoevsky "has left us magnificent models of anti-religious propaganda." As a matter of fact, Dostoevsky in his novels frees himself from his antireligious temptations. Shortly before his death, commenting on the criticisms which his last novel, *The Brothers Karamazov*, had received, Dostoevsky wrote in his journal: "These dolts have ridiculed my obscurantism and the reactionary character of my faith. These fools could not even conceive of so strong a denial of God as the one to which I gave expression. . . . You might search Europe in vain for so powerful an expression of atheism. Thus it is not like a child that I believe in Christ and profess Him. My hosanna has come forth from the crucible of doubt."

Dostoevsky was not too much concerned with the search for God up to the time of his penal servitude. He was at first imprisoned in St. Petersburg, in the Fortress of St. Peter and Paul, and from there he wrote a letter to his brother asking for some books and, in particular, for the Bible. Soon thereafter he was deported to Siberia. There the convicts were allowed no books except the Bible. When Dostoevsky finally came under a less rigorous regime, he immediately asked for the works of the Church Fathers, to aid him in his scriptural studies.

While he was in prison, Dostoevsky's faith in Christ and in Christianity struck very deep roots. He speaks of this in the first letter he wrote after his release, a letter addressed to Madame Wisine: "If anyone had told me that Christ is outside the Truth, and if it had really been proven that the Truth is outside Christ, I should have preferred to stay with Christ rather than with the Truth." He even put into the mouth of Kirillov, that fanatical atheist, a hymnic praise of Christ. And the inscrutable Stavrogin utters words which express Dostoevsky's own profession of faith.

In *The Possessed* the idea recurs again and again that the reason why the West is moribund is that it has lost Christ. And in the notes which served as a preparation for this novel, we read:

True, it is possible to argue . . . that Christianity will not fall to the ground if Christ is regarded as a mere man, as a philosopher who went about doing good, and that, moreover, Christianity is neither a necessity for mankind nor a source of life . . . but that it is *science* that will be able to vitalize life and to set up a perfect ideal. . . . But we know . . . that all this is utterly absurd; we know that Christ, considered as merely a man, is not the Savior and the source of all life; we know that no science will ever realize the human ideal and that, for mankind, peace—the source of life and salvation and the indispensable condition for the existence of the entire world—is contained in the saying, "The Word was made flesh."

Among the atheists we meet in *The Possessed*, Kirillov is the one who has most in common with the author of this novel. He exemplifies the Nietzschean temptation of the man-god in its purest form. Kirillov is a mystic who has a fervent admiration for Christ and also a self-sacrificing love for his neighbor. "In him extreme atheism is joined with sainthood," writes Jacques Madaule. But Kirillov is actually a madman. The idea from which he starts out is that life presents itself to contemporary man in its aspects of suffering and terror, and this is what leads him astray. "Man is not yet but he will one day become," says Kirillov. "There will be a new kind of man, happy and proud. . . . The one who overcomes suffering and terror will himself be a god. And the God above will no longer exist." That God above has, Kirillov argues, never really existed except as a figment of man's mind: He has grown out of man's fear of death, a fear which keeps man in bondage and from which he must free himself. Then the second phase of human history can begin and will begin—its divine phase. The first phase began with the ape, the second will begin with the annihilation of God. But someone must dare make a start; someone must have the courage to kill himself in order to kill the fear of death, that is, to kill God. But nobody has as yet dared. True enough, there are millions of suicides, but never for that reason. Men kill themselves in fear, not in order to kill fear itself. The man who will kill himself solely in order to kill fear will immediately become a god.

Kirillov is, in the opinion of Henri de Lubac, S.J., the representative and spokesman of atheistic humanism. He intends to proclaim the man-god, and he is trying to be a second Christ. He will complete

Christ's sacrifice by killing himself. "I shall be a savior," Kirillov says in his rantings. "This is the only thing that will save all men and transform them physically . . . for in their present physical state it seems to me that it is impossible for men to do without the old God. . . . " Stavrogin and Verkhovensky are greatly amused: "I am prepared to bet," says Stavrogin, "that when I return I shall find you already believing in God." And Verkhovensky, more brutally: "You are even fuller of belief than a Russian Pope!"*

Kirillov's atheism, like that of Nietzsche, illustrates the fact that the human will by its very nature aspires to the good in its plenitude, that is, to pure goodness. This striving can be fully satisfied only in a Being who is in himself this infinite plenitude of the Good. This means that every will, even the most perverse, desires God under many errant forms (or desires "to become God," as Sartre would say). "Atheism," writes Jacques Maritain, "if it could be lived down to its ultimate roots in the will, would disorganize and kill the will metaphysically. . . . Every absolute experience of atheism, if it is conscientiously and rigorously followed, ends by provoking its dissolution, in suicide" (Maritain, *True Humanism*, (New York: Scribner's Sons, 1959), p. 53).

Kirillov tries to live atheism down to its metaphysical roots. A few minutes before he commits suicide he argues:

If God exists, all things depend on Him, and *I* can do nothing outside His will. If He does not exist, then all depends on *me*, and I am bound to demonstrate my *independence*. . . . For three years I have been searching for the attribute of my divinity, and now at long last I have found it: the attribute of my divinity is my *absolute independence*. That is all I can do to prove in the highest degree my absolute autonomy and my new and terrible freedom. For this freedom *is* terrible. I shall kill myself to prove my independence and my terrible new freedom.

The profoundest metaphysical attribute of the Deity is *aseitas*, that is, total self-sufficiency of being. And it is this attribute which

*See Henri de Lubac, S.J., *The Drama of Atheist Humanism* (New York: Sheed and Ward, 1950), *passim*.

Kirillov, the atheist, must manifest in himself: he must subordinate his own existence to his own absolute independence (Maritain, *ibid.*).

The Possessed was written with a polemic purpose. Dostoevsky stayed at Dresden in Germany when he was told by his brother-in-law of the recent murder of a student named Ivanov by a band of fellow terrorists, the Netchaevians, who had suspected him of treachery. Dostoevsky was deeply shocked, and his hatred of the revolutionary socialist ideas was increasing with every passing day. He finally resolved to strike a decisive blow, and he set to work at once. The murder of Shatov in the novel is modelled upon the murder of Ivanov. Peter Verkhovensky, the head of the band of terrorists, is at once a double and a caricature of Netchaev. Stavrogin, too, shows several features that are borrowed from the character of Netchaev. Gradually, however, the novel assumed truly epic proportions, and this carried it far beyond the original polemic purpose. The novel thus became a descent into the darkest depths of the human psyche and at the same time a warning prophetic message addressed to all of Western Europe. Dostoevsky's ferocity towards the revolutionaries whose portraits he sketches is matched only by an equal lack of pity for the world which they intend to undermine, namely, the bourgeois world.

The revolutionary Socialists are portrayed as the heirs of those Liberals who had been the first ones to espouse atheism. "To annihilate God" was the first point in their program, and now the Socialists merely drew the logical radical conclusions from the liberal premises. The Socialists were no longer content with a vague belief in progress: they were actually trying to build a new humanity without God. The first phase of their work had to be wholly destructive: the old society must be destroyed, especially everything in it that owed its origin to a faith in God. Nothing in man must permit a recourse to some supernatural origin or some so-called sacred destiny. Once this preliminary spadework was done, the new social structure could then be erected on the basis of pure science. Eventually the happiness of mankind must be thoroughly scientifically organized.

But now the question arises: How free will the man be who has freed himself from God? Only one of the companions of Verkhovensky has given some serious thought to this question, and he has worked out a complete plan for what is to follow the revolution. This man is Shigalev. His system is really very simple: "Having set out from *unlimited freedom,* I have ended up with *unlimited despotism.*" Shigalev is, of course, a maniac but he is also a "realist." He has arrived at the conclusion that "all the former framers of social systems . . . have been dreamers, tellers of fairy tales, simpletons who contradict themselves and know nothing of natural science, nothing about that strange animal called man. One must simply divide mankind into two sections: one-tenth will exercise absolute authority over the other nine-tenths. This is the one necessary condition for the establishment of the *earthly paradise.*" Shigalev likes the suggestion that it would be even more logical to liquidate the other nine-tenths; then there would be nothing left but "a handful of educated men who, organizing themselves according to scientific principles, would live happily ever after." But, alas, it may prove a little too complicated to put this grandiose idea into practice. So Shigalev prefers his own idea of the earthly paradise.

The idea which Dostoevsky wants to convey to his readers is that social systems which have no religious basis inevitably become systems of violence and enslavement. For Dostoevsky, the fatal mistake which these pretentious builders of the Tower of Babel make lies in the fact that they believe the basic need of man is the sort of happiness that can be found in such an earthly paradise. But far more than he needs happiness, man, according to Dostoevsky, needs to know and believe that there is something infinitely great before which man can stand in wonder, awe and reverence. Even the atheist pays homage to this infinite Something or Someone when he sets up his human idols for worship (see the tomb of Lenin, for example). The emancipated Nihilist is at the same time an idolator like Peter Verkhovensky, who tells Stavrogin: "You are my idol . . . . You are the sun, and I am your earth worm." In other words, if man rejects God, he will sooner or later have to kneel before an idol of wood or of gold or even of poor human flesh. As Martin Luther expressed it with profound psychological insight, "Man is made in such a way that he either worships God or an idol."

Kirillov feels that he is different from all the rest. He is obsessed with his own idea: "I cannot think of anything else. I spend my whole life thinking of this same thing. God torments me, I think of nothing but that." And Kirillov thinks he has discovered the reason why he is different from all the others: "The others are flitting from distraction to distraction; *they forget to be themselves*. If this were not so, they would all see and confess that God is tormenting them."

Stavrogin drops in for a visit, and he finds Kirillov playing with a baby girl, and Kirillov confesses that he loves children, that he loves life. If this is the case, why is he determined to blow his brains out?

KIRILLOV: "Why, what is the connection? Life exists and death does not exist."

STAVROGIN: "So you do believe in a future eternal life?"

KIRILLOV: "No, not in a future eternal life but in an earthly eternal life. There are moments . . . when suddenly time stands still and becomes eternity."

STAVROGIN: "And you hope to attain to a moment like that?"

KIRILLOV: "Yes."

Kirillov points out that in the Apocalypse the Angel announces the coming of a day when time will be no more. When humanity attains happiness, time will no longer be necessary. "Time is not a thing but a concept. It will vanish from the understanding."

Kirillov has a foreknowledge of that day because he has already attained occasional glimpses of ineffable happiness. And it is the same with respect to goodness, he rationalizes. Men are not good because they do not know that they are good. Thus they must be taught that they are good, and then they will become good immediately. This kind of man, this kind of teacher will be instrumental in bringing the world to an end. And he, Kirillov, will be that teacher, that man-god. For he knows now that he is happy and he knows that he is good. His faith cannot be shaken, for it rests not only on logic but on experience:

It sometimes happens that for a few seconds . . . you suddenly feel, in an absolute way, the presence of an eternal harmony. It is not like anything *earthly*, and I don't say that it is heavenly either, but I do say that man in his earthly form cannot endure it. He must be transformed physically or die. . . . When God created the world, He said, according to Genesis, at the end of each day, "Yes, that is true, that is good, indeed very good." You do not *forgive* anything, because there *is* nothing to forgive. Nor do you *love*—this is something much better than love.

But for poor Kirillov these blissful states of mind are merely the premonitory symptoms of an approaching fit of epilepsy. In those blissful states which precede the epileptic attack, he feels a tenfold intensification of life and of awareness; his mind is illumined with an intense clarity; all his anxieties die and give way to a supreme calm, while reason rises to such a pitch that it can "even grasp final causes."

Shatov, too, is a mystic of sorts. After having joined Peter Verkhovensky's gang of terrorists, he tries to extricate himself from the conspiracy. He has come to realize the madness of this entire socialist venture, which proposes to build a universe exclusively on reason and science. He knows from history that reason and science have never performed more than minor functions, that nations and civilizations always act on the compulsion of forces whose origin remains mysterious. Is this higher force not "the spirit of life" of which the scriptures speak? "I will merely say," Shatov concludes these reflections, "that this force is the *search for God.* . . . There has never yet been a nation without religion, that is to say, without a definite idea of good and evil . . . and reason alone has never been capable of distinguishing between good and evil . . . as for *science,*

it has only been able to supply very crude solutions . . . superficial
science is a tyrant the like of which has never been known until
our own times."

To Stravrogin's argument that Shatov intends to reduce God to
an attribute of the Russian people, Shatov replies: "On the contrary,
I am trying to raise the Russian people to the level of God! The
people are the body of God. . . . A nation remains a nation only as
long as it has its particular God and fiercely disapproves of all other
gods."

Shatov distinguishes two classes of nations: on the one hand, "the
great nations of the world" and, on the other hand, mere "ethno-
graphical material. . . . A great nation is a nation which believes
that it is the sole repository of the Truth, that it is the only one
called and the only one capable of . . . saving the world by its
particular truths; as soon as it ceases to believe that, it is done for."
"As there is only *one* truth, there cannot be more than one single
nation which possesses the true God. . . . The only people 'bearing
God' is the Russian people . . . ." This, in short, is Shatov's religion.

Shatov embodies some tendencies in Dostoevsky's own thinking.
Dostoevsky himself believed in Russia as a "God-bearing people,"
and he almost identified the Russian people with God; he remained
convinced that Russian thought had the mission to regenerate the
world. His "messianic orthodoxy" tended to fuse with the Pan-
Slavic idea. Nonetheless, Dostoevsky did not (like Shatov) confuse
mystical nationalism with Christian faith. Shatov's answers to
Stravrogin's intensive questioning are always evasive. Stavrogin, as
usual, goes to the heart of the matter: "I should like to know this:

Do you yourself believe in God? Yes or no?" "I believe in Russia," Shatov
replies, "in its Orthodoxy. . . . I believe in *the body of Christ*. I believe that
it is in Russia where the new advent will take place. . . . I believe," Shatov
stammered, as if he were raving.

STAVROGIN: "But in God, do you believe in God?"
SHATOV: "I . . . shall believe in God."

Verkhovensky, Shatov and Kirillov are all three, as it were, the offspring of Stavrogin, who, "an extinct force, casts off his own unutilized possibilities," each of which becomes incarnate in another creature. But they are also to some extent incarnations of Dostoevsky's own ideas. However, for Dostoevsky the spiritual world, the realm of eternity, was and remained enshrined in and sanctioned by sacred scripture, and the only way to enter this world of the spirit is by conversion (*metánoia*), that "new birth of which the Gospels speak." It is the mystery of the Cross which both guards and opens up this realm. All nature is for Dostoevsky a sign and symbol of the spirit. And Christ abides as the center of this spiritual world.

Dostoevsky thus became the prophet of a "resurrection" which presupposes the experience of death. He had been granted in an extraordinary way a double anticipation of this experience: we know that in the experience which precedes an epileptic seizure there is a striking similarity with the last moments in the life of a condemned man, when the executioner's axe is about to fall. And Dostoevsky speaks of the singular light which that fatal moment casts upon the totality of existence. He had actually experienced that moment when, as a young man, in Semenevsky Square in St. Petersburg, he was at the point of being executed by a firing squad. From that crucial point onward he saw the world from the perspective of death, that is, from the perspective of eternity. He remained in this world like a man who has come from a strange planet. He saw things differently from everyone else. He had reached what Karl Jaspers would call the "extreme limit-situation," the frontiers of humanity.

Dostoevsky, like Kierkegaard, Nietzsche and Heidegger, visualizes the ultimate consequences of the situation of modern man. They all described the frightening experience of the radical finitude of man and the world. In the world view of antiquity and of the Middle Ages the finitude of the world and of man was sustained and permeated by the infinite and the eternal: the world and everything in it was regarded as a symbol or manifestation of the divine. The finite thus partook of the eternal and was therefore more than mere finitude. Everything in the world was seen as hierarchically ordered, either in the form of a pyramid or in some harmonious arrangement of spheres. Man was regarded as a microcosm, that is, as a small universe mirroring the macrocosm, the large universe, or as the center of the universe, or as its crown, or as the high priest of the created world.

From the fifteenth century onward the world begins to expand. The consciousness of being enveloped by the sheltering and sustaining divine power, goodness and beauty was gradually lost. The things of the world were losing their symbolic signification. They thus assumed the character of radical finitude. Man and world were supposed to be self-sufficient, absolutely autonomous. And man tried to find the meaning of his existence in his own self; he established himself resolutely in his finite situation, and in doing so he tried to appropriate more and more of the attributes of divinity: in short, he tried to absolutize himself.

One province of civilization after the other proclaimed its autonomy: politics, economics, art, literature, science, ethics, philosophy. The State became for Hegel the mouthpiece or the substitute of the divinity. The conscious experience of radical finitude caused at first a feeling of abandonment and of anguish, but later man discovered in his finiteness a new value and even a moral foundation of his existence, a new source of self-responsibility (for example, Feuerbach, Nietzsche and Sartre). In the eighteenth century there came into being a sort of "titanic finitism" (Romano Guardini). Finally, finiteness itself was deified: God was "dead" (Nietzsche). And thus finite reality remained as the one and only "real" reality. Mankind, it was proudly proclaimed, found its ultimate meaning within itself. If "everything is permitted," then everything becomes possible. There was no longer a supreme law, since there was no longer an Absolute Lawgiver.

It is against this cultural and intellectual background that the character of Stavrogin becomes intelligible. At the end of *The Possessed* there remain hopeless and universal desolation and destruction. And the reason for all these breakdowns can ultimately be traced to the personality of Stavrogin. What sort of a man is he? He has been spoiled and even adored by his ambitious and thoroughly frustrated mother, Varvara Petrovna Stavrogina. She lives only for her "prince," but she really does not understand him: she alternately fears him and worships him. And she feels in the end nothing but emptiness and despair. Varvara's foster daughter, Darja Pavlova Shatova, the sister of Shatov, is in love with Stavrogin. She hopes she may be able to save him by her complete self-surrender. Lisaveta Nicolaievna Tushina, too, loves Stavrogin. She is proud, passionate, but inwardly discordant. She feels safe and calm as long as she stays with the honest and loyal Mavriky Nicolaievitch Drosdov. In half-despair she finally yields to the aggressiveness of Stavrogin, but Lisaveta learns to her sorrow that Stavrogin's coldness is invincible. Now everything is lost, and when she is struck down during the conflagration (that was set by Fedka, the ex-convict, to destroy the corpse of Stavrogin's crippled and mentally deranged wife, Marja Lebedkina), it seems almost like a merciful stroke of fate. Poor Marja Lebedkina herself bears in her crippled body the soul of a romantic princess as well as the soul of a timid child and a visionary. Her feverish imagination has transformed the image of Stavrogin into that of a shining white knight, but she sees through her illusion before her tragic death. Shatov's wife, Marja Ignatievna Shatova, is another of Stavrogin's victims. He seduced her when they met abroad, and she returns to her husband, pregnant with Stavrogin's child. But during the short hours preceding Shatov's assassination she is instrumental in giving back to her husband, that enthusiastic dreamer, his faith in love and his sense of reality.

The male characters in the novel are equally infected by the evil that lurks in Stavrogin. Kirillov's mania and suicide are but the sprouting of a seed which Stavrogin had planted in his soul.

Stavrogin is also responsible for the destruction of Shatov's life: he is the seducer of both Shatov's sister, Darja, and Shatov's wife, Marja. It is Stavrogin, the man without faith himself—neither faith in God nor faith in the Russian people—who has generated in Shatov the demoniac pagan worship of the deified Russian people. It was supposed to be "an experiment in belief." Finally, there are all those other "demons," all creatures and puppets manipulated by the evil genius of Stavrogin: Peter Verkhovensky, the son of Stepan—ruthless, unscrupulous, cynical, destructive and vile. Peter has only one great superstition: a strange faith in the fantastic realm of an Emperor-Messiah whose still unknown ruler (or Czsarevitch) is to be Stavrogin; there is Captain Lebedkin, for whose violent death Stavrogin is responsible; there is Fedka, the ex-convict, to whom Stavrogin suggests the idea of the double murder of Marja and her brother, the Captain. Then there are Liputin, Lyamshin, and all the other "possessed."

Chapter 5 of the novel bears the title "The Subtle Serpent." In Section 5 of this chapter the reader witnesses Stavrogin's homecoming after a prolonged stay abroad. In his mother's house he comes upon a strange gathering of people: Lisaveta, Darja (who has just returned from Switzerland, where she had associated with Stavrogin), Marja Lebedkina (who has revealed her secret marriage to Stavrogin). Then Stavrogin enters. The narrator relates:

I was struck by the first sight of him just as I had been struck four years before, when I saw him for the first time . . . apparently he was exactly the same as he had been four years ago. He was as elegant, as dignified, and he moved with the same air of consequence as before, indeed he looked almost as young as at that time. His famed smile had the same graciousness and complacency. His eyes had the same stern, thoughtful and pre-occupied look. In fact, it seemed as though we had only parted the day before. But one thing struck me. In old days, though he had been considered handsome, his face was "like a mask," as some of our sharp-tongued ladies had expressed it. . . . I don't know why he impressed me at once as absolutely beautiful, so that no one could have said that his face was like a mask. Perhaps he was a little paler and rather thinner than before. Or was there, perhaps, the light of some new idea in his eyes?

Stavrogin's father had died prematurely, and he grew up under the loving care of his mother. His education was entrusted to his tutor, Stepan Verkhovensky. The young Nikolay was a rather weak and sickly boy, strangely calm and pensive, but later on he distinguished himself by extraordinary physical strength. At the age of sixteen he entered the lyceum and thereafter joined a cavalry regiment of the Imperial Guards. His mother supplied him with plenty of money. He was a great social success, but "suddenly the wild beast showed its claws. . . ." Suddenly, the narrator informs the reader, "our prince became guilty of incredible outrages. . . . He acted utterly silly and mischievous, quite unprovoked and objectless."

There is no doubt that Stavrogin is mentally ill. But what is the psychological and theological meaning of this illness? He hurts, humiliates and disgraces others with absolute calm and indifference. He observes the consequences of his actions as a detached spectator, or like a scientist who observes the results of his experiments. He wants to find out how the other person reacts to offenses, humiliations and disgrace. He travels abroad, visiting Europe, Egypt, Palestine; he takes part in an expedition to Iceland; he spends one winter studying at a famous German university; then he returns to Russia.

Stavrogin is physically strong. He also has a strong willpower. He demonstrates his physical powers in his encounter with Fedka, and his willpower in his conversation with Shatov and in his duel with Gaganov, an elderly high official in the military establishment. But Stavrogin is also very indolent. The narrator tells the reader that "he was lazy and perhaps even bored." However, his is the laziness of a beast of prey; he shakes it off whenever he springs into action. He knows himself that his inertia has deep roots in his being. Nikolay's inactivity is in part also due to the fact that he is a member of the lordly leisure class and that there is no compelling reason for him ever to be gainfully employed. Thus his strong potentialities remain without an object, without direction and without a goal. When occasionally he does spring into action, it is from sheer boredom, irritability, or perhaps from existential despair.

Inwardly, Stavrogin is cold and indifferent. It is the realization of this cold indifference that drives Lisaveta to her death. Stavrogin knows about his frigidity, and his indifference is prone to make him despair, but he is unable to shake if off.

The individuals who revolve about Stavrogin suspect that there must be some hidden treasures in his soul. And the manuscript of his "confession" reveals that they are not altogether wrong. There lives in the depth of his soul some indefinite and perhaps infinite longing, a dream of beauty:

I had a dream, which was totally surprising to me because I had never dreamed anything like this before. In the Dresden Gallery there hangs a painting by Claude Lorraine, called in the catalogue *Acis and Galatea*, but which I always like to call *The Golden Age*. . . . I went to the gallery simply in order to look at it, and it was perhaps for that reason alone that I stopped at Dresden. This picture appeared to me in a dream as though it were an actual scene.

As in the picture, I saw a corner of the Greek archipelago the way it was some three thousand years ago: caressing azure waves, rocks and islands, a shore in bloom, the magic panorama, a beckoning sunset—words fail me. European mankind remembers this place as its cradle, and the thought filled my soul with a love bred of kinship. Here was mankind's earthly paradise, gods descended from heaven and united with mortals. . . . Here lived beautiful men and women, . . . happy and innocent; the great overflow of unspent energies poured itself into love and simple joys. All this I sensed and at the same time I envisaged as with a second sight their great future, these three thousand years of life which lay before them unknown and unguessed, and my heart was shaken with these thoughts. Oh, how happy I was that my heart was shaken and that at last I loved! . . . Oh, marvelous dream, lofty illusion! The most improbable of all visions, to which mankind throughout its existence has given its best energies, for which it has sacrificed everything, for which it has pined and been tormented, for which its prophets were crucified and killed, without which nations will not desire to live, and without which they cannot even die! All these sensations I lived through in this dream. . . . All that I seemed to see and I woke up and opened my eyes for the first time in my life literally wet with tears. I do remember these tears, I remember that I was glad of them, that I was not ashamed of them.

What does this dream tell us? It reveals a deep longing for the saving power of light, beauty and love. For the first time in his life Stavrogin weeps tears of love, tears of despair and, perhaps, even tears of remorse. But, alas, it is only a dream. In his conscious life the emptiness remains and it becomes in the end all-pervasive. Stavrogin, as we already know, possesses a keen, penetrating reason, a powerful physique, a strong power of will, but his heart is and remains desolate and frozen. He feels neither joy nor grief, only their pale derivatives: lust and the tortures of a clear insight into his own condition. He knows that his heart is dead, that his mind is cold and empty, that his body is poisoned by inertia and animal sensuality. This is why he is unable to communicate with others, why others cannot communicate with him. He is homeless, estranged from his own self. He is closed, shut up with himself. He does not possess himself and thus is unable to give himself to others in devotion and in love.

Because Stavrogin's heart is frozen, both fear and anguish are equally foreign to him: "Nikolay Stavrogin," says the narrator, "was one of those natures who do not know fear. During a duel, while his adversary took aim, he stood with absolute cold-bloodedness. When it was his turn to shoot, he aimed and killed with a calm which was almost animalistic."

The different characters of the novel are mere refractions of Stavrogin's personality or, like his mother and his tutor, they serve to explain his personality structure. Peter Verkhovensky, Kirillov, and Shatov in particular reflect specific aspects of Stavrogin's character. Peter and his gang embody Stavrogin's skepticism and nihilism with respect to the existing social order, his rebellious instincts, his sadistic enjoyment of social manipulation and experimentation. Shatov reproaches him for having planted in him, the one-time Socialist, the idea of the divinity of the Russian people. Shatov fanatically believes in this idea with a grim seriousness, but for Stavrogin it remains just another intellectual whim. Kirillov's romantic-Promethean revolt, his religious brooding and his defiant rebellion against Christianity are likewise ingredients and reflections of Stavrogin's ideas.

Stavrogin himself becomes never engaged or involved in the problems of existence. He remains "the stranger," the "outsider." He is impelled by a demoniac force to exert his influence on others, to implant in them ideas, to start movements. And he is driven on by an irrepressible urge to dominate and manipulate the lives of others, to torture and destroy. However, this strong urge itself deteriorates eventually into a mere coldly calculating and experimenting curiosity.

Shatov intimates that Stavrogin is responsible for the madness of Kirillov: "You have confirmed him in his lies and calumnies, you have driven his reasoning power into insanity. Go and look at him now, he is your creature." "I was the pupil," says Shatov of himself, "and you were the teacher." But Stavrogin refuses to assume any responsibility for his own teachings. All he is willing to admit is that when he wanted to instill in Shatov the ideas of Pan-Slavism, he was more concerned with himself than with Shatov. Since Stavrogin himself has no faith, he tries to suggest certain beliefs to others, in the vain hope that perhaps in this roundabout way he may in the end convince himself. But Stavrogin recognizes that his experiment has failed. Shatov does not believe. It all remains an abortive, fantastic and fanatical ideology. Soon, to be sure, Shatov will believe: when his wife returns, pregnant with Stavrogin's child, the miracle of love and of the new life opens and inflames Shatov's heart. All of a sudden Shatov has faith, shortly before he goes to meet his death.

The tragic story of the rape and suicide of little Matryosha and Stavrogin's marriage to Marja Lebedkina reveal the sadistic elements in his character. In his "confession" to Bishop Tihon he says of himself:

Every extraordinarily ignominous, humiliating, vile, and especially every ridiculous situation into which I entered during my life, produced in me, aside from an excessive rage, an incredibly lustful pleasure. And the same thing happened in those moments when I committed some infamy or when I found myself in mortal danger. . . . When I was struck in the face (and this happened twice in my life) I was, aside from the terrible rage which I felt, overwhelmed by the same lustful sensation. . . . I am convinced that I might have spent my whole life as a monk, although there is innate in me an animalistic sensuality which I whipped up again and again. But if I want to I am always master of myself. Let me state that I do not wish to excuse myself by shifting the responsibility to either my environment or my illnesses, but that I am taking upon myself the full responsibility for all of my crimes.

It is a sordid mixture of sadism and masochism which is articulated in this telling self-examination. The narrator adds that the evil in Stavrogin was "cold and calm, or, if I may say so, completely rational and thus the most repulsive and horrible thing that can be imagined."

In the pathologic-visionary hallucinations of Stavrogin the satanic or Luciferian element of his character comes into profile: "And suddenly . . . he began to speak of how he suffered, especially at night, from certain strange hallucinations; how he sometimes saw or felt close beside him an evil being, derisive and 'rational': 'it shows different faces and assumes different characters, and yet is always the same and always infuriates me. . . . ' "

TIHON: "And how long have you been subject to this?"

STAVROGIN: "About a year, but it's all nonsense. I'll go to see a doctor. It's all nonsense, frightful nonsense. It's myself in various forms, nothing else. . . . You must surely think that I still have some doubt as to whether it's I or whether it's not really the devil."

TIHON: "And . . . do you really see him?" . . . "do you really see a definite image?"

"It is strange that you should persist in asking me when I have already told you that I do. . . . Of course, I see him. I see him just as plainly as I see you. . . . Sometimes I do not know who is real, he or I. . . . It is all nonsense. And you, can't you imagine that it really is the devil? . . . It would be more in keeping with your calling."

THE BISHOP: "It is more likely a disease, although . . . " "Although what?" "Devils undoubtedly exist", says the Bishop, "but our conceptions of them differ widely."

STAVROGIN: "I am slyly putting a question to you: does he [the devil] really exist, or not?"

TIHON smiles vaguely.

STAVROGIN: "Well then, let me tell you plainly that I am not at all ashamed, and . . . I will say boldly and in all seriousness: I do believe in the devil, I believe canonically, in a personal devil, not in an allegory, and I don't need confirmation from anybody."

Then STAVROGIN suddenly asks: "Do you believe in God?"

THE BISHOP: "I do believe."

STAVROGIN: "It is written, isn't it, that if you have faith and bid a mountain remove itself hence, it will do so. . . . I am curious to know: can you remove a mountain or can't you?"

TIHON: "If God commands, I will remove it."

STAVROGIN: "Well, but that would be the same as if God Himself removed it. No, you—you—will you be able to do it, as a reward for your faith in God?"

THE BISHOP: "Perhaps I shall not."

STAVROGIN: "Perhaps? . . . Ha! ha! You are still a doubter then?"

THE BISHOP: "I doubt, because my faith is imperfect."

STAVROGIN: "What! Even *your* faith is imperfect? Well, I wouldn't have supposed it, to look at you."

THE BISHOP: "Yes. . . . Perhaps my faith is imperfect," answers Tihon.

STAVROGIN: "Is it possible to believe in the devil without believing in God?" asks Stavrogin with a laugh.

THE BISHOP: "That's quite possible. It's done right and left."

STAVROGIN: "And I am sure that you consider such a faith more estimable than utter lack of faith. . . ." Stavrogin bursts out laughing.

THE BISHOP: "On the contrary, outright atheism is more to be respected than worldly indifference."

Finite man, immersed in temporality, who no longer acknowledges his ground and origin in the infinite and eternal, becomes the prey of anguish and of nothingness. If that happens, there rises from within, in the words of Pascal, boredom, ennui, satiety, disgust, nausea, meaninglessness. The whole of existence is poisoned by the nothingness and emptiness within.

The reader is tempted to ask: Is there a potential for good in Stavrogin? Is there a possibility that this potential might acquire a positive meaning? Stavrogin's "confession" results from a strong desire to lay bare the innermost recesses of his soul. Nonetheless, everyone who places his trust in him or takes him seriously is in the end defrauded. Stavrogin not only permits this to happen but he cooperates with the deception by his silence when he could clarify the situation by speaking up.

During his visit with the Bishop, Stavrogin cynically denounces Tihon's "psychology," and he protests against his being "analyzed." But at the same time he speaks of his search for a man who is stronger than he, a man whose faith "can move mountains," whose faith can help him to liberate himself from his own loathsome ego. But even in this search there is an ever-present rebellion. Bishop Tihon does not believe in the sincerity of Stavrogin's repentance. His "confession" he finds replete with vanity, the vanity of the "immoralist." And Stavrogin is all the time filled with resentment against his listener, and his unbearable self-humiliation turns eventually into hatred and selfrighteous pride.

"There is no forgiveness for me," Nikolay finally says gloomily. And, referring to the rape of the girl Matryosha, "In your book it is written that there is and can be no greater crime than to offend 'one of these little ones.' In this book here!" and Nikolay points to the Gospels. "I will come back again some time," Stavrogin says with an air of extreme fatigue. "I appreciate very much both the pleasure of this talk and the honor . . . and your sentiments. . . . I understand why some people love you so. Please pray for me to Him whom you so love."

"I know," says the Bishop, "an old man, not far from here, a monk and a hermit, and of such Christian wisdom that you and I could hardly understand it. . . . I will tell him everything about you. Will you permit me? Go to him, become a novice under him for some five or seven years, for as long as you find it necessary. Take a vow, and with this great sacrifice you will purchase all that you desire and even more than you expect, for you cannot understand now what you will receive." Stavrogin, flushed and intent, replies, "You bid me become a monk and enter a monastery?" "You do not have to enter a monastery," the Bishop says. "You do not have to take orders. Simply be a novice, secretly. You can do this, living in the world." "Quit it, Father Tihon," Stavrogin interrupts. He rises from his chair and the Bishop does likewise.

"What is the matter with you?" Stavrogin exclaims, staring almost fearfully at Tihon. Tihon "stood before Nikolay, his palms pressed together and thrust forward, and a morbid convulsion, apparently caused by an overwhelming fear, momentarily contorted his features."

"I see clearly," exclaims Tihon, grief-stricken, "that never, poor lost youth, have you stood nearer to a new and a more terrible crime than at this moment."

Alarmed, Stavrogin tries to reassure him. "Perhaps I will postpone. . . . You're right. . . . I will not publish the sheets. Compose yourself."

"No," the Bishop exclaims, "not after the publication, but even before it, a day, an hour perhaps, before the great step, you will plunge into a new crime as a way out, and you will commit it solely to avoid the publication of these sheets. . . ."

Stavrogin "veritably shook with anger and almost with fear."

" 'Cursed psychologist!' he suddenly cut the conversation short in a rage, and, without looking back, left the cell."

In the meantime, Peter Verkhovensky has already planned the assassination of Marja Lebedkina. Stavrogin has given money to Fedka, the ex-convict, who is to commit the murder. It is not a direct order to kill, but only a suggestion, only an encouragement.

Stavrogin's visit with the Bishop presents the last opportunity for a decisive change. Everything that follows, from the double murder to Stavrogin's suicide, is but a logical consequence of Stavrogin's refusal to make positive use of this last opportunity. His psychological knowledge and sophistication are so far advanced that no argument can prevail any longer. The psychological and theological implications of the distintegration of Stavrogin's character point to the descriptive analyses presented in Kierkegaard's most gloomy work, *The Concept of Dread:* Here the author depicts with masterly psychological insight the progressive forlornness of the human person in the advancing dread of nothingness and the concomitant or subsequent emergence of the *demoniac* forces. In the end there remains nothing positive at all. Everything disintegrates under the impact of the powers of evil, the work of "the possessed," the work of those "devils" who carry out the designs of their master, Stavrogin. This demoniac world circles about nothingness, meaninglessness and despairing emptiness.

CHAPTER TWO

Léon Bloy

Pilgrim of the Absolute

LÉON BLOY was born at Périgueux in the South of France in 1846. When he told his father that he wanted to be a painter, he was sent to an architect's studio in Paris. Here Bloy immediately severed all his relations with the Catholic faith. Fascinated by the militant aggressiveness of atheism, he acted like a precursor of the Bolsheviks.

In 1868 Bloy became acquainted with the French poet Barbey d'Aurevilly. As the latter's secretary, he came across the writings of Joseph de Maistre, the passionate enemy of the ideas of the French Revolution and the advocate of the infallibility and the absolute sovereignty of the Pope and the political ideas of French romanticism. In 1869, at the age of twenty-three, Bloy returned to his abandoned Catholic faith. His correspondence with Barbey d'Aurevilly gives evidence of a strong leaning toward mysticism. Barbey d'Aurevilly introduced him to the writings of the Spanish social and political philosopher and diplomat Donoso Cortés, the implacable enemy of socialism, liberalism and enlightenment. Cortés demanded as a remedy against the maladies of the age a restoration of the political power and influence of the Church. For Cortés the only alternatives were either a "dictatorship of the dagger," or a "dictatorship of the sword."

In 1877 Bloy met Anne-Marie Roulé, a poor prostitute, whom he loved passionately and whom he tried desperately to convert to Roman Catholicism. To escape the torments of his own sensuality,

Bloy sought refuge and solace in a retreat at the Trappist monastery at Soligny. After his return to Paris in 1878, Anne-Marie Roulé finally embraced the Catholic faith.

During the next four years (1878–1882) Bloy's life was completely dedicated to Anne-Marie. He tells of her and of his own mystical experiences, and he says that from that time on he "lived almost constantly in the dark night of pure faith," so that in his future writings he had to do nothing but give literary expression to the divine light he had received and retained in his heart during these four years. After Abbé Tardif de Moidrey had introduced him into the mysteries of an eschatological exegesis of the Bible, Bloy passed through a phase of religious experiences which came close to religious mania. He anticipated the impending end of the world and was filled with "a consuming longing for the glorious revelation of the Kingdom of God."

Bloy and his friend, the writer Ernest Hello, felt themselves as the chosen prophets of the coming realm of the Holy Spirit. Early in 1882 Anne-Marie descended into the night of insanity and was confined in the asylum of St. Ann. In utter despair Bloy fled into the solitude of La Grande Chartreuse, the famous Carthusian monastery in the French Alps near Grenoble. But when he was told that he had no vocation for the monastic life, he returned to Paris and threw himself into a feverish literary activity. In 1886 he completed his partly autobiographical novel *Man in Despair* (*Le désespéré*). This work was received with shocked silence, and the French critics and writers as well as the general public began to treat Bloy as if he were a leper.

In August 1889, Bloy—who had just returned from the burial service of his friend, the poet Villiers de l'Isle-Adam—met Jeanne Molbech "in the shadow of death, as it were." Jeanne became his wife, and the couple was linked in close friendship with Bloy's many godchildren whom he had converted to Roman Catholicism and some of whom were to become leaders of the Catholic revival movement (the *renouveau catholique*) in France and in Europe. Two of the four children to whom Jeanne gave birth died of hunger and privation.

Salvation through the Jews (*Le salut par les Juifs,* 1892) and *The Soul of Napoleon* (*L'âme de Napoléon*), the works which embody Bloy's philosophy of history, were the fruit of many years of intense study. Jeanne Molbech was at Bloy's side when, on November 3, 1917, he passed on "like a child that joyfully anticipates a great journey" (Karl Pfleger).

Two main themes can be discerned in what Bloy's wife and his friends termed his "prophetic mission." The first is his anticipation of the epochal catastrophe which he envisaged as the sequel of the modern defection from Christ and Christianity. The second is the praise of poverty as the only legitimate imitation of Christ. In the novel *Le désespéré* Bloy says of himself that "as a perpetual dreamer I was never able to see things as they actually are" and that "there existed perhaps never a more helpless and inept individual whenever it was a question of seizing opportunities."

It is interesting and rewarding to consider briefly the principal concepts of Bloy's philosophy of history. Like Nietzsche, he was looking in history for the revelation of the mystery of existence. For him, however, history was above all the history of the divine will. Historical facts were for Bloy the raw material in which "the style of the divine Word" documents itself with an iron necessity. History was a mysterious and symbolic divine language which told of the ways in which man was being tried and tested by his Creator. Through "the chaotic sea of facts" he wanted to penetrate to the recognition of the "boundless solidarity of everything that has happened in different times and at different places." Bloy's many shocking accusations and condemnations of the bourgeois, the rich, the landlords, the popes, the Jews, the Freemasons, philosophers, technocrats, musicians, writers, journalists, Englishmen, Germans, and Protestants are manifestations of the disgust with which this worshipper of the Absolute looked upon all those who are satisfied with less than the Absolute—upon all those, including himself, who are not saints. His revolt grew out of a depth of resentment and existential anguish as did the similar outcries of revolt of a Kierkegaard, a Nietzsche and an Unamuno. Their common starting point is the great lament over the agony of Christianity and the apostasy of modern man. Bloy tried to persuade his contemporaries that they were living in that world-historic hour when professing "Christians" were crucifying the Holy Spirit.

In *Le désespéré* we read that the present civilization of "Christians" and "good Catholics" is "the snow-like leprosy of religious sentimentalism." Looking at modern Christendom, "we must ask ourselves whether Sodom and Gomorrah were not devout and saintly in comparison with this modern sewer of innocence." Our "good Christians dishonor God more than the most fanatical enemies of Christianity were ever able to."

Léon Bloy was, in short, an author so overpowered by his own existential anguish that he lost more and more the freedom of a personal perspective and therewith also the possibility of taking a personal, critical decisive stand with respect to his own ego. Above all, he lacked completely a redeeming sense of humor, and it was perhaps this lack which caused him to take himself and his sufferings much too seriously. His constant gesticulating and his often pompous and fuzzy prose are expressions of a discordant and split psyche which is striving for powerful self-assertion and self-assurance at any price.

What Bloy—despite basic differences—has in common with the present generation of Roman Catholic writers (for example, Mauriac, Julien Green, Waugh and Graham Greene) is the realization and conviction that the time is past when one could naively and safely call oneself a Christian and actually live the life of a pagan. Bloy was the first among European Christian novelists to point out the dangers of a provincial pharisaical denominationalism, and he was one of those few who defined religious faith in terms of risk and resolute daring in personal existential action.

Jeanne Molbech, Bloy's wife, was the daughter of the renowned

Danish poet, Christian Molbech. Jeanne had renounced her Protestant faith and become a Roman Catholic. In 1922, after her
husband's death, she published his letters, covering the period of
their engagement (*Lettres à sa fiancée*). Jeanne's entry into Bloy's
life marked the beginning of a happiness he had never known before.
Courageously she shared his poverty and his loneliness. She understood and loved him as he was, with all his virtues and all his faults.
Twice they travelled to Denmark and, while there, Bloy met the
Danish writer, Johannes Joergensen, also a convert to Roman
Catholicism. After his return to France, Bloy spent those sordid
"four years of captivity" in the small town of Lagny-sur-Marne
amidst the mediocrity of provincial bourgeois philistines (see *Quatre
ans de captivité à Cochons-sur-Marne;* freely translated: *Four Years of
Captivity among the Swine on the Marne River*). The inhabitants of the
town were hated bourgeois merchants, tepid priests and "respectable" women. They all filled Bloy with loathing and disgust. When
he returned to Paris he established himself at Montmartre, in the
shadow of the Basilica of Sacré Coeur. And it was there, a few years
later, that the recently married couple, Jacques and Raïssa Maritain,
paid him a visit, an encounter which proved decisive, especially for
the Maritains, who had come a long way from agnosticism to Roman
Catholicism.

Bloy's life was a prolonged odyssey of wanderings, quarrels with
landlords, struggles for his daily bread. In a letter to his fiancée,
dated September 24, 1889, he wrote: "I am without any resources,
earning absolutely nothing. . . . This involves me in desperate
expeditions across the city (Paris), in ghastly disappointments,
humiliations, in exhaustion and death-like anguish. . . . Ah, those
worldly people who happily are sure of their daily bread . . . and
who, wanting to turn their backs on Christ, have never for a single
instant pondered the idea of suffering for their brothers or of
sacrificing themselves for the unfortunate."

Many of his critics have reproached Léon Bloy for his incapacity
to earn a living. But he believed that it was his special vocation

to live entirely by faith, hope and the love of God. This belief he embodied in Clotilde Maréchal, the heroine of the novel *The Woman Who Was Poor* (*La femme pauvre*), who ended her days as a beggar.

In 1892 the first volume of Bloy's *Journal* was published. "Bloy's diaries," writes Rayner Heppenstall in his study of Léon Bloy's life and works, "personify him by their titles. He is in turn the ungrateful beggar, the provincial caged lion, the man who cannot be sold, the old man of the mountains . . . the pilgrim of the Absolute, . . . standing before the apocalyptical threshold, and venturing finally through the gateway of the humble."*

In the first volume of the *Journal* (titled *Le mendiant ingrat*) Bloy endorses exclusively the integral Roman Catholic point of view: "Everything that is not exclusively and unconditionally . . . Catholic, belongs to the gutter" (p. 209). Or: "In my justified pride I possess the boldness of bragging about the many enmities which I have made among the professional pundits by my aggressive need for independence" (p. 60). "I have the honor of being the most feared and therefore also the most maligned writer of my time" (p. 145). "The unbelievers curse me because I scoff at their sophistries, and the believers detest me because I dare hurl their cowardice into their faces" (p. 224).

Bloy reproaches the Church and certain members of the clergy for their crass materialism and for their soft, sentimental piety: "Every Christian who is not a hero is a pig." He regarded it as his divinely appointed task to be or become the "pilgrim of the Absolute." Bloy was one of the first to call attention to the weakening of religious faith in France, especially among the working class and the peasantry. And yet he again and again emphasizes his own unworthiness while at the same time asserting the total integrity of his motives: "Actually, I am one of the meek and obedient. This is why as a writer I regard it as my task to be inexorable in the defense of truth and to bear witness to the God of the poor. That is

*Rayner Heppenstall, *Léon Bloy* (Studies in Modern European Literature and Thought; Cambridge: Bowes & Bowes, 1953), p. 9.

all. The most violent pages of my books were motivated by love, were often written with tears of love, in hours when I felt surrounded by an unfathomable peace."

Bloy spent the last years of his life at Bourg-la-Reine, in the house which had once belonged to Charles Péguy, who died on the field of battle at the beginning of World War I, in 1914. Toward the end of his life Bloy became somewhat calmer. He died in the presence of his wife and a few faithful friends, among them his favorite godson, the neo-Thomist philosopher Jacques Maritain.

It was Charles Péguy who first made the distinction between *poverty* and *destitution* (*les pauvres et les misérables*). Destitution, Bloy asserted, degrades and dehumanizes because the destitute bears witness to the horrible injustice of which he is the victim. Poverty, on the other hand, ennobles because the poor bear testimony to Christ, whose poverty they emulate: "I daresay that a society without the poor is inconceivable from the Christian point of view. . . . You call for a society without the poor? What you will get in the end is nothing but an inhuman society, or perhaps you have gotten it already. The innocent poverty which you have tried to destroy reappears under other, more terrifying forms." In the words of Georges Bernanos,

The modern world has two enemies, *childhood* and *poverty*. . . . The freedom of the saints is without doubt nothing but the freedom of the poor totally supernaturalized. You say you have no longer any need of either the saints or the poor? . . . You shall see, and you can see already what this society of tomorrow—a society without the saints and without the poor—will look like: for every missing poor man you will have a hundred monsters, and for every missing saint you will have a hundred thousand monsters. . . . You dare assert that poverty is the worst of evils? But who among you would not prefer a thousand times to die in the flesh of a beggar resigned to the will of God rather than in the flesh of an honorable but egotistic, complacent, and comfortable bourgeois? . . . Our hideous mechanized civilization has in effect not only proletarianized *men*, it has proletarianized the *human conscience*. It has allowed . . . the formation of a *mass-conscience*.*

*Georges Bernanos, "Dans l'amitié de Léon Bloy," in Luc Estang, *Présence de Bernanos* (Paris: Plon, 1947), pp. xiv ff.

In *The Woman Who Was Poor* Bloy depicts that most desolate and abject poverty which surrounded him in Paris and which he himself experienced through most of the years of his life. This is why he could say: "We do not enter paradise tomorrow or the day after or ten years hence; we enter it today *if* we are poor and crucified." The novel is autobiographical, especially in its second half, in the portrayal of the tragic life and love of Clotilde and Léopold. The theme of poverty as it is presented here shows a peculiar fusion of medieval and romanticist ideas. Bloy, as has been pointed out, associates the degradation of the human person with the civilization of the nineteenth and twentieth centuries. Man has become drunk with his material success, with scientific progress, and his greed for money and pleasure has increased proportionately. As a consequence the poor are deprived of the last vestiges of their human dignity. The thesis which Bloy advances pleads for the restoration of the poor to their proper place in society as creatures formed in the image of God. Bloy hated every thought of mediocrity, and it was mediocrity that he saw embodied in the "bourgeois." Even more, if possible, he despised the "respectable woman" (*la femme honnête*). She, too, is too mediocre: neither hot nor cold, neither a saint nor a real sinner: "Woman has only two ways of living, either a life of sanctity or a life of sensual pleasure. . . . Between these two there exists only *la femme honnête*, that is to say, the female of the bourgeois—the ultimate reprobate whom no sacrifice can redeem." In this sense the reader must interpret the shocking portrayal of Mademoiselle Planude in *La femme pauvre*. She is a practicing Roman Catholic woman and as such "very respectable," but she is at the same time a landlady and thus a hardened *petite bourgeoise*. And nothing could be more despicable, nothing more hypocritical: "Mademoiselle Planude would kneel at the Holy Table with a little bag worn next to her chaste skin, in which title deeds and IOU's were tied up jointly with religious medals and scapulars."

The novel analyzes the underlying reasons for the moral and spiritual decadence of the Catholic laity. Bloy holds the clergy

responsible for this spiritual decline, particularly what he calls the
"clerical confectionery of Saint Sulpice."* "A saintly clergy,"
Bloy writes, "produces a virtuous laity, a virtuous clergy produces
a respectable laity, and a respectable clergy produces a profane
laity." As a matter of fact, too many priests, Bloy contends, favor
their wealthy parishioners. The typical average homily distinguishes
carefully and often with cautious casuistry between the *commandments*
and the *counsels* of the Gospels in order not to offend the average
bourgeois churchgoer. While the commandments simply state the
minimum required to get by, the counsels stipulate the maximum
as enunciated in the Sermon on the Mount.

Part I of *The Woman Who Was Poor* is titled "Flotsam of the
Shadows"; Part II bears the title "Flotsam of the Light." Clotilde's
story in the first part of the novel shows her wretched life in the
company of her widowed mother, who lives with a drunken black-
guard who terrorizes both his mistress and Clotilde. The young girl,
who is profoundly unhappy, has been seduced by the first man she
had met, an insignificant fellow who soon abandons her. In her
loneliness and desolation, there keeps passing before her mind's eye
a picture which she had once seen and which she longs to possess.
It shows a scene in a brothel, where a group of thieves are drinking
with some prostitutes. The wall on the right has disappeared to
give place to a luminous vision: Christ in His Glory, as He appeared
to Mary Magdalene on the day of His Resurrection, stands there
with an expression of divine pity on His sorrowful face and He
stretches out His hands in forgiveness to one of the women who has
left the group and is kneeling at his feet. The woman's face expresses
both agonized sorrow and a glimmer of hope. This woman, thinks
Clotilde, has given her only treasure beyond recall. And though she
may anoint the feet of Christ like Mary Magdalene, it would not
be within her power to draw a single thorn from His tortured brow.
It is only after much cruel suffering that Clotilde achieves peace

*Saint Sulpice is the name of the seminary for the education of priests, founded in
Paris in 1641 by J. J. Olier.

of mind by living, in abject poverty, a life of prayer and meditation. After a brief moment of great happiness with Léopold, she enters into complete solitude: "Clotilde even learns to understand . . . that woman only *exists*, in the true sense, if she is without food, without shelter, without friends, without a husband, without children; that only thus can she compel her Saviour to come down." This sentence reminds us of a very similar one in Simone Weil's *Cahiers*.

In the second part of *The Woman Who Was Poor*, Bloy places side by side two sermons on the Gospel of the twenty-first Sunday after Pentecost (Matt. 18: 23-25):

The kingdom of heaven may be compared to a king who decided to settle his accounts with his servants. When the reckoning began, they brought him a man who owed ten thousand talents, but he had no means of paying, so his master gave orders that he should be sold, together with his wife and children and all his possessions, to meet the debt. At this, the servant threw himself down at his master's feet. "Give me time," he said, "and I will pay the whole sum." And the servant's master felt so sorry for him that he let him go and canceled the debt. Now as this servant went out, he happened to meet a fellow servant who owed him one hundred denarii; and he seized him by the throat and began to throttle him. "Pay what you owe me," he said. His fellow servant fell at his feet and implored him, saying, "Give me time and I will pay you." But the other would not agree; on the contrary, he had him thrown into prison till he should pay the debt. His fellow servants were deeply distressed when they saw what had happened, and they went to their master and reported the whole affair to him. Then the master sent for him. "You wicked servant," he said. "I canceled all that debt of yours when you appealed to me. Were you not bound, then, to have pity on your fellow servant just as I had pity on you?" And in his anger the master handed him over to the torturers till he should pay all his debt. And that is how my heavenly Father will deal with you unless you each forgive your brother from your heart.

The assistant parish priest, who himself is poor and whose duty it is to deal tactfully with those who are well off, is taking a shortcut. He passes over in silence the severe punishment that awaits, according to the Gospel, the pitiless creditor, and he thus misinterprets the entire parable.

What a text to paraphrase, on the eve of the day when so many poor beggars are seized by the throat and strangled. All those who have been acquitted and pardoned are there, all the proprietors in the land, and it might not appear altogether impossible to touch the consciences of some of them. But the assistant priest, who is himself a poor devil and who has orders not to offend the well-filled bellies of the parishioners, is afraid to speak about "the seizing by the throat" and the "strangling," and thus he interprets the parable . . . as a precept of infinite elasticity, as a license to pardon any kind of offense and injury, thus drowning in a mush of concessions the indiscreet and blunt lesson taught by the Son of God.

Then a cloud descends upon Clotilde, and she falls asleep. And now she hears the voice of another priest speaking:

"Here you have the Gospel, my brothers, and here are your hearts. At least I venture to presume that you have brought them with you. I wish I could feel sure that you have not forgotten them, buried in your cash registers or under your counters, and that I am not speaking to corpses. You must allow me then to ask your hearts if they have understood anything of the parable which I have just read to you.

"Nothing at all? Really? I thought so. Most of you probably were too busy with adding up the sums of money you expect to receive tomorrow from your tenants. . . .

"At that passage of the Gospel where we hear that the servant who was let off by his master took by the throat that other unfortunate man who owes him a modest amount, the hands of some of you must have *clenched* instinctively and almost unknowingly, even here, before the Tabernacle of the Father of the poor. And when, without listening to the poor man's prayers, the servant sends him off to prison, then no doubt you were all of one mind in the conviction that he did exactly the right thing. . . .

"This, I think, is about all the fruit you derive from this Sunday's lesson, a lesson to which only your Guardian Angels have listened with trembling. Your Guardian Angels, your grave and invisible Angels, who are with you in this house and who will still be with you tomorrow when your debtors will bring to you their children's bread or beg you in vain to have patience with them. . . .

"The rest of the parable is not meant for you. Or is it? The possibility that your Lord might ever seize *you* by the throat and strangle you, that is just an invention of your priests. You owe nothing to anybody; your books are in order, and your fortunes, big or small as they may be, have of course been acquired honestly and righteously, and all the laws, even the Law of God, are stacked in your favor. . . .

"You have no idols in your homes; I mean you don't burn incense and worship images made of wood and stone. And you don't blaspheme. As a matter of fact, the Name of the Lord is so far removed from your thoughts that you would never even dream of 'taking it in vain'. . . . You honor your fathers and mothers; I mean you don't fling dirt into their faces from morning till night. You do not kill, at any rate you don't kill with daggers or with poison, because this would be very displeasing to men and it might even scare away your customers. And you don't indulge in debauchery so openly as to cause great scandal. Nor do you tell lies as big as mountains. You don't steal—not on the highways, where you might easily get hurt, and you don't rob banks, which are always so admirably guarded. . . .

"In short, then, you are above and beyond reproach; your souls are neat and clean, and there is absolutely nothing you have to fear. . . .

"But God, my brothers, is terrible when it pleases Him to be terrible. . . . God, who made Himself poor when He made Himself Man, is in one way or another always being crucified, always being abandoned, always dying in torture. But what are we to think of these people here who never feel pity, who are incapable of shedding a tear and who do not consider themselves irreligious? . . . Have I spoken to a single soul who is truly Christian? I doubt it very much. . . .

"We know that often the Master was Himself among the poor, and when we cause suffering to a fellowman in affliction we know not which of the members of the Saviour's body we may lacerate. . . .

" 'What time is it, Father?' His poor children have been asking God throughout the centuries, for we watch 'without knowing the day or the hour.' When will our suffering end? What time is it by the clock of your never ending passion? . . .

"Ah, Lord, I am a very bad priest! You have entrusted me with this sleeping flock and I do not know how to awaken them. . . . Here I am, falling asleep myself. I fall asleep as I speak to them, I fall asleep as I pray for them, I fall asleep at the bedside of the dying, by the biers of the dead. I fall asleep, oh Lord, as I consecrate the Bread and the Wine of the awesome Sacrifice. . . ."

Clotilde "woke up" at the very moment when the humble priest was leaving the pulpit. Their eyes met, and because her face was bathed with tears he must have thought that it was his sermon which had made them flow. Without doubt he was right, for this woman, endowed with the gift of vision, had sunk into a sleep so deep that she might well have heard the *real* words which the priest had not dared to pronounce save in his heart."*

*Léon Bloy, *La Femme pauvre* (Paris: Mercure de France, 1937), pp. 281–285.

In the novel *Le désespéré* the story was told of Caïn Marchenoir, his early life and conversion and his relations with a prostitute, Véronique, who, on the verge of sainthood, becomes insane in the end. We meet Marchenoir, who is a self-portrait of Léon Bloy, again in *The Woman Who Was Poor*. The rather sinister character of Marchenoir is interwoven with the fate of Clotilde and Léopold. After Marchenoir's and Léopold's violent deaths (Marchenoir is run over on the way back from the asylum where he had to confine Véronique, and Léopold dies in the conflagration of the Paris Opéra Comique) there remains for Clotilde only one witness to her past life, the painter Lazare Druide: "From time to time she comes and distills into the soul of the painter a little of her own peace, of her own mystical greatness, then she goes back to her vast solitude, to the streets crowded with common people." The novel concludes with a sentence which might have served as an epigraph for the story of Clotilde's life: "There is only one misery," Clotilde says during her last meeting with the painter, "and that is—Not To Be Saints."

Léon Bloy was either loved or hated. To remain indifferent in the face of his life and work seems to be impossible. The following comments of both friendly and unfriendly critics as well as some of Bloy's closest friends may serve to illustrate this point.

Graham Greene, in one of his essays, called it a waste of time to criticize Léon Bloy's work as a novelist because "this irate man lacked creative instinct" and remained forever preoccupied with the molding of his own Self, using as his raw material his very personal resentments, humiliations and hatreds. Greene adds that every sin against good taste reveals a flaw in Christian thinking. Jacques Maritain, on the other hand, in his introduction to his late wife's selections from Bloy's works (*Pages de Léon Bloy*) recalls his first visit with the author (June 25, 1905): "As soon as one stepped over the threshold of his home, all values, as by an invisible mechanical device, were transmuted. One knew or one felt it as a certainty that truly there was '*only one misery, not to be saints.*'"

Discussing the merits and demerits of *The Woman Who Was Poor*, Raïssa Maritain writes that in this novel she and her husband

found themselves for the first time face to face with the reality of Christianity. . . . Certain exaggerations of style are compensated for by an obvious sincerity, . . . a genuine, profound and inexhaustible lyrical dynamism and by the singular tenderness of a heart which seemed created to love in an absolute sense. . . . What struck us at the first reading of the novel was the boundlessness of this devout soul, its thirst for justice, courage and spiritual independence.*

In the opinion of Graham Greene, *La femme pauvre* is "a grotesque and badly constructed novel," and as far as the entire literary work of Léon Bloy is concerned, Greene says that Bloy's message which astonishes us by its noble sentiments and insights is given the lie by the uncultured and selfish core of his intellect. Greene intimates that though Bloy may have been a devout man, he was a man without humility, a social reformer without personal unselfishness and that his self-pity and his petty hatreds prevented him from becoming a first-rate novelist or a first-rate mystic.

Raïssa Maritain, in turn, points to the decisive role which Léon Bloy played in the situation in which Christianity found itself at the turn of the century and in her own life as well as in the life of her husband. She might have pointed with equal justification to the role Bloy played in the lives of such prominent artists and writers as Georges Rouault, the painter; Johannes Joergensen, the Danish writer and recipient of the Nobel Prize for Literature; or Pierre Termier, the well-known geologist. In Termier's notes we find the following sentence: "I divide my life into two sharply and deeply separated halves: that which preceded my meeting with Bloy and that which followed this encounter."

Nicholas Berdyaev, too, attributes to Bloy a key position in reestablishing the interrelationship of modern literature and Christianity. The French critic Joseph Bollery, who from 1924 to 1939

*Raïssa Maritain, *Les grandes amitiés. Souvenirs* (New York: Editions de la Maison Française, 1941), p. 171.

edited a periodical exclusively dedicated to the study of Léon Bloy (the *Cahiers Léon Bloy*), solemnly declared that Bloy "was not only closer to life and of greater vitality than many of the greatest of his and of our time" but that, despite his faults and errors, "he always was and still is in the right in the impressive unity and faultless logic of his work."

Hubert Colleye, in the several volumes of his study titled *L'âme de Léon Bloy*, says that the despair of Bloy has nothing to do with the romantic literary despair espoused by such authors as Rousseau and Byron, but is intimately related to the experience of the absolute naught which tormented Baudelaire, Verlaine and Dostoevsky. Daniel-Rops regards Bloy as the commanding mind in the French and European "Catholic rebellion in the spirit of Kierkegaard" and as the spiritual ancestor of Georges Bernanos. The latter said of Bloy that he was the only writer who knew "how to administer the sacrament of literature." What links Bloy with Bernanos is their common distrust of all the achievements of modern civilization. Bloy, in the opinion of Bernanos, being a true Frenchman, responded like Joan of Arc when the call of God reached him. Against the levelling bureaucratization of human existence he had protested "that the lot of the freedom of man in this world is mysteriously linked with the lot of the poor." Both Bloy and Bernanos took upon themselves the fate of the beggar—Bloy reluctantly, Bernanos voluntarily—because in their polemic protest against worldly possessions they wished to emphasize that the only thing that mattered for a Christian was the salvation of immortal human souls.

The following two passages may illustrate the parallelism in the thinking and writing of Bloy and Bernanos with respect to their evaluation of poverty. In *The Woman Who Was Poor*, Léon Bloy writes:

Does not mankind belong to poverty? There is no beast of the field so naked as man. . . . When the chaos of this fallen world is sorted out, when the stars are begging their bread, and only the most despised dust of the earth is permitted to reflect the Glory; when men know that *nothing was in its place,* and that the rational species lived only on enigmas and illusions, it might well be that the torments of unhappy, unfortunate man, may reveal and display the wretched poverty of the soul of a millionaire. . . .*

And in Bernanos' *The Diary of a Country Priest* the Curé de Torcy, the clerical friend and superior of the country priest, states:

Have we kept God's word intact: *The poor you have always with you?* Does that sound like the slogan of a demagogue? But it is God's word and we have received it. . . . It is the saddest saying in the Gospels, the most burdened with sadness. And firstly it is addressed to Judas. . . . Judging by that last deal of his, he'd hardly have made a first-rate broker's clerk, old Judas wouldn't. . . . Fact is Our Lord knew all about the power of money: He gave capitalism a tiny niche in His scheme of things. He gave it a chance. . . . It is so magnificent! God despises nothing. After all, if the deal had come off, Judas would probably have endowed sanitoriums, hospitals, public libraries or laboratories. Remember he was already interested in the pauper problem, like any millionaire. *The poor you have always with you, but Me you have not always with you,* answered Our Lord. Which amounts to this: don't let the hour of mercy strike in vain. You would do far better to cough up that money you stole, at once, instead of trying to get My apostles worked up over all your imaginary financial deals in toilet waters, and your charitable enterprises. . . . I am not attached to My paupers like an English old maid to lost cats or to poor bulls in the Spanish bull-ring. I love poverty with a deep, reasoned, lucid love—as equal loves equal. I love her as a wife who is faithful and fruitful. . . . The poor you have always with you just because there will always be the rich, that is to say, there will always be hard and grasping men out for power more than possession. These men exist as much among the poor as among the rich, and the scalawag vomiting up his drink in the gutter is perhaps drunk with the very same dreams as Caesar asleep under his purple canopy. Rich and poor alike, you would do better to look at yourselves in the mirror of want, for poverty is the image of your own fundamental illusion. Poverty is the emptiness in your hearts and in your hands. It is only because your malice is known to Me that I have placed poverty so high, crowned her and taken her as My Bride. If once I allowed you to think of her as an enemy, or even as a stranger, if I let you hope that one day you might drive her out of the world, that would

*Léon Bloy, *The Woman Who Was Poor* (New York and London: Sheed & Ward, 1947), p. 218.

be the death-sentence of the weak. For the weak will always be an insuffer-able burden on your shoulders, a dead weight which your proud civilizations will pass on to each other with rage and loathing. I have placed My mark upon their foreheads, and now you can only confront them with cringing fury. . . . If My arm were to be lifted for only an instant, slavery—My great enemy—would revive of itself, under one name or another, since your law of life is debit and credit, and the weakling has nothing to give but his skin. *

When Léon Bloy insisted that pain was the essence of poetry, he echoed Kierkegaard's words which we find in the first of his *Diapsalmata*, at the beginning of *Either/Or*.

What is a poet? An unhappy man who conceals deep torments in his heart, but whose lips are so formed that when a groan or a shriek streams out over them it sounds like beautiful music. . . . And men are gathered in a crowd around the poet and say to him, "Sing again at once"—which is as much as to say, may new suffering afflict your soul, and may your lips continue to be fashioned as before; for the shriek would only distress us, but the music, that is delicious. And reviewers come forward and say, "That is just right, just as it should be according to the rules of esthetics." Well, of course, a reviewer in fact resembles a poet to a hair—except that he has no torments in his heart and no music upon his lips. I tell you I would rather be a swineherd . . . and be understood by the swine, than a poet and be mis-understood by men. †

Pain was for Bloy the mysterious affinity in man which made of him the eternal companion of divine beauty. Human pain he saw enclosed and enshrined in the divine pain, in the folly of the Cross.

While the theory of art for art's sake symbolizes for Bloy the poet in his ivory tower, he saw poetry always as a result of suffering and therefore capable of contributing its weighty share to the religious work of redemption, a redemption bought with the poet's blood. Thus, for Bloy, poetry and art were linked closely with the eternal destiny of Man: *L'art pour le salut*, that is, he regarded it as the destiny of art to contribute to man's salvation.

*Georges Bernanos, *The Diary of a Country Priest*. Trans. by Pamela Morris (New York: Doubleday Image Books, 1954), pp. 47 ff.
†See Walter Lowrie, *Kierkegaard* (London, New York, Toronto: Oxford University Press, 1938), p. vi.

Bloy never regarded himself primarily as a writer. His one and only aim was to serve God, and he tried to serve Him with his writing, which he regarded as his greatest gift: "I am a pilgrim of the Holy Sepulcher—I am just that and nothing else."

The main sources of Bloy's thinking and writing were quite consistently the Bible and the liturgy of the Church. He likened himself to the Old Testament Prophets, and he thought he had inherited from them the voice of one who calls his people to repentance. But he realized well enough that he was only a feeble tool used by Providence: "Rest assured that I am simply a poor and humble Christian, nothing else, nothing more. It has pleased God to bestow on me a gift for literary expression such that I was an old man before I recognized my sad soul under this disguise" (see *Le vieux de la montagne*). He quite consistently lived in a self-created world of absolutes. From that dizzy height he looked down upon the world and upon men and judged it and them. He would not tolerate contradiction and he disliked debates and discussions with other members of the literary guild.

There obviously were striking contrasts and contradictions in Bloy's character. On the one hand, he was incredibly stubborn, vain and apparently self-assured, lacking in a charity which would have made him at least respect those with whom he disagreed. On the other hand, he rediscovered the strength and the truth of an integral Christianity whose immortal values he wished to impart to his fellowmen. He did not and could not offer a palpable practical solution for the social injustices of his age, but he did insist on the inherent dignity of the human soul and especially on the human dignity of the poor as the ones who were closest to Christ. With respect to the two extremes of individualism and socialism, he proclaimed the social solidarity of all the members of the Mystical Body of Christ, in which individualism and socialism appear, as it were, harmonized in a higher synthesis.

In conclusion, it may be appropriate to give the word once more to some of those who knew Bloy best. Raïssa Maritain wrote in her memoirs:

In reality, Léon Bloy spoke like a man who has to fulfill an extraordinary mission, from which nothing must deter him . . . who hastens toward the single goal, defying all obstacles, like a torrent which drags the rocks and trees from its banks and carries them headlong with the mud and the pebbles.*

And in Johannes Joergensen's autobiography we read: "Never did he write a line to please any public. . . . When I saw him in Denmark he was already looking like an old man. . . . Wherever I happened to be in the world, when I see Bloy's name on the cover of a new book in a bookseller's window, I feel the irresistible urge to go in and buy it. And through three hundred pages I am again under the old magic spell: I grow enthusiastic, I hate, I love, I rebel, I am angered, I glow, I melt, I weep. . . ." Pierre Termier, in his *Introduction à Léon Bloy,* states: "He only writes to bear witness to the truth, to unveil, to dispel and humiliate lies. He was fully conscious of having to fulfill the double mission of denunciation and praise; and that is why in every one of his books, almost on every page, he changes abruptly from invective to prayer, from the outcry of wrath to the call of love." Finally, Karl Pfleger, a German literary critic, taking an overall view of the life, the work and the mission of Léon Bloy, offers this evaluation: "If the Catholics of his time and his country had but shown him half the sympathy and understanding which they reserved for minds of incomparably lower literary and spiritual worth, Bloy would have been the pioneer of a powerful religious movement. He was aware of this himself."

*Raïssa Maritain, *Les grandes amitiés. Souvenirs* (New York: Editions de la Maison Française, 1941), p. 157.

CHAPTER THREE

Georges Bernanos

THE DIARY OF A COUNTRY PRIEST

GEORGES BERNANOS was born in Paris on February 20, 1888. His ancestors on his father's side came from Lorraine, those on his mother's side from Central France. His father was an interior decorator, a typical *petit bourgeois*. In 1898 the father bought a country home in Fressin on the Channel coast. Here the boy spent the most memorable years of his youth. With his elder sister, Marie-Thérèse, he grew up on the white plains near the seashore. The family entertained friendly relations with the Catholic clergy of the region. Georges grew up as a practicing Roman Catholic, and he never wavered in his faith. He was an avid reader and had at his disposal the many books of his father's library. His favorite authors were Balzac, Barbey d'Aurevilly and the anti-Semitic writer Edouard Drumont (1844–1917).

The years Bernanos spent in primary school and in one of the Jesuit boarding colleges remained a hated and dreaded memory all through his life. He also retained a lifelong aversion to the Jesuit order. In retrospect he speaks of "the black winters, the stinking classrooms, the dining halls with their fatty smell, the never ending blaring high-masses, where a tired little soul has nothing to share with God but his own boredom" (*Les grands cimetières sous la lune* [*A Diary of My Times*], Paris: Plon, 1958, p. 79).

The boy's first Holy Communion had a decisive influence on the writer's future development: death and the fear of death suddenly invaded his being and remained ever-present realities. He resolved to dedicate his future life to God and for a while considered the possibility of studying for the priesthood and of a possible vocation as a missionary, but he soon arrived at the conclusion that his "life and his death" were to be offered to God in the vocation of a layman because, as he writes in one of his letters, a layman "has to fight battles in many fields in which the priest remains ineffective." The calling of a writer appealed to him now as the only way in which he personally would be able to express himself "that is, to live."

At college Georges was known as a shy, reticent and sensitive boy. From 1901 to 1903 he attended the Junior Seminary of Notre- Dame des Champs, and in 1904 the Junior Seminary at Bourges, where he felt more at ease and where he befriended two young priests who were also friends of his family. In 1906 he received the degree of *bachelier*. From 1907 on, short stories from his pen began to appear in Royalist periodicals.

As a law student in Paris, Bernanos became a member of the political-religious party *Action Française*, which represented the extreme chauvinist Catholic right wing, and he showed himself an ardent and noisy champion of the monarchist idea. He was frequently involved in political controversies and in demonstrations and public riots.

Upon the request of Léon Daudet of the *Action Française*, Bernanos assumed the editorship of the small polemic paper *L'Avant-Garde de Normandie* in Rouen. In every issue he wrote the political editorial, and in the pages of this paper he also published his first three novelettes.

Bernanos became engaged to and soon married the chairman of the women's section of the *Action Française* in Rouen, a direct descendant of the family of Joan of Arc, Jeanne Talbert d'Arc. He was a devoted husband and a loving father to his six children, and he presided in the role of a patriarch over a large group of family relations and friends. With his entire clan he moved restlessly from place to place and finally across the Atlantic to South America, making his home in Brazil.

Bernanos' family life was not without conflicts: there occurred frequent clashes between him and his children. All in all, he bore a full measure of unrest, sorrow and suffering. Most of the time he found it very difficult to make ends meet and to feed himself and his large family from the meager proceeds of his writings.

In World War I Bernanos served from the beginning to the end, having enlisted as a volunteer in the Sixth Regiment of Dragoons. He rose to the rank of *brigadier* (the lowest rank of commissioned officer in the French cavalry).

At the age of thirty-eight, Bernanos published his first novel, *Under the Sun of Satan*. In the war letters addressed to his confessor, to his fiancée and to several comrades in arms he displayed a somewhat forced blend of storm and stress and haughty aristocratic bearing. He tried to press a volcanic content into a rigid form.

When the war ended, Bernanos returned from a heroic mode of existence to the rank of the ordinary citizen. His attitude with respect to war became more and more ambivalent and ambiguous. On the one hand, he speaks of the purifying and even sanctifying effects of a soldierly existence (see the character of Olivier in *The Diary of a Country Priest*). The life of a soldier, he feels, faces ultimate realities, such as death and the prospect of divine judgment. On the other hand, he laments the "impurities" of war, its necessary concomitants whenever a war is not inspired and consecrated by the faith of a people but when it is the cold calculation of diplomats and the greed of financiers which provide the chief incentives. The author became more and more distrustful of the attempts made on the part of "Christians" to justify the atrocities of war by means of casuistry or on the supposed basis of "natural law."

The end of the war compelled Bernanos to ponder his future course of life, and after three anguished years of uncertainty he realized the need for a steady income that would enable him to take care of his growing family, and so in 1922 he accepted a position as a life-insurance agent.

It is truly paradoxical to picture Bernanos, the fierce opponent of all bourgeois security, the advocate of risk and daring, a man who all his life never knew how to deal with money or with any practical household problems, traveling across the French countryside, trying to persuade people to buy life-insurance policies. Bernanos could make such an existence tolerable only by submerging himself ever more deeply in the world of his dreams. We see him at work, trying to translate his dreams into the written word, indefatigably writing, in railroad cars, in waiting-rooms, in hotel rooms, in the cafés.

From these years dates Bernanos' life-long friendship with Robert Vallery-Radot, the writer and lyric poet, to whom we owe some of the most authentic information on the author: "He asserted that he had read practically nothing, which was a gross exaggeration. His admired masters were Balzac, Léon Bloy, Barbey d'Aurevilly, Dostoevsky, and Joseph Conrad." He did read few of the contemporary writers, aside from Charles Péguy and Léon Bloy. He happily discovered Pirandello and Marcel Proust. He suffered, according to Vallery-Radot, "from nervous states of anxiety which often made him start up during the night and which seemed to give him a presentiment of the agony of death. He loved firearms, swords, horses, the hunt, good food, French wines of good vintage years, and was fond of all natural joys and pleasures." Vallery-Radot also tells us that Bernanos never read for the sake of reading but rather "to rediscover the dream which dwelled within him. This is why he was so fond of detective stories: he saw in them parables of the spiritual life, signs and symbols of other worlds." For the same reason Bernanos frequented the cinemas: "The motion picture was for him the dark-room of dreams."*

Bernanos had read the story of the life of the Curé d'Ars, Jean-Baptiste-Marie Vianney (1786–1859). "This saint," Vallery-Radot writes, "had charmed the poet by the pure simplicity of his child-

---

*Bulletin trimestriel (edited by the Société des Amis de Georges Bernanos), I, 9–10. This Bulletin contains a number of short texts by Bernanos: letters, lectures, articles, essays, novelettes, and so on.

like heart which loved only God and the souls of sinners. Bernanos wanted to depict a country priest in the twentieth century who, without being a slavish double of Vianney, was nonetheless to bear his main features—a counter-thrust against religious conformism and godless science, he also wanted his hero to relive his own anxieties" (*Bulletin trimestriel*, II–III, 25).

Somewhat head over heels, Bernanos severed his association with the insurance company: "I have no longer any interest," he wrote in a letter, "in insuring the lives of my contemporaries, lives which in most instances are not worth the trouble." He had high hopes of being able to live on his royalties. In 1926 he established his family at Bagnères-de-Bigorre, where soon afterwards his father died of cancer of the liver. Cancer became for Bernanos a symbol of evil, "a symbol of the monstrous fertility of evil in souls." Bernanos, too, was to suffer and die from cancer of the liver.

The novel titled *Under the Sun of Satan* was followed by the double novel *The Fraud* and *Joy*.

These productive years, however, had in store some bitter humiliations. Bernanos had dedicated the better part of his youthful enthusiasm to the Royalist movement, but he was more and more repelled by the intellectual leader of the Royalist party, Charles Maurras—by Maurras' lack of Christian charity and his attempt to transform a fluid intellectual movement into a rigidly organized political party. In 1919 Bernanos withdrew from the *Action Française*. The complete incompatability of the respective points of view had become glaringly evident to him. The leaders of the *Action Française* subsequently launched a violent attack of vilification, but Bernanos always retained for Charles Maurras a high personal regard. Underneath all the distortions he thought he could still discern the original and essential purity of the Royalist ideal.

The double novel was followed in 1931 by the publication of Bernanos' first critical work, *The Great Fear of the Right-Thinking People* (*La grande peur des bien-pensants*). The original title had been *France Capitulates*. This treatise presents a critical intellectual history of France and in particular of French political Catholicism during the period which followed the French defeat in the Franco-Prussian War (1870–71).

Bernanos and his family moved from place to place, to Clermont-de-l'Oise, Toulon, La Bayorre, always haunted by financial worries and often near destitution.

As early as 1926 Bernanos began to speak of his "wild desire to leave everything and escape to America." He was fed up with Europe, with France and, above all, with the conditions in the Church. There followed an accident which left the author crippled for the rest of his life. Bernanos, the arch foe of modern technology, had been an enthusiastic motorcyclist. Near Montbéliard, trying to avoid a collision with a car, to spare the life of a child on the other side of the road, he threw himself and his motorcycle against a stone wall and broke both legs. Henceforth he had to walk on crutches.

Vallery-Radot has left us a description of Bernanos' external appearance:

At the age of thirty, he was of a radiant beauty. The light blue, sky-blue eyes under a high and straight forehead were always illumined by a child-like smile. . . . He had not yet the corpulence which later on weighed heavily on him, but rather the elegance of a cavalry officer in civilian clothes. . . . He loved grandiose hour-long soliloquies . . . during which he conjured up the spirits of Ezechiel, Aeschylus, Aristophanes, and Rabelais, while he would walk back and forth without pause with a gigantic, roaring laughter. . . . pulling his lion's mane with both his fists and relighting his pipe a hundred times (*Bulletin trimestriel*, II–III, 29).

While he was living at La Bayorre the attacks of anguish recurred more frequently and in aggravated form. Anguish was for Bernanos a medium of poetic vision, and these anxieties were his companions from the days of his childhood. According to his friend in Brazil, the German Benedictine Father Paul Gordan,

the eruptions of his tremendous temperament, the explosive power of his mind was easier to bear than the heavy and leaden torture of those mysterious states of anguish which often enough haunted this man who at other times was so full of sparkling vitality: they evidently were the price he had to pay for his prophetic visions. . . . These mental states showed all the symptoms of *agony* and were accompanied by the physical nightmares of a rapidly progressing fatal disease. . . . He loved medical science and always sought the company of physicians; he delved deeply into this science which he regarded as indispensable for the psychologist (*Erinnerungen an Bernanos*, Hochland, 1949, pp. 522–523).

All of Bernanos' works abound with medical terms and metaphors as well as with medical analogies of surprising precision. In most of Bernanos' novels a physician is placed in the center of the action as the counterpart and antagonist of the priest. These physicians are usually materialists without any religious faith, and as such they are contrasted with the priestly physician of the soul who is equipped with sacramental power as a supernatural aid in his healing office. Bernanos' physicians are, however, almost without exception men of great nobility of character (cf. the similar characterization of the physician Dr. Rieux in Albert Camus' *The Plague*).

In 1934 Bernanos quite abruptly departed from France, leaving behind his house, his furniture, his father's large library and many of his manuscripts. On Majorca, the largest of the Spanish Balearic Islands, he tried to establish for himself a new basis of existence. A contract with his publisher guaranteed him a modest income in return for a regular specified number of manuscript pages. This perpetual pressure, in combination with a strictly enforced intellectual self-discipline, bore fruit within the next two years in the trilogy of novels, *A Crime, An Evil Dream,* and *The Dead Community* (better known as *Monsieur Ouine*), Bernanos' gloomiest works. Following these, he published *The Diary of a Country Priest.*

When he conceived the plan for this latter work, he felt a sense of liberation:

It seems to me that I can now write with a clean slate again; I am without anger. I believe that after having written about the adventures of my friend [the Country Priest] I shall now write the memoirs of his youth. With these two books I shall have fulfilled my destiny (*Letters*). If I do not like to speak about this book, it is because I love it so much. . . . I love it as if if it were not my own work. My other books I did not love. *Under the Sun of Satan* is like fireworks which burn themselves out in the evening in the midst of a thunderstorm. . . . *Joy* is a mere whisper, and the anticipated song of praise remains unsung. *The Fraud* is a countenance of stone weeping real tears. But if I were confronted with this book [*The Diary of a Country Priest*] on the day of judgment, I should not dare say, "I know thee not," for I know full well that this book contains a part of my very own mystery (*Le Cahier*, letter of November 1936).*

The characters in *An Evil Dream* and *Monsieur Ouine* are not human wrecks, as are the protagonists in Graham Greene's novels. They are human beings who have lost the meaning of their lives and who despairingly gesticulate in the void, prior to their extinction.

On the island of Majorca Bernanos experienced the outbreak of the Spanish Civil War as a personal tragedy, as a new personal crisis and a profoundly soul-shaking event. His disillusionment with the rightist politicians in France was now followed and intensi- fied by an even greater disillusionment with the Catholic Falangists in Spain. *Les grands cimetières sous la lune* is a document of the indig- nant outcry of a Christian conscience in view of the hypocrisy of a supposedly Catholic political movement that was conspicuous only by the heinous crimes committed in the name of religion. The great compassion that is prepared to descend with fellow humans into any kind of hell breaks forth in Bernanos with elemental force under the impact of the horrors of the Civil War. While he was working on a new book (*La nouvelle histoire de Mouchette*), he saw in passing trucks, surrounded by armed men, poor wretches, crowded together like cattle, "their hands on their knees, their faces covered with dust, yet upright, their heads held high with that dignity which is peculiar to the Spaniard even in the most abject misery. The following morning they would be shot—that was the only thing which was clear to them. Everything else remained incompre- hensible. . . . Well then: what most impressed me was the fact

Bernanos par lui-même, collected and arranged by Albert Béguin (Paris: Editions du Seuil, 1954).

that these poor people found it totally impossible to understand the abominable game in which their lives had been caught" (letter of June 17, 1937).

In 1938, Bernanos returned to Toulon and shortly afterwards, disgusted by the capitulation of the Allies at Munich and anticipating the Nazi invasion of France which the author had already prophesied in *Les grands cimetières sous la lune,* he carried out his intention to emigrate to South America.

In July 1938, Bernanos started out on a journey to Paraguay, a land of which he had been dreaming as a sort of utopia in his early youth. After some disappointing experiences in Paraguay, he, his family and the several relatives and friends who were his companions on all of these travels moved on to Brazil, where he stayed at different locations until the summer of 1945.

These Brazilian years were on the whole happy ones. Without the author's knowledge a group of friends and admirers settled most of his ever-recurring debts. They paid for several of his homes and thus repeatedly rescued him from the failures in which his experimental adventures usually ended.

Bernanos stayed longest in the vicinity of Barbacena, at a hamlet named Cruz das Almas (Cross of Souls), a name which he used as a title for a collection of his essays. With passionate interest he followed world events and commented on them in weekly newspaper articles and soon also in impassioned radio appeals addressed to the French and the Allies. Through the medium of these broadcasts from overseas, the self-exiled author became one of the pillars of the French *Résistance* in his homeland.

Living in virtual seclusion on his *Fazenda,* he expressed himself more and more frequently in the form of diary notes. In this he followed the model of Léon Bloy. In *Les enfants humiliés* (Paris: Gallimard, 1949), one of Bernanos' most beautiful books, which was published posthumously in 1949, there are profound reflections and meditations on the main themes of his life and work. His other critical works include his *Letter Addressed to the British* (1942), *Medita-*

tions on the Present Age (1942–45) and *France against the Robots* (1944).

Bernanos loved the people of Brazil and this love was reciprocated. He made many friends among the laity as well as among the clergy. Among the latter, Father Paul Gordan, O.S.B., came to know him most intimately. But even in this new environment Bernanos was frequently depressed by the conflicts and clashes in his own home and family, and the usual states of mental anxiety remained his steady companions.

In 1945 Bernanos and his family returned to France. The author was received enthusiastically in Paris, but he withdrew almost immediately to the seclusion of the countryside. From there he hurled—during the period of national liberation—stirring articles into the metropolitan press of France, manifestoes intended to purify the consciences of his fellow countrymen and to force them to take an unequivocal stand with respect to the intellectual, moral and sociopolitical problems of the day. He lectured in Belgium, at the international conclaves in Geneva, at the Sorbonne and in several cities of Switzerland. His main themes were always the the same: the defense of the honor and dignity of the free human personality, the dangers threatening from technocracy and, above all, totalitarianism in any form and under any disguise. His remaining hope was actually no longer of or for this world. (See *La Liberté pour quoi faire?* Edited posthumously by A. Béguin [Paris: Gallimard, 1955].)

Looking at postwar France, Bernanos felt disgust and nausea: France had evidently learned nothing from the tragic experiences of the war and of the occupation. The author finally decided to go to Tunisia, and there he attempted for the last time to work out a design for his own life, trying to collect himself for the creation of a final climactic work on the life of Christ. Shortly before his death he vowed to dedicate all his remaining strength to the completion of this work.

The request to write dramatic dialogues to a scenario by Father R. L. Bruckberger O.P. on Gertrud von Le Fort's *The Song at the*

Scaffold (see also the opera by the modern French composer Francis Poulenc, dealing with the same theme) became the occasion for Bernanos' last and perhaps purest creation, *The Dialogues of the Carmelites*, which he completed shortly before his death and which was a great success on the stage. It is essentially an apotheosis of mystical anguish and love, set in the frame of the Carmelite pattern of spirituality.

Bernanos' liver ailment necessitated his immediate return to Paris, where he died after an unsuccessful operation at the American Hospital at Neuilly, on July 5, 1948. To Abbé Daniel Pézeril we owe the report on Bernanos' last days and hours. He retained to the end his incomparable spontaneity and the immediacy of his childlike heart. On the eve of his death he said to his wife, "Now I am entering into the holy agony" (see Georges Bernanos, *Essais et témoignages, réunis par Albert Béguin*, Paris: Plon, 1955, pp. 341–358). In a letter addressed to Father Paul Gordan, Abbé Pézeril writes: "He died in a state of extraordinary peace. All his physical and mental anguish he had overcome in his faith. . . . He had once again become the child which in his innermost essence he had never ceased to be."

Because Bernanos was so absolutely certain of his own faith as a pure gift of grace, he could afford to be free from all complacency, from pharisaism, hypocrisy and arrogance in contemplating the almost universal phenomenon of the unbelieving masses. He never gloried in not being like those without faith. The fact that he believed and the others did not never prevented him from feeling a strong solidarity with believers and unbelievers alike. For similar reasons he remained aloof from the intellectual climate of the numerous French converts to Roman Catholicism.

The truth is that the faith of Bernanos was neither logical nor systematic but rather dynamic and synthetic. And his faith made it possible for him to envisage clearly and deeply the "mystery of iniquity," to penetrate with his glance into the depths of evil and sin. The characters of his novels emerge from the mysterious abysses of either iniquity or grace and thus completely lack the distinctness and transparency of Cartesian logical constructs.

Bernanos' primary concern remained man: man in his dignity, forever consecrated because Christ had become man. And man, himself redeemed, was called to redeem others. But to be able to do this he must be free: he must show forth what Martin Luther called "the freedom of a Christian man." And the ideal type of a free man was for Bernanos the Christian knight, or, in an even more purified incarnation, the Christian saint, the saint of the type of Joan of Arc. In her fate and her fight he found above all the most convincing argument for his own fight against political clericalism.

A true Frenchman, Bernanos saw in France the embodiment of the patrimony of Christianity, understood as a community of free men united in Christ. He visualized the true France that had been buried under rubble and rubbish, and he wanted to believe in its resurrection, hoping against hope.

For Bernanos, the Christian man and writer, the mystery of poverty was and remained a deeply experienced and painfully loved reality. Like Léon Bloy, he was himself a poor man, and even in the days of a relatively comfortable existence he retained an indifferent and freely detached attitude with regard to money. Moreover, he was conscious of the spiritual value of poverty, which he, like Bloy and Péguy, sharply distinguished from the misery of destitution. He was actually haunted as by a nightmarish phantom by the possibility that some totalitarian despot might one day succeed in abolishing poverty, thereby committing a terrible assault on the dignity of man. For Bernanos had preserved a profound understanding of the meaning of the scriptural saying that man cannot serve two masters, that he must choose between God and Mammon.

When Bernanos at times hoped for a rebirth of Western Christian civilization, he did not expect such a renascence from power but from powerlessness, not from affluence but from poverty. Most important, however, was for him the restoration and re-formation of the individual human being. Without this all attempts at social and economic reform will be doomed.

When World War II ended, Bernanos expressed the conviction that those who had lost the war were Germany *and* France. These two ancient nations had left as victors only those powers which had at their disposal huge masses of men, materials and money—the United States and Russia. Ancient Christian nations such as France and Germany could never submit to this "new order" without betraying themselves, their past and their future. The national rivalries between Germany and France, he thought, had become ridiculous anachronisms in the postwar world. What these two nations had in common was of much greater significance than what separated them. In comparison with the Great Powers, they had become very poor indeed, but their poverty was their treasure because it protected most effectively their human and Christian character as nations. To France and Germany he saw ultimately entrusted the salvation of Europe.

Bernanos loved and castigated his own people with the passion and the wrath of an Old Testament Prophet. And yet this volcanic individual with the explosive speech, with his intolerant indignation, was in his heart of hearts a patient sufferer. He could be very angry and wrathful, but he was unable to hate: his wrath sprang from a hurt and disappointed love.

To his friends Bernanos left in an album this message:

When after many years you read again these lines, please remember in your prayers the old writer who believes more and more in the powerlessness of the mighty, in the ignorance of the scholars, in the stupidity of the Machiavellis and in the incurable frivolity of all grave people. Everything beautiful in the history of the world has originated without anyone's knowledge, from the mysterious accord which exists between the humble and burning patience of man and the gentle mercy of God.

The novels of Bernanos are much more than mere narratives: they are authentic interpretations of human existence as it unfolds within the frame of contemporary life. The author asserted repeatedly and emphatically that he did not regard himself as a theologian and that for this reason (if for no other) faith could never assume the form of a tranquilizing intellectual systematic construct. He regarded the "systematic mind" as a sort of insanity. When philosophers and theologians pretended to simplify matters by systematizing them, he thought that by making this attempt they merely confused everything. Life, contrariwise, which seems to confuse things, actually simplifies all complexities.

Bernanos' faith enjoined him to love his neighbor whoever that neighbor might be, and loving presupposes understanding. Understanding the other, therefore, seemed to Bernanos the surest and the most decent way to loving him. He thus tried to see the truth in its simplest terms, to express it as accurately as was humanly possible, and to live in conformity with it. He thoroughly distrusted the "intellectuals" because he was convinced that their intellectualism abounded with abstract and preconceived theories and therefore saw reality colored or distorted by their theories.

Bernanos had a strong sense of history and tradition. He was, however, not interested in the dead relics of the past but rather in its lasting and timeless values and accomplishments. "I honor the past," he wrote, "because it has made us what we are. . . . I honor the past, but I think only of the future, whereas our little communist or fascist intellectuals think only of the present, that is, of themselves" (*Le Chemin de la Croix-des-Ames,* 4 vols. Rio de Janeiro, 1942–1945; in one vol., published by Gallimard, Paris, 1948. pp. 245 ff.). Like Péguy and Claudel he had his roots in the historical classical France of Louis XIV, of Joan of Arc, of Corneille, Racine, Rabelais and St. Francis of Sales. These kindred souls provided the standard by which he measured his rootless and shiftless contemporaries.

It was during his stay in Brazil that Bernanos wrote:

I am an author who has ceased writing novels, that is, who has ceased doing what he loved more than anything else, in order to attempt instead to say things which others could presumably say much better if only they had the courage. But they prefer to become ministers of state or members of the Academy, or maybe even archbishops. . . . I am not interested in becoming a minister of state or a member of the Academy. As far as becoming an archbishop is concerned, I cannot say, for I have never been approached (*La Liberté pour quoi faire?*, p. 298).

And again: "I have lost my fatherland, and I shall probably never see it again, for the ocean crossings are expensive. Be that as it may, I possess all the freedom of which a penniless writer and the father of six children can dream. And I am free to have my own opinion concerning Señor Franco" (*Nous autres Français* [Paris: Gallimard, 1959], pp. 67 ff.). And in the same context:

I have the right to look upon the clerical circles with little sympathy, and I know that thousands of priests and religious are of the same opinion without daring to admit it. . . . Should we not assume that after two thousand years of Christendom a Christian would be allowed to breathe the air of freedom? But the fact is that during the past two or three centuries even your vocabulary has become that of people living in a beleaguered fortress . . . a vocabulary of conservation, of defense, of sheer togetherness— anything but the vocabulary of conquerors. . . . Though he may be correct as far as his creed is concerned, the Christian of today presents—from the social and human point of view—an unspeakably pale image of what was formerly called a Christian man (*ibid.*, pp. 211 ff.).

Bernanos points to the fact that with the advancing technical organization and mechanization of the modern world listless *conformism* becomes the norm for Christians and non-Christians alike. Those *free spirits* who two or three centuries ago were still typical of the Christian personality are disappearing ever more rapidly.

In the pages of *Les Grands cimetières sous la lune* we read:

I am writing my books in café houses at the risk of being regarded as a drunkard, and I might actually have become one if it were not for the fact that our mighty republics have mercilessly imposed heavy taxes on all comforting spirits. In their place I have been swallowing for years those sweetish *café-crèmes* with a fly swimming on top. I am writing in taverns because I am unable to do for any length of time without the human face and the human voice. . . . I am writing in taverns as I formerly wrote in railroad cars, in order not to fall victim to imaginary creatures, in order to regain with a glance at the passing stranger the proper measure of joy and sadness.

More than any other modern Christian literary artist Bernanos was the poet and eulogist of both grace and freedom. Like Léon Bloy, he was "a pilgrim of the Absolute." He pictured himself as standing "between the radiant and the dark angel," as looking at both ultimately "with a mad hunger for the absolute." He thus embodied in his creations not only the praise of the grace offered human beings but also the demoniac rebellion of those who stubbornly, yet freely, resist the offer. However, when he depicts the tortures of the sinner and the rebel, he does so to show in the extreme bitterness of a seemingly lost heart and soul a latent receptivity for the overwhelming sweetness of grace. What Bernanos wrote to a young French author applies to himself: "If God demands of you that you bear witness, be prepared to suffer much, to doubt yourself unceasingly, in success and in failure. For thus understood—as a testimonial—the calling of a writer is no longer a trade but an adventure, above all a spiritual adventure. But all spiritual adventures are Golgathas" (*The Patience of the Poor* [*New Letters*]).*

In the *Bulletin trimestriel* we find the following telling passage:

Don't say too many bad things about the vagabonds. You all will be like unto them, at least at some moments of your lives. They are people who start out, not knowing where they will find rest in the evening, adventurers on a journey of discovery, headed toward a new world. And what a world! Without having ever seen it, you will suddenly recognize the invisible universe to which your bodies have no access, from which you carefully turned away your mind's eye. But it is there where you feel the breath of those great passions of which most of you know no more than the surface ripples of your impoverished lives (pp. 12, 24).

Yet Bernanos was convinced that at the hour of death the almost extinguished flames of these poor souls will see themselves as they

*See German edition: *Das sanfte Erbarmen*. Edited and Introduction by A. Béguin, Johannes-Verlag, 1951.

really are—"monstrous underdeveloped cripples, mere stumps of men." From this same conviction derives Bernanos' scorn of all depersonalized forms of "togetherness," of congresses, academies, mass meetings and a host of other merely external associations; likewise his profound distrust of all church organizations that are trying to impress the world with a sheer weight of numbers and collective aggregations: clubs, committees, mass communions and religious sodalities. In his opinion they will all of necessity reflect the spiritlessness of mediocrity and of the human average. "I am writing down dangerous truths," he says in *Chemin de la Croix-des-Ames.* "I am writing them down without pleasure. I am writing them down merely because I know that thousands of priests and simple believers in all the world think as I do . . . without being permitted to express their thoughts. I, on the other hand, can and dare say it" (p. 51). And in *Nous autres Français*: "I say, I repeat, and I shall not tire of repeating that the present state of the world is a cause of shame for all Christians. . . . We constantly reiterate with tears of exhaustion and inertia . . . that the world is becoming less and less Christian, but the fact is that Christ was not given to the *world*; He was given to *us for* the world, and it is from our hearts that God withdraws His presence; it is in *us* that this de-Christianization is taking place" (p. 36).

La France contre les robots (*France Against the Robots*) is one of Bernanos' most stirring manifestoes. Here he says that "capitalists, Fascists, and Marxists all resemble each other." While Fascists and Marxists deny freedom, the capitalists still pretend to believe in freedom, "but whether or not they believe in it is quite unimportant because none of them knows any longer what to do with it" (p. 47).

In *Cimetières* the author qualifies his critique of the Church and its human representatives and officials: "If I find myself compelled," he says, "to accuse the Church, I certainly do not do so with the laughable intention to contribute to its reform. . . . I do not even wish to see the Church perfect: it is a living organism and, like its poor naked souls, it stumbles from this world to the next; it commits faults, and it atones for them" (pp. 114 ff.).

As far as the actually realized existential truth in the Church is concerned, Bernanos points out that the priest stands no higher than the layman, and the layman not higher than the priest. The only one who could claim preeminence in rank is also the one who will never claim it: the saint. "I do not speak in any manner as a theological expert: here as at other times I speak in accordance with the letter and the spirit of the beginner's catechism" (*Cimetières*).

Bernanos had a very exalted opinion of the writer and the poet. In *Cimetières* he expresses this conviction most succinctly: "Every vocation is a call—*vocatus sum*—and every such call must be handed on to others. Those whom *I* call are not numerous, to be sure; they will not change the course of the world. Yet it is for them that I was born." And the same idea is expressed in the *Bulletin trimestriel*: "The older I grow, the better I understand that my modest calling is truly a *vocation: vocatus sum.* The dear Lord has to call me each time He needs me. . . . When He does, I get up, not without protest, and after the thing is done I return to my very ordinary everyday life" (p. 5).

Bernanos repeatedly asserts that he is not a rebel. "I am not a rebel in any manner of speaking," he says in *Nous autres Français*. "In the spirit of rebellion there hides hatred or contempt of human beings" (p. 32). But more dangerous than the spirit of rebellion are disappointment and disillusionment: "While *revolt* is a transitional phase, disappointment no longer has a share in this world: it is filled and satiated like hell" (*Les enfants humiliés*, p. 195). Only he who has never understood the dark miracle of the world can be disappointed.

Life speaks a single word, and it keeps its promise. I am unable to help those who deny this. They are either frauds or cowards. *Human beings,* of course, are often disappointing, they alone. And again I am unable to help those who allow themselves to be poisoned by this kind of disappointment. Their soul's metabolism does not function properly: they are unable to eliminate the toxic substances. As for myself, human beings have *not* disappointed me. . . . I was always prepared for something much worse (*Cimetières*, p. 280).

Bernanos vouched for the virtual identity of poetic and religious truth, that is, for the ultimate identity of aesthetics, ethics and religion. The authentic poet's glance upon the dark paths of human creatures is simultaneously a glance upon the Creator who provides the standard and measure of poetic, artistic and religious truth. And even where the poet and artist are most angry and indignant, they must never try to swim against the current of divine life. The only unfailing remedy, however, for anger or passive resignation in the face of adversity and evil is prayer.

It is interesting to note that for Bernanos, as for all Christian mystics and contemplatives of the past and present, faith did not imply an absolute certainty but rather a "dark light" that had to be rekindled again and again: "It is not true," Bernanos wrote in *Chemin de la Croix-des-Ames*, "no it is not true that faith is *security*, at least not in the human sense of the word. Faith cannot be compared with those evidences of which the 'two times two equals four' presents the most common form." The evidence of faith rests on the presence and choice of God, and it is from this kind of evidence that the calm and security of the poet and artist derive: "God sees and judges. The experienced certitude which He sees and judges has upheld me all my life. This is the reason why I was always able to look calmly into the faces of legalists, scribes and Pharisees, without contempt and anger but also without illusions" (p. 132).

All the literary and plastic arts, it seemed to Bernanos, pointed at something transcending them; they were to him symbolic expressions of man's never-ending search for Being. Marcel Proust, André Gide and all those who tried to explore the abysses of the human psyche by applied psychology or by the merciless *dénouement* of the evil in man, remained in the end stranded in absolute ennui, locked in meaninglessness and emptiness. Bernanos was convinced that the authentic writer and artist must proceed from the opposite pole, starting out from God. This is why he thought it impossible for the genuine artistic creator to do without theology, that is, without revealed truth.

In the letters addressed to Jorge de Lima, the author's Brazilian friend, we read:

The modern world has mutilated and disfigured art by concentrating on insignificant detail, reducing art and literature to ironic anecdotes, small confectionary. . . . What is lacking is *the principle of incarnation*. Art has no longer its home either in heaven or on earth or in hell. Our present day literature is a literature without a world; it is out of joint like eveything else. It is without passion and without insanity, like the devil. It lacks the stormy majesty of great passion, and the deeper reason for this lack is that men have lost the vision of those immense spaces which are traversed by the Saints—the Saints who appear on the surface so tranquil, so waterproof. But there is hidden in all human inwardness an oceanic mobility, a striving for perfection, which is a way without end, the way of the entire creation, with eternity as the goal. It is a way of messages, of universal communications, of participations in truths, in beauties, in fruitful anxieties (published in *Esprit*, August 1950).

In another letter to the same friend he wrote: "I venerate the clarity of Racine, and I detest the verses of Cocteau, just as much as I detest a certain pious and episcopal type of poetry, pseudo-Catholic and exclusively for clerical use. We can have either world-open reality-saturated Catholic literature or closed world-estranged sectarian, Jansenist pseudo-literature, whether it be clerical or abstract-surrealist."

In the last analysis, the vocation of a writer was for Bernanos an "impossible" vocation. He had learned from bitter experience what it meant to be a writer in a material as well as in a spiritual sense—*only* a writer, and a *Christian* writer at that: one who dreams himself into the most sublime realities. For what does his own miserable little life amount to, compared with the lives of those saints and heroes whom his pen creates? What are his dreams worth unless he be permitted to pay for them with his very existence, with his lifeblood? The Roman Catholic ruling circles had given

him "what they are willing to give to one who does not flatter them
—exactly nothing." Bernanos was thus content to have gained the
approval of a small group of kinsmen and friends. But did they
really understand him? Were these literary men who admired his
glorious style really the readers for whom he wrote? "What bitter
irony," he exclaimed in *Cimetières,* "this pretense of the will to
persuade, to convince when, after all, it is my deepest certainty
that the still redeemable part of the world belongs to no one but *the
children, the heroes,* and *the martyrs.*"

Bernanos despised the prudent methods of a well-intentioned
apologetics which tries to lead the opponent to truth step by step.
He preferred to hurl his reader into the incomprehensible mystery
of faith, into its darkest luminosity. With such a method and intent
he could of course never hope to gain a large reading public. All
he could hope for was that spark of grace which here and there
might strike some lonely individual reader. This then was what he
called his "impossible" task: to build lasting edifices with the most
fragile and ephemeral material, to build monuments of the supernatural with the tools of a trade which like no other was marked
by human vanity and pride. For he knew full well that he was *only*
a writer, no saint, no extraordinary human being. He also knew
that he was not of the race and type of those men whom he portrayed
in his novels. He regarded himself as a "street singer, living in exile
in a land without streets" (in Brazil).

In the final section of *Les enfants humiliés* Bernanos contemplates
his Brazilian hut, and it turns for him into a symbol of the "open
house" of his life. Many unknown persons are passing by and are
looking in:

My house does not live up to their expectations, but it nonetheless belongs
to them; it is open to them. I am glad that I have built my life so poorly
that one can enter into it as into a mill. And if I may further pursue this
simile, I do not regret having journeyed so far across the sea, because
even though I may not have found here the house of my dreams, I have
found at least something that closely resembles my life. The doors have

no locks, the windows no panes, the rooms no ceilings. No one will deny that this *is* an open house. ... We are in the hands of every passer-by as in the hands of God (pp. 209 ff.).

We have had occasion before to call attention to the fact that for Bernanos *The Diary of a Country Priest* (*Journal d'un curé de campagne,* Paris: Plon, 1936) was the favorite among all his works, the only one which he personally endorsed from beginning to end, simply because he had written it with his very lifeblood. No false modesty prevented him from regarding this book as a true masterpiece. No doubt ever assailed this conviction, whereas on *Monsieur Ouine,* for example, he had worked for ten years, constantly tortured by doubting his talents as a writer. Those letters, on the other hand, in which Bernanos refers to the progress of his work on the *Diary* are filled with confidence, for he knew immediately and as if by intuition that success was certain.

Thus the *Diary* represents one of those rare instances where a writer finds a fully adequate external form for his inner vision. It had, after all, been the author's fondest dream ever since he had become engaged in the art of the novelist to create the profile of the "saint," that is, of a Christian man (or woman) in whom the Christ-life had in a very real sense become incarnate. This early dream became a reality in the country priest of Ambricourt—a priest destined by Providence to live his humble life in a small French village which, to use the words of the *New York Times Book Review,* "becomes almost a microcosm." This young priest, of humble peasant stock, sickly in his body and none too brilliant in his mental endowments, is presented in the pages of his diary in his great spiritual strength which shines through the frailty of his burdensome somatic condition. And the interiority of this seemingly average human being becomes the battleground of the gigantic struggles of good and evil that are besetting our bleeding world on this tiny planet set amidst the immeasurable macrocosm of as yet unknown and uncounted galaxies.

The humble servant of God at Ambricourt was, as Bernanos

confessed, so close to his heart and his mind that he could not even think of giving him a specific name, for this would have indicated at least a modicum of the objective distance of the observing spectator. Thus this young priest, in all his awkward insecurity and often oppressively real incertitude, comes close to existential despair, from which he is saved only by that faith which can truly "move mountains." The priest loves the people whose souls are entrusted to his feeble hands but who, in their turn, are unwilling to take him seriously and who subject him to all those either robust or subtle cruelties which human malice is capable of and against which people of this type are defenseless. But, as the author explains the plight of his hero, "his naïveté overcomes everything; when he believes that everything is lost, he discovers that he has served his God precisely to the extent that he thought he had completely failed. . . . In peace he will die of cancer" (of the stomach). This is the kind of Christianity that Bernanos likens to the divine and still unspoiled nature of children and childlike human beings.

The Country Priest clearly recognizes that it is prayer which provides the *juste milieu*, that rarefied atmosphere, in which absolute truth can live and breathe. This is the reason why the young priest never desists in his effort to extend prayer into the life of every day and every hour, so that all thinking and doing may be transformed into "a conversation between God and myself." He is encouraged in this effort by his wise but somewhat crusty superior, the Curé de Torcy. The latter tells him that when he has an idea, he tries to place it before God, and then the idea will undergo such a remarkable change that one may no longer even recognize it as one's own. The same reflection, the Curé de Torcy insists, applies especially with regard to the *mysterium iniquitatis* (the mystery of iniquity), the problem of evil. A Christian should try to look at evil not with his own eyes but, as it were, with God's eyes, that is, in that state of mind which is generated by prayer. Man cannot force evil to retreat by looking at it with a fixed stare, for if he does he will never escape its strange and seductive fascination. "And never look at it without praying." For, the Curé de Torcy continues his fatherly discourse, there is a mysterious connection between prayer and the understanding of our fellowman.

Upon listening to these words, the country priest asks himself whether there could be a similar connection between the life of the religious contemplatives, those cloistered monks, those "day-dreamers," and their often uncanny insight into the psyche of human beings.

This kind of vision is for Bernanos not only the characteristic of the authentic religious vocation but also the paradigm of the vision of the artist and the poet. And the significance of prayer, the author insists, applies equally to both types of vision. In short, prayer is for him the only means by which any human being can authentically partake of spiritual reality and of the vision of God.

While the country priest meditates on the revolt of sinners and broods about the dark mysteries of demoniac possession, he feels an overwhelming desire to be able to look at all "these crippled creatures with angelic eyes." And the Curé de Torcy turns this lonely meditation into a fruitful dialogue with his question, "Do you pray to the Angels?" He implies that people do not usually pray to the Angels. And why not? Because the theologians are a little afraid of them, "and yet the world is full of Angels." But not far removed from the Angels are the children and, more especially, that child which each and every human being once was, that child which eventually will sit in judgment over our lives. "I wish," retorts the Country Priest, weaving the thread of the same theme, "I could speak the language of childhood." Now and then, he admits, he succeeds in reawakening some of the long forgotten cadences of that wondrous tongue. There is one abiding wish that fills his soul, the wish that to the end he may remain loyal to the child that once he was and that lies dormant like a remote ancestor.

This book met, probably to Bernanos' own surprise, with a rather enthusiastic reception on the part of the French reading public which hitherto had shown but little appreciation of the genius

of the great novelist. It was awarded the Grand Prix of the Académie
Française.

Aside from the theme of prayer and the discourses on the problem
of evil to which we have already referred, the work contains other
striking observations on certain aspects of contemporary life and
civilization which command the attention of the discriminating
reader. In some instances the spokesman is the Curé de Torcy,
but in the majority of the most notable passages it is the pages of
the Diary itself that tell the story.

One problem which never failed to arouse Bernanos' interest
and to evoke his comments is that of science and technology. In
this novel the author uses the Curé de Torcy to express his doubts
and reservations. The priest is by no means hostile to science and its
spectacular exploits: he does not propose to arrest or even retard
scientific and technological progress, but he asks the pertinent
question what it would profit the scientist if he could even create
life in a test tube in an age when human beings seem to have lost
all sense of the meaning of life. "Might as well blow your brains
out among your test tubes."

The Curé de Torcy has given some thought also to the problem
of poverty and to those "wars" that are being propagated for the
abolition of poverty. He seems convinced that scripture was not
far off the truth when it stated that the poor will always be with us.
He reminds the Country Priest that they were trying their hand at
this noble experiment in Russia. And he does not think that the
Russians are any worse than the rest of us. In his view, "they are
all mad, mad dogs, the people of today—but those Russian bastards
have at least got some guts. . . . They can stomach anything. Give
them another century or two and they will be able to swallow a
polytechnic engineer—and keep him down."

The Country Priest too has often found himself thinking about the
Russians, and he does so "with a strange sort of inquisitiveness and
tenderness." He knows from bitter experience the meaning of real
poverty, "its joys, mysterious, incommunicable—Russian writers

can bring tears to the eyes. . . . Sufficient to have once heard . . . the cry of a people, a cry different from that of any other nation. . . . There is something of everything in it . . . the howling of a moujik under the rods, the screaming of a beaten wife . . . and the growlings of animal joy." For, alas, "poverty and lust seek each other out and call to each other like two famished beasts. . . . And yet I feel that such distress . . . that has ceased to reason or to hope, that lays its tortured head at random, will awaken one day on the shoulder of Jesus Christ." Here then we have, with the poor of Russia serving as illustration, a powerful resumption and restatement of Léon Bloy's ruminations, protestations and rantings on the blessings and the curses of poverty.

And just as the poor will always be with us, so will the rich: there will always be hard and greedy men and women who crave possessions, but even more they crave power. Such men and women are, alas, found just as often among the poor as among the rich. So perhaps we had better take a good look at ourselves in the mirror. For what, after all, is poverty? "Poverty is the emptiness in your hearts and in your hands." Weak men and weak women will likewise be with us at all times, and Christ meant to tell us that the weak will always be a prodigious burden on our fragile shoulders, "a dead weight" which "our proud civilizations will pass on to each other with rage and with loathing."

The Curé de Torcy contributes his own share to the younger priest's meditations on man's obligations toward his brothers by reminding him of a famous saying of the medieval Flemish mystic Jan van Ruysbroeck (1293–1381), surnamed "the Admirable": "Even though you were caught up in ecstatic rapture, and there was a sick man to ask you for a bowl of soup, leave your seventh heaven and give him what he asks for." This means that the contemplative and the active life should be intertwined or, as other Christian mystics expressed the same thought, that "Martha and Mary must work together" in a cooperative effort for the benefit of all.

This consideration evokes once more a reflection on the nature of prayer. The pages of the *Diary* return to this theme again and again. The usual idea of prayer the country priest regards as quite absurd. For if prayer amounted to nothing but formalized chatter or a superstitious kind of petition for the good things of this world as well as of the next, how could thinking people find such abundant joy in prayer? Or is prayer, perhaps, as some scientists and psychologists tell us, nothing but autosuggestion? They surely can never have met some of those old and wise monks who were aglow with their passionate insight and at the same time showed a great tenderness in their humanity. True prayer does not stand in need of many words, for silence is often more eloquent than any words, and listening is a great art that requires a good deal of experience and mastery. The Country Priest calls prayer a truly extraordinary "opiate," one that does not turn an individual back upon himself and isolate him but rather unites him with all human beings in universal love.

And yet the Country Priest realizes only too clearly the weakness and caducity of his own prayers. For, more often than not, when he needs a response to his prayer most, it remains unanswered: God does not come to him. Thus, without even remotely suspecting the parallel, the priest frequently experiences those days and hours of failure and total abandonment which the mystics described as "the dark night of the soul"—a sensation of complete dryness and a feeling of utter futility and meaninglessness. He knows of course that many saints had similar experiences of failure and forlornness, "but never this dull revolt, this spiteful silence of the spirit." What then threatens is the abyss of nothingness: "I breathe, I inhale the night; it is entering into me through some ... crack in my soul. I myself am the night." This is when the horrible thought strikes him that he might perhaps never again be able to love, and he lies prostrate at the foot of his bed, his face downward: "I only wanted to make the true gesture of complete acceptance. . . . I waited to be picked up."

This kind of self-analysis fits perfectly Kierkegaard's description of "existential despair." But, as the Danish philosopher-theologian reminds himself and his reader, such despair is not necessarily a "sickness unto death" because it can be healed by faith. How? "By virtue of the absurd." And therefore the one who is seemingly fully and consciously in the abyss of despair "is already beyond despair." But first the bitter cup has to be emptied to the dregs. The person thus abandoned, the Country Priest notes in his diary, has lost even the capacity to suffer! "I feel so horribly well. No fear of death," for death has become just as indifferent to him as life. He feels as though he had gone right back all the way he had come since God first had drawn him out of the void. First he was no more than a spark or an atom of the glowing dust of divine love. And now he feels he is that again, lost in the darkest of dark nights, nearly extinguished.

These diary jottings contain of course profound psychological insights. They are of a nature which perhaps only the highly trained psychologist or, at the other end of the scale, the *docta ignorantia* of the childlike pure soul of the saint can describe, the former by way of experiment and rationalization, the latter by personal experience and intuitive knowledge.

The climax of this kind of psychological insight is embodied in that unforgettable episode in which the Country Priest records in his diary his decisive encounter with the Countess, who with her profligate husband and her family lord it over the poor villagers. Typical representatives of a decadent aristocracy, they present a stark contrast to the lives of those whom Dostoevsky called "the humiliated and offended."

This scene stands out as a classical and typical example of the healing of a severe neurosis, not by an experienced psychotherapist but by a humble and unlettered priestly physician of the soul. It would be a serious mistake, however, to engage in unwarranted generalizations or to draw unjustified conclusions concerning presumed successful priest therapists. The sobering fact is that most priests and ministers who dabble in psychotherapy are as a rule no more successful than psychiatrists and psychotherapists who dilettantishly engage in "spiritual guidance." Both are running the risk of doing more harm than good, except perhaps in a few shaded areas in which psychotherapy and spiritual guidance overlap or even coincide. This is much too serious a territory to permit the intrusion of bunglers, regardless of their possible intellectual acumen.

Keeping this cautionary remark in mind, we may now proceed with a brief analysis of the problem facing the Country Priest: For some time he has had the impression that his mere presence was, in a manner of speaking, summoning the evil in others to the surface. It had seemed to him as if the "enemy" face to face with such an insignificant adversary could afford not to hide himself, as if sin and the sinner chose to defy him and make ridicule of him openly and unashamedly. This is precisely what happens in several encounters with members of the Count's family, but especially and in a most aggravated form in the final decisive encounter with the Countess herself. At one of their meetings in the grounds of the château the noblewoman remarks with biting irony that priests often have such strange notions of family life, and she wonders why she feels a compulsion to reveal to this stranger to reality the dark secrets of her life.

The Countess once had a son, the fulfillment of all her longing. He lived only eighteen months. Her daughter, whom the bad example set by her father, the Count, has corrupted when she was still in the tender years of childhood, had hated that little brother from the moment of his birth. On the day of the little boy's death the girl went out with her father for a walk. When they returned the boy was dead. From that day on the Count and his daughter became inseparable. The girl acted as if she were the real mistress of the house and began to treat her mother as if she were one of the servants in the household. The Countess, meanwhile, lived locked up and locked in with the memory of her son.

What had happened to the Countess? In her loneliness and in the knowledge that her husband had been unfaithful to her all through her married life, she had begun to idolize her dead little boy, while at the same time she has nothing but hate for her husband, for her daughter and evidently also for herself. In medical terms, the Countess is suffering from a severe "neurotic fixation" which totally dominates her and completely distorts her sense of reality. Bernanos can well afford to convey his meaning without resorting to psychiatric technical language, merely by allowing his hero to tell his story in the simplest possible terms.

The priest tries to persuade himself to feel nothing but pity for this unfortunate woman, and as a rule he has found it very easy to share sympathetically in another person's depravity, but what complicates matters in this case is the contrast between the graceful external appearance of the château and the dark and cruel secrets it harbors. As a result, instead of compassion he feels indignation at the sight of these foolish human beings with their stubborn malice. They are the ones, he thinks to himself, who do their level best to give all the powers of evil and of death a free hand.

When the Countess meets the priest's admonitions with the haughty assertion that "hers is a *Christian* household," the measure of his exasperation knows no more bounds. This phrase "hits him like a bullet in his chest." But the Countess, unaware of the priest's state of mind, continues in the same vein. She observes casually that the little priest naturally reasons like all the members of the working class and that, of course, every family has skeletons in their closets. Does it do any good, she asks, to wash one's dirty linen in public? The priest, however, can now speak without restraint, straight from the shoulder. He tells the Countess that the most stupid and the most blind are the self-satisfied members of the possessing and possessive classes, and it is precisely the poor man who can smell from afar the hidden vices of the rich. And, somewhat more calmly, he points out to the Countess that actually we are all members of one and the same large family, the family of the human race, and that there is only one family-head, Christ.

To all appearances, these last words have hit the mark. The Countess tells the priest that he is a very queer sort of man; she has never met another one like him, and she suggests that they part as friends. Yet the priest has already gone too far to retreat. He sees through the sham of this faked conciliatory mood. More than that, he feels the hardness of heart and the stubbornness of mind that hide behind the façade of a polite rejoinder. His patience has reached the breaking point. "God will break you," he shouts, and she responds with an agonized moaning sigh, not a sigh of submission, however, but of ultimate defiance. Has God not broken her already when He took her son? What more can He do?

From here on the struggle between these two headstrong personalities becomes desperate. When the Countess tells the priest to hold his tongue, he replies, "No, Madame, too many have held their tongues." In this case silence would be cowardice. Does she insist on creating her own hell? For what else is hell but "not to love any more"? Hell is to cease loving and to relinquish the will to understand—and yet to go on with the external motions of life. Actually, however, both time and movement have stopped for these crippled creatures: they are fixed and frozen forever. This thought of Bernanos of course brings to mind the case history of Dostoevsky's Stavrogin, who too was "frozen" and thus had condemned himself to eternal "fixation." And we might also think of the three "frozen" individuals in Sartre's image of hell as he sketched it in his play *No Exit* (*Huis-clos*).

The Countess in a hysterically passionate scream asserts that nothing either in this world or the next can ever separate us from what we have loved most, loved more than life itself, more than life eternal. The priest then goes straight to the heart of the matter. He is certain, he tells the Countess, that God has permitted him to see the danger that threatens her, her alone. And he asks of her the seemingly impossible—complete resignation to the will of God, that is, free and unreserved acceptance. The initial effect of this frontal assault is open rebellion, "authentic rebellion." How can he dare accuse her of any sin? Does she not attend mass? Does she not fulfill what the Church commands? She would consider it beneath her dignity to neglect her religious "duties." This argument the priest calls much worse than any blasphemy could ever be. Her words are replete with "the callousness of hell." Has she not at least lived in a semblance of "peace" until this accursed accuser had sown seeds of doubt in her conscience? God had become indifferent to her. If she is now ready to admit that she hates God, "will you be any better off, you idiot?" But the "idiot" suggests that she is already beyond hate, for hate equals precisely indifference. At this moment, however, the priest is seized with an undefinable fear: for "this woman had lived for many years in the horrible quietness of desolation, and desolation is of all the forms of despair the most atrocious, the most incurable and the least human. Such suffering, however, is of a kind which priests should only approach with fear and trembling."

It is during this fearful struggle against doubt and terror that with great sweetness and gentleness—and when least expected—the spirit of prayer returns to the priest's heart. The Countess, exhausted from this ordeal, has sunk into a chair, her head resting between her hands. At last she takes a medallion which she has been wearing around her neck on a silver chain. The medallion contains a lock of yellow hair. The priest now realizes that the end of this strange "therapy" is in sight. All that is left for him to do now to free this woman from her "fixation" is to convince her that what the Lord really demands is *all* or *nothing:* "Give Him everything, and He will give you back even more."

Now peace begins to flow in from all sides, a peace which this earth cannot give because it surpasses all human understanding. The priest sees himself "standing there alone between God and this tortured human being." The priest's final words carry no threat and no reproach. He merely reminds the Countess that it really may concern God very little when we shake our fist at Him, when we spit into His face, when we scourge and crucify Him. And why should it concern Him so little? Because "my daughter, it has already been done to Him."

As in almost every therapeutic process, there remains one last obstacle to be overcome. The technical name for it is transference. The mentally ill or disturbed person transfers his or her idolization from its original object (or subject) to the therapist, in our "case history" to the priest. "It is to *you* I surrender," says the Countess. And the priest, inexperienced in the art of therapy, exclaims unbelieving and almost in terror, "*To me?*" And the Countess repeats that she will *not* surrender unless it be to him who is the one who has torn the inveterate hate out of her heart. However, the spirit of prayer is an invaluable aid in inducing a final "transference," namely, from the priest to his Master. And so the Countess is ready and willing to give to the Master her one and her all—everything. The priest sees "her eyes shining strangely, but it was already too late to stop her. She flung the medallion into the midst of the glowing logs."

This is really more than the priest would have dared to ask for, for God is no "executioner." He "wants us to be merciful with ourselves." The end is or seems to be the peace which the priest had asked for and the Countess had longed for in her heart of hearts. "The peace I had invoked for her had descended also upon me. . . . She has asked me to hear her confession tomorrow. I have made the promise to tell nobody what passed between us, and on my side I have vowed absolute silence. 'No matter what may happen,' I said; and my heart sank with these last words, and again sadness overcame me, 'God's will be done.' "

When the priest returns to his modest abode, he is handed a small parcel from the Countess. He already guesses what is inside—the empty medallion with its broken chain. But there is something more, a letter. It reads: "I have lived in the most horrible solitude, alone with the desperate memory of a child. And it seems to me that another child has brought me back to life again. . . . Now I hope again." What new and strange kind of hope is this? "No more what philosophers call 'hope' than the word 'love' is like being loved. This hope is flesh of my flesh, I can't even express it. I should have to speak as a little child."

There is one terse postscript to this last diary entry: "*Half-past six.* Madame la Comtesse died last night. . . . 'Be at peace,' I told her. . . . Oh, miracle—thus to be able to give what we ourselves do not possess, sweet miracle of our empty hands! . . . Lord, I am stripped of all things, as you alone can strip us bare, whose fearful care nothing escapes, nor your terrible love!"

After this grandiose psychological-theological drama of conversion, rivalled only by some of the masterly psychological analyses in Dostoevsky's *The Brothers Karamazov, The Idiot,* or in the *Notes From the Underground,* the themes subsequently meditated upon in the *Diary* are almost anticlimactic. There are, however, a few notable exceptions. One of these is the encounter of the Country Priest with the brutal fact of his own impending death, on the occasion of his often-postponed visit to Dr. Delbende in the city of Lille. This episode is much more than a documentary of Bernanos' lifelong fascination with medical science and with the characters of its practitioners. Like Dr. Laville, another physician whom the priest has previously consulted, he is himself endowed with a thirst for the *libido sciendi.*

While in the office of Dr. Belbende the priest does not know yet that he is dying of a carcinoma of the stomach. Now he meets with another man who is also among those condemned to death by their somatic condition. The physician suffers from a malignant lymphogranulomatosis, a term that sounds quite outlandish and forbidding to the priest. Symptomatically this disease is characterized by deep ulcerations of the skin of the genitals, and it is evidently caused by a microorganism sometimes referred to as Donovan body. This illness is generally believed to be caused by venereal infection. The priest feels most uncomfortable in the presence of this man of science who may hold his death warrant, and he is seeking for an excuse to get away. But the physician feels—despite

his avowed agnosticism—as if he had met a twin brother. They
both never had spared themselves, and Delbende is certain that the
priest was just as untiringly dedicated at the seminary as he himself
was at the Provins *lycée*. The one "hurled" himself on Religion as
the other had hurled himself upon Science. And now they are
facing the same ultimate end. When the doctor says that he will
be dead in six months, the priest believes he is referring to suicide,
and the other can easily read this thought in the priest's mind.
But suicide, the doctor remarks, is not for men of his kind.
Suicide is "a game for lords and poets," a luxury which a scientist
can ill afford. However, in the face of certain death, he is not
willing to turn his back on "the goal," that is, on his vocation.

Then the physician mentions another grave problem, a problem
which sooner or later confronts every practitioner in the healing
arts. Should a physician tell the truth to a patient who is in the
terminal stage of his illness? Is it advisable and permissible to lie
to a patient? The doctor thinks it is: "Lying to my patients is a
necessary part of my calling." And when the priest replies that
perhaps Delbende is lying too much, the doctor observes that it is
very difficult for him to kill a patient's hope with one devastating
blow. It is different, he thinks, with theologians because they put
their trust in the future and thus escape the predicament of the
awful present; their trust "has folded hands." He too, however,
knows that hope dies slowly and reluctantly, and he compares it
with a wild beast, powerful and fierce. Therefore it is better to
allow it to die very slowly.

Up till now the priest had engaged in this discussion more or less
theoretically. Probably his subconscious mind had kept from him
the realization that it is his own illness and his own death that are
the real subject matter of this dialogue. This is why the physician,
with a gesture of sincere compassion, places his hand on the priest's
shoulder while he tells him that perhaps a doctor does owe the
truth to people of his kind. And now the truth comes to the priest
with such force that even before Delbende has finished speaking

he realizes that he is already like a dead man among those still living. Almost absentmindedly he listens to his sentence: "*Cancer, cancer of the stomach!*"

The presence of the physician is forgotten. The priest is alone, facing his death. The visible world is slowly fading away, and many dazzlingly beautiful images begin to emerge, pictures of the past and also some pictures of the present. It had all been so very beautiful! Is it possible that he actually has loved this life so much, loved this world so much? And suddenly he realizes that he is crying bitterly and happily. Happily, because he feels like a man who is an unhappy-happy lover. The tears may be the tears of a coward, but they are tears of love nonetheless!

His youth rises up before the eyes of the priest's mind; youth which is always God's precious gift. Are not the ones who appreciate the gift of youth most those who do not survive it? No doubt the priest is one of these. He sometimes used to wonder what he might do or what he might be like at the age of fifty. It was only natural that he never found an answer because there simply never was a man of fifty in his psychophysical being. He was one of those who are and remain eternally young.

How does such a young man, such a young priest, face death? The *Diary* simply records that he does not confront it bravely, but that he has tried to face it with open eyes and with the readiness for total surrender. To do this well, however, one would again have to become like a little child. He has loved human beings very deeply, and this is why to depart from them is a sad and tearful business. Nothing, he knows, is farther from him than stoic indifference. Is he really terribly afraid? If he is, then there is no reason why he should be ashamed to confess his fear. Taken all in all, the priest can truthfully say that he does not hate himself, that he is reconciled to himself, that he is willing to accept himself as he is, without pride and without pusillanimity.

This theological novel which is really nothing but the straight and simple autobiographical journal of one of Christ's "little

people" is precisely for this reason also the diary of a saint. It closes
with a letter written by Monsieur Louis Dufrety, a defrocked
priest, and addressed to Monsieur le Curé de Torcy. The letter
tells of how Dufrety found his former schoolmate and friend, the
country priest—to whom he had given shelter in the messy household which he shares with his paramour, after the priest's visit to
the office of Dr. Delbende—unconscious on the floor of his room.
Later he vomited blood but finally regained consciousness. But he
did not speak. He did not have to speak nor was he able to. Only
his eyes spoke of a great anguish. However, when Dufrety came
closer he heard distinctly the whispered words: "Does it matter?
Grace is everywhere." Then he died. Somewhat earlier he had told
his friend, the renegade priest: "If some day I might have the great
misfortune of becoming disloyal to the vows of my ordination, I
would rather have this happen because of a great love for a woman
than because of what you choose to call 'intellectual growth.' "
Thus the Alpha and Omega of the life of the Country Priest was
and remained to the end *love*—love of God and love of man, whether
man be sinful or holy.

CHAPTER FOUR

François Mauriac

VIPERS' TANGLE

IN THE POSTSCRIPT to his novel *Galigaï* François Mauriac wrote: "Perhaps I was created and placed on this small piece of earth to give testimony of the guilt of man before the boundless purity of God." Early in 1952 Jean Cocteau addressed to Mauriac the following indictment: "I accuse you of acting as a judge who secretly has nothing but tender love for his culprits. . . . I accuse you of depicting only that which is ignoble and of trying to restrict all nobility to another world. . . . I accuse you of acting from petty motivations which you drape up as moral principles." We shall make an attempt to find out to what extent these and similar indictments by representatives of the literary intelligentsia are justified.

Mauriac was born at Bordeaux in 1885. His parents belonged to the middle class of the French bourgeoisie. They were moderately affluent and, as most of the inhabitants of the Gironde, were at least nominally of the Roman Catholic faith. Order, thrift and hard work were characteristics of the men, while it fell to the women to uphold the tradition of religious devotion. The men, too, adhered to some external religious observances: they usually attended Sunday Mass from force of habit, while also habitually they never denied themselves any of the pleasures of this world. As a rule of prudence, they showed an external decorum, to avoid giving scandal and possible public reprobation. There were, however, always a few among them in the towns and villages who were dissatisfied with this kind of double standard of morality. They were the freethinkers, the anticlericals, the "radicals." The members of the peasantry were actually pagans at heart and had retained but few links with the Church, aside from clinging to the ritual that marked the most decisive events in human life: birth, marriage and death. Almost customarily the men regarded their priests as a sort of parasites who were in a material sense unproductive and lived at the expense of their parishioners.

Mauriac's family did not quite fit into this general pattern. His father died when François was not yet two years old. He left behind his widow, four sons and one daughter. The father had been a freethinking rationalist, while François' mother was a devout and dedicated Christian woman. François resembled his father both physically and in his moral disposition. And like his father, only to a much greater degree and probably with much less justification, he was almost perpetually tormented by scruples of conscience. This was obviously due to a more or less conscious Jansenistic mentality which had been kept alive in the family tradition. The result was that—whether they were freethinking skeptics or believers —their lives were dominated by the triple threat of a terrifying God, an all-pervasive sense of guilt and sin, and the certainty of death which would exact retribution and judgment when it was least expected. What mitigated somewhat the harshness of this eschatological prospect was the beauty of the surrounding landscape with its vineyards stretching alongside the banks of the Garonne and the wide expanse of the forests.

It is the combination of elements of inherited characteristics, environment and psychological influences and experiences that give color as well as contrasts to the novels of Mauriac and account for the complexity of his character portraits, portraits of entire families whose lives are so replete with hatreds, depravities and all the deadly sins that nothing but unmerited and unmeritable divine grace can intervene occasionally as a redeeming force.

Is there any other trait in Mauriac's novels that could be cited as mellowing the forbidding pessimism of a Jansenistically dis-colored human nature? In 1952, in the acceptance speech Mauriac delivered in Stockholm on the occasion of the awarding of the Nobel Prize for Literature, the author gave an answer to this question: "Nothing grieves me more," he said, "than the fact that my critics and my sometimes too hasty readers tend to disregard the position which children occupy in my novels. The dream of a child holds the key to all my books. . . . They see the vipers in my novels, but not the doves. And yet, childhood is for me the lost paradise and the entrance gate to the mystery of iniquity."

Mauriac's delicate physical constitution kept him apart from his classmates at school, and his loneliness, paired with a rich imagina-tion and a superior intelligence, were conducive to melancholy. He complained that his teachers did not emphasize sufficiently the education of the intellect and put too much stress on the emotions. To this he attributes in part his preoccupation with the thought of his personal salvation as well as his growing alienation from the external world, a world which, he suspected, was populated with people who were not "in the state of grace." During the years of his adolescence he felt a growing personal conflict between carnal desires and puritanical-Jansenist precepts. He experienced more and more frequently anxieties and states of anguish because he believed himself separated from God and isolated from his fellow humans. At times he sympathized with the strongly anticlerical views of Anatole France, despite the fact that his religious faith remained unshaken. However, he had discovered with deep excitement an entirely new realm of literature, of a kind that was generally pro-hibited *terra incognita* for young Roman Catholics. It was inhabited by such poets and writers as Baudelaire, Verlaine and Rimbaud. The latter two became, in a sense, Mauriac's friends.

When, in 1905, François departed for Paris, he said of himself: "At the age when the blood awakens, all my disquietudes and anxieties turned into scruples; everything seemed to crystallize around the concepts of purity, sin, and the state of grace." At the

age of seventy-eight, in 1962, appeared Mauriac's definitive autobiographical confession, titled *What I Believe* (*Ce que je crois*).* It
not only contains his credo but also describes the odyssey of his
spiritual life. In these pages the "Christian radicalism" of his earlier
years has mellowed while, on the other hand, his existential realism
as well as his agonizing struggle with the *mysterium iniquitatis*
persist. The central preoccupation of the author remains the metaphysical and theological problem of sin and salvation. With fear
and trembling and even more with awe he ponders the mystery of
human guilt in the face of the inscrutable omniscience of God.

The pages of this book vibrate with an almost morbid soul-
searching long familiar to Mauriac readers. But the conclusion of
this confession strikes a note of childlike simplicity and total
acceptance. The main themes of Mauriac's creed are the same as
those one encounters in the confessional documents of his spiritual
ancestors—St. Augustine, Kierkegaard, Dostoevsky, Unamuno and,
above all, Pascal.

"This book," says Mauriac in a prefatory statement, "is not
intended for scholars or philosophers or theologians. I hoped in the
most simple and direct way possible to answer the question, 'Why
have you remained faithful to the religion into which you were
born?' " The answer to this question is—paradoxically—both
difficult and easy. In the years of adolescence Mauriac had un-
hesitatingly examined all the objections to the Church and the
Catholic faith raised by historical criticism and by Modernism.
But, he says, the final choice "was determined in advance": it was
"less the choice of a certain religion, of a certain Church, than the
choice of *Someone* with Whom I communicated thanks to that
Church and that religion." What ultimately confirmed Mauriac
in the faith of his youth was the fact that, thanks to the body of the
Church (more often than not presenting indeed aspects that were,
to use Nietzsche's phrase, "human, all too human"), "a certain

*Translated and with an Introduction by Wallace Fowlie (New York: Farrar,
Straus and Co., 1963).

Word has come down to us." Actually, there are *two* such sayings which Mauriac underscores: "Your sins are forgiven you," and "This is My body given for you."

What generated Mauriac's act of faith—notwithstanding those aspects of creation which appeared both bewildering and unacceptable to his intelligence—was neither the beauty of Christianity (that is, the aesthetic components of Catholicism) nor the liturgy, but solely the reality of the God-Man. "The closer I live to God . . . the less need I feel for ceremonies. . . . I am neither shocked nor scandalized by the pomp of the Vatican. But neither am I dazzled or really enchanted. I am grateful to the institution for what it has saved and protected and maintained." Mauriac does not minimize in this confession his misgivings regarding the temporal history of the Church, "its relationship with Caesar," but he looks beyond this foreground to "the soul of the Church, manifested for me no better in Saint Peter's at Rome than in the poorest village church where the small lamp burns and which I prefer. For Saint Peter's was built with money from indulgences which cost the Church half of the people who joined the Reformation. This was putting architecture at too high a price" (*What I Believe,* p. 10). He recalls the presence of Pope John XXIII and the beginning of Vatican Council II. Through this gentle old man who spoke "the words of mercy which I always wanted to hear in Rome," the Holy Spirit itself addressed the world, "the spirit of love and consolation. . . . He pronounces no anathema, no curse, and all nations turn toward the prow of the ancient boat, more impressed by the sight of the fisher of men than they were . . . by the explorers of the cosmos. . . . Thus the sixth Pope to whom I have been obedient, the humblest of all, has scattered the cloud of distrust, the vague resentment in which I lived" (p. 137).

Mauriac continues:

Nothing is less natural to me than the impulse which encouraged Père Teilhard de Chardin to enlarge Christ to the dimension of the cosmos. . . . I belong to another race of men. In my eyes, the deepest mystery is that of the Creator reduced to the dimensions of each creature, the least of whom is infinitely more important than the cosmos, which is blind and deaf and without conscience. I do not see what the knowledge gained by these last generations would add to what Pascal said concerning the two infinities.

The particular *pensée* of Pascal to which Mauriac refers here, begins with the well-known words, "All material bodies, the firmament, the stars, the earth and its satellites are not worth the humblest human being. For man knows all that, and he knows himself. But the material bodies know nothing." But Pascal, to whom Mauriac "owes everything," who was his "master" even at the early age of sixteen, possessed an intellectual dimension which remained inaccessible to Mauriac: Pascal, the scientist—the mathematician and geometrician—eluded Mauriac. The same was not true of Teilhard de Chardin, whose mind and heart were wide and open enough to embrace the entire Pascal, his existential as well as his scientific testimonial. With great candor Mauriac admits: "The strangest part of this story is that there is no writer about whom I am less capable of speaking than this Pascal ... because one whole part of his genius eludes me" (p. 104). Why, then, did Mauriac feel so close to the spirit of Pascal? His answer: "We knew what Christ had said to the saints, to Saint Teresa of Avila, to Saint John of the Cross; but we were not able to believe that what concerned those heroic souls could also concern us. Yet Pascal, despite his greatness, remains one of us" (p. 106). One passage in particular in Pascal's writings struck root and lived on in "the most intimate and most secret part" of Mauriac's being: "It was to this brother that the Lord spoke the words, 'I thought of *you* in my suffering. Be consoled. You would not be looking for me if you had not already found me. For *you* I have shed a drop of blood.' " In short, Pascal owned what his late modern disciple obtained only in his old age: "He knew he was loved. . . . He possessed certainty, peace, joy, and the triumphant happiness of grace" (p. 112).

These pages illustrate Mauriac's agonizing struggle on the way to final certitude. But, as in the case of Pascal, there remains almost to the very end a Jansenistically inspired distrust of the wounded human nature and also an almost totally negative evaluation of technology and science: "I have no regard for the miracles of technology if they unfold in a materialistic prison, even if the prison has the dimensions of the cosmos. I have no interest in reaching the planets if what the . . . rocket carries is this poor body destined to rot away" (p. 33).

In Chapter IV Mauriac shows himself still obsessively pre-occupied with the theme of purity, a theme which had haunted him since the days of his childhood and on which he had elaborated most extensively in the essay titled *Souffrances et bonheur du chrétien* (1929); it concluded with the words of Léon Bloy, "There is only one misery—not to be a saint." Mauriac in his old age has at long last been able to rid himself of those spectres which had turned much of his youth into a nightmare: "We should not scorn the flesh. It is not the enemy I was taught to be ashamed of and to be afraid of. . . . This body of ours was sanctified by the Son of Man who Himself took it on" (p. 58).

The life of Mauriac was a life of loneliness, of a solitude which was in part self-chosen and in part attributable to what Kierkegaard in his similar predicament had referred to as his "crazy upbringing" which caused the Christian religion itself to become "a scandal" to him. "All my life," writes Mauriac, "I have felt within the visible Church a sentiment of redoubled solitude. . . . I have never been truly associated with the life of a parish. . . . I have been incapable of participating and have always disliked it. . . . In this I am guilty, and I confess that I have been the creator of my own solitude within the Christian flock. . . . The magic impassable circle which my own temperament has drawn around me . . . has condemned me to grow old and to die alone" (p. 65). Mauriac then tells of the great loneliness which often overwhelmed him even when breaking the Living Bread with fellow Catholics "who perform certain gestures but who have no authentic religious life" and of the companionship he often felt in the presence of "true Israelites" or "holy Moslems" or "certain souls who do not belong to any definite confession but who live, as Simone Weil lived, just outside the Church" (p. 68). Even in the souls of "avowed militant atheists" there is frequently a great longing "for the Kingdom of God and His justice. I recognize all the signs of the love of that Christ whom they do not know" (p. 69 f.).

But life's ambivalence seems to be and to remain so all-pervasive that we will have to have recourse again and again to that saying of St. Teresa of Avila which Mauriac chose as epigraph for his best novel, *Vipers' Tangle* (*Le Noeud de vipères*): "Lord, consider that we do not understand ourselves and that we do not know what we want, and that we go infinitely far astray from that which we really desire." The practical wisdom of these words reverberates in Mauriac's creed: "At my age . . . we discover that we do not detest the men we think we detest and that . . . they do not detest us. We often confuse hate with exasperation" (p. 76).

Who are those enemies who, with Nietzsche, have proclaimed that "God is dead"? "They were once Christians and are Christians no longer. . . . Whose fault is this? The truth of the matter is that Western Christianity has failed in its vocation" (p. 80). And since modern man "has cut off communication with God by . . . negation," the spirit of evil has been given an unparalleled chance.

Summing up the articles of his credo, Mauriac, like Unamuno, invokes from the Gospel of Mark (9:23) that anguished exclamation of a father whose son was possessed by an evil spirit but who was cleansed and healed by Christ: "Lord, I believe. Come, help my unbelief." What more can be said? "Lord, why didn't you abandon me? . . . Something in me must have disarmed you," although "that doorway which the saints went through I have never even approached"; and yet "my old age is sanctified by my communion on the Living Bread. . . . *What I believe?* I believe that I am loved such as I was, such as I am, such as my own heart sees me, judges me, condemns me" (p. 126).

In Paris, the ecclesiastical controversies, the political battles and the social conflicts between the "rich" and the "dispossessed" drew Mauriac's attention to problems with which he had hitherto been unfamiliar. He was himself one of those who could live with relative ease without being compelled to look for a gainful occupation. For a while he became involved in the rather short-lived religious-social *Sillon* movement which was founded in 1893 by Marc Sangnier. Its members were Roman Catholics who sought to bring about a solution of the "social question" in line with "Christian-democratic" principles. The movement died an untimely death after its condemnation by the Church (1910) because of its "liberalistic" tendencies.

Gradually Mauriac had come to a point where it became necessary for him to examine seriously the intellectual basis of his faith. In 1913 he had married Jeanne Lafont. He found in her *la grave compagne* of whom he had dreamed. One year later, World War I started and Mauriac served in Salonika in the early phase of that campaign.

To the young people of the post war period of 1920 Mauriac addressed these words: "There is no reason whatever for being so proud of our ignorance in matters of theology. . . . There is in the world no more foolish chimera than the pretense that we are capable of attaining happiness without paying any attention to metaphysics and theology."

"It seems to me," Mauriac stated later on, "that there was never anything so tragic as these early months of 1919, when the exhausted nations, following their blind leaders, were embarking upon the route to another inferno, worse than the one from which they had just emerged and which they wanted to forget at any price. . . . All around us we see young people, drunk and foolish, preferring their sad pleasures to true happiness."

It was Mauriac's conviction that God alone could give to man that happiness to which his being aspires. To demonstrate this thesis, Mauriac now attempted to portray human love in its most tragic and sordid aspects—mere carnal love, adulterous love, marriages of convenience, wrecked marriages, marriages that illustrate the dilemmas of adolescence and the loneliness of the marriage partners. By depicting human beings totally deprived of a religious sense of life, the author succeeded in exposing the emptiness of their hearts and souls.

In the period between 1925 and 1928 Mauriac created a series of characters who have no consciousness of sin at all. To explain their conduct he made use of the discoveries of biology, psychology and especially of psychoanalysis. He adopted the Freudian view concerning the decisive effects of early childhood experiences on the adult life of individuals. He also stressed the influence of heredity which in many instances predisposes or predetermines an individual for "vice." Both of these factors tend to diminish personal responsibility. This point of view gave Mauriac an opportunity to criticize society and the mediocrity of character it fosters, because, he insists, it is society which mutilates the potentialities as well as the free responsible actions of the individual. As the special enemy of the healthy development of the human being he singles out the family.

That Mauriac grew up without a father and a "father image" may account for the fact that the fatherly type is rarely encountered in his novels. Instead we find an abundance of widowed mothers and domineering grandmothers with a conspicuously pharisaical self-righteousness. Their sons or their grandsons are usually tortured by Mauriac's own moral dilemma—the struggle between carnal passion and the moral precepts and prohibitions imposed upon them by institutionalized religion, a religious frame of reference into which they were cast without having had a say in it. A case in point is Mauriac's first novel, written between 1909 and 1912, *Young Man in Chains* (*L'Enfant chargé de chaînes*). Though lacking the spiritual depth of the author's more mature works, the novel is nonetheless a genuine documentation of Mauriac's genius as a writer.

As we already know, Mauriac had never claimed to be either a theologian or a philosopher. Each of his novels expresses a view of life and reality distinctly his own and born of unmistakable personal experience. Each of them accentuates a specific facet of his total philosophy of life as well as a personalistic or existential reaction to some unique situation. Perhaps the one all-pervasive theme, a sort of leitmotif, is the experience of loneliness with its concomitant mood of melancholy. All of Mauriac's novels are marked by a decisive conquest of certain aspects of reality which were lacking in the traditional and conventional Catholic novel, aspects and dimensions which were fractionally embodied in the works of Zola, Flaubert, Stendhal, Gide and Proust, wholly incarnate perhaps only in the religious experience of Pascal. What was missing in the works of the French naturalists and symbolists was, according to Mauriac, the dimension of *the eternal*.

Notwithstanding the fact that Mauriac, as has been pointed out, realized and emphasized the significance of the massive influences of environment and heredity, he was convinced that what was needed to counteract and counterbalance these determining factors was *un surnaturalisme* which alone could eventually break down the prison walls erected by biological and social determinants and could thus aid the individual in his struggle for self-determination, liberation, emancipation and salvation. Mauriac fought his way through to a clear visualization of the nature of grace: only divine grace could resolve the otherwise hopeless entanglement of man in the thickets of depravity and perversion. Mauriac came to regard it as the vocation of the Christian writer to unveil the divine image in sinful man—a task which could be fulfilled only if the writer refrained from sentimental idealization and adhered to the strictest kind of natural-supernatural "realism."

"The giving of one's self," Mauriac wrote in an essay dealing with the art form of the novel, "the taste of purity and perfection, the hunger and thirst for justice, these too are part of the patrimony of man; and we novelists must bear witness to it. . . . We must dedicate ourselves to the discovery of the inner life, and we are not permitted to hide any of our discoveries." Mauriac had stated furthermore that the true cornerstone of his work was "the physical presence of grace." The simple and profound meaning of this phrase is—in the words of Bernanos and Graham Greene—that "grace is everywhere," regardless of whether the individual human being chooses to acknowledge or to ignore this omnipresence.

As is the case with several of Mauriac's novels, *Young Man in Chains* is in part autobiographical. Like the young Mauriac, Jean-Paul Johanet, the protagonist, is alone with himself as a student in Paris, feasting intellectually on the exultation he derives from his indulging in the literary masterpieces of the *fin de siècle* (Baudelaire, Verlaine, Rimbaud, etc.). This is the kind of life of which Mauriac speaks in his *Mémoires intérieurs* (1960): "All that I write today had its beginnings fifty years ago in that little club room of the Bordeaux *Sillon*. . . . I was filled with intellectual pride, as a young man so often is who has led an isolated existence in a remote countryside."

Jean-Paul is one of the idle "rich" whom nothing and nobody compels to look for gainful employment. Yet Jean-Paul is profoundly nauseated by an acute sense of personal failure and uselessness. The scenes he encounters on his annual expensive travels are powerless to console him or to mitigate the painful experience of being an "outsider": "All cities look alike. . . . The little world which I carry within myself never changes." Jean-Paul's relationship to his fellow-students is decidedly asocial and non-existential, although he enjoys watching them live their lives, giving them advice, even acting as their leader: "He turned their feet from the primrose path by telling them of his own struggles of conscience . . . and of the orgies in which he had participated before his conversion. . . . In this circle of young Catholics, Jean-Paul turned theologian. He spiced his talk with a grain of modernism," and his familiarity with Kantian philosophy "allowed him to demonstrate that St. Thomas Aquinas was no longer enough. He spoke with irony of the Encyclical *Pascendi* . . . and declared that the time had come to revert to the great mystical tradition."

Jean-Paul's chance meeting with Vincent Hieron, a former schoolmate, leads to his temporary affiliation with the members of *Amour et Foi,* the religious-social movement which we have already referred to, a movement which in the novel is fanned by the fanatical zeal of Jérome Servat, its "leader." Here again the autobiographical element is quite transparent. Aside from such occasional references to actual historical events and constellations and frequent personal introspective meditations of great complexity, the plot of this novel is of lapidary simplicity. What there is of a "love story" concerns the relationship of Jean-Paul, the sophisticated "amateur of souls," to Marthe Balzon, his cousin. Her love for Jean-Paul is an unquestioning self-giving which in its pristine purity becomes an unfailing medium of existential communication. Despite the physical frailty of the earthly vessel, this kind of love is capable of building bridges from soul to soul. It is a love as yet untainted by the gloom of the later Mauriac, who, in referring to Pascal's relationship to his sister Jacqueline, could say: "In brotherly love, as in any other kind of love, the one wounds, and the other is wounded." In Mauriac's first novel, this ordinary and therefore all the more luminous love is capable of breaking the "chains"—forged by heredity, environment, education, and temperament—of Jean-Paul, the "young man" with his sad "pleasures" and his melancholy ecstasies.*

The *oeuvre* of Mauriac can be divided into two distinct periods, the earlier one characterized by the metaphysical pessimism born of a Jansenistically discolored religious experience, and a later one that shows evidence of a decisive change to a more balanced and more humanistically oriented Weltanschauung. The first period reached its climax in the mid-Twenties of our century, when the author had completed the fourth decade of his life and when the powers of darkness and the prevalence of evil cast their deepest

---

*See the recent English translation of *Young Man in Chains* by Gerard Hopkins (New York: Farrar, Straus and Cudahy, 1965). This completes the English edition of Mauriac's narrative works.

shadows over his life and work. At that time the conflict between Jansenism and orthodox Catholicism had become so acute that an either-or seemed unavoidable: *either* the Jansenist doctrine of predestination and grace with a concomitant break with the Roman Catholic view of nature and reality, *or* a "conversion" to a Catholic realism that left room for at least a modicum of "natural" morality and free human cooperation with a supernaturally offered and infused grace. Mauriac made his choice about 1928.

It was then that Mauriac wrote upon request a critical Postscript to Bossuet's famous *Traité de la concupiscence*. Bossuet, the Court Theologian of Louis XIV and the educator of the French Dauphin, had written: "Tainted from the day of our birth and conceived in iniquity, in the ardour of a brutal concupiscence, in a revolt of the senses and an extinction of reason, we must fight to the day of our death the evil we have contracted in being born." Bishop Jansenius himself could not have been more explicit in denigrating human nature and in describing its alleged total perversion and corruption. However, Bossuet was officially regarded as one of the most authentic and respected spokesman of the *magisterium* of the Church. Mauriac, in his critique, cannot quite hide his own sense of "revolt," a revolt that had come into being almost imperceptibly but which asserted itself all the more strongly.

While Mauriac's original essay dealing with Bossuet's *Traité* had borne the title *Souffrance du Chrétien* (*The Suffering of a Christian,* first published in *La Nouvelle Revue Française*), he now wrote a sequel with the title *Bonheur du Chrétien* (*The Happiness of a Christian,* 1929). In this latter essay Mauriac states that the law of the spirit is the same as the law of the flesh. For when Christ said that He is "the Life" and that He is a true nourishment, He meant to say that He is literally the life and nourishment of mind and body alike. This meant, furthermore, that a true ennoblement was possible for man as a whole, as a composite of body and spirit or body and soul.

In comparing traditional Christian doctrine with the religion taught by Mohammed, Mauriac concludes that Mohammedanism is more realistic in that it does not demand of man the impossible. For example, he finds that it is beyond human power to remain blind to the beauty of human bodies. This is of course true. What is wrong with this comparison and with the entire argument is that Mauriac's perspective òf authentic Christian-Catholic theology is still somewhat askew. What he demands of man is more than his Church demands. What he interprets as a general maxim of Roman Catholicism is the ideal of an austere form of asceticism and monasticism, based on the Evangelical counsels of perfection and embodied in the monastic vows. This merely goes to show how deeply a certain Jansenist extremism was ingrained in Mauriac's mentality. Thus, even after his "conversion," Mauriac remained convinced that, as he asserted in *Dieu et Mammon,* (*God and Mammon,* 1929), "every human love acts as a block; it stands opposed to the exclusive love of God" (p. 128). In other words, he believes that the Christian God does not merely want to be loved: He wants to be loved *exclusively.* It would follow from this premise that from the Christian point of view human love can be justified only when it is cleansed of all carnality and has been transformed into a purely spiritual love. It took the author another three decades to rid himself (in his previously discussed autobiographical *confessio*) of this misconception.

According to Dom Cuthbert Butler, O.S.B., a fully authentic Christian life shows four essential characteristics: first, the public or social element, manifesting itself in congregational life, in cult and sacrament; second, the intellectual element as embodied in tradition, dogma and doctrine; third, the mystical element, reflecting a personal existential experience of the supernatural; and fourth (and most important) the element of charity or love, which becomes visible and tangible in the Christian's service to his fellowmen. It is Butler's contention that if one of these four is missing, one cannot speak of an integrated and well balanced Christian life.

If Butler's stipulations are regarded as valid, then we will have to admit that, as far as the *social* element is concerned, its function in Mauriac's work is largely negative, and to this extent he seems to fall short of the Christian ideal.

On the other hand, it is Mauriac himself who repeatedly and freely admits his hesitation to lead his characters farther than to the threshold of such an ideal Christian life. Often they gain their final insight only at the very end when they are facing death, that is, in what Karl Jaspers calls the "extreme limit-situation." For Mauriac the definitive assurance of the meaningfulness of human existence lies in the efficacious experience of grace. In the absence of this experience, there remains nothing but doubt, anguish, and even despair—the "dark night." For this reason Mauriac considered it his appointed task to convince those whom he addressed through his writings that their pleasures were illusory. Why? Because communion with God by virtue of infused grace was the only enduring pleasure, the only one, therefore, worth living and striving for.

Before turning to a discussion of the novel *Vipers' Tangle,* it appears necessary to round out the picture of Mauriac, the man of letters, by a few additional lines. In his analysis of such masters of style in French literature as Racine, Pascal, Jacques Rivière, and Lacordaire, he points to a common denominator in these authors—their constant preoccupation with the problem of the relationship of man to God and to his fellowmen. They all were of the conviction that love of God and love of neighbor were inherently interdependent and that therefore the one could not be conceived without the other. Conversely, Mauriac finds in Zola, Flaubert, Stendhal, Gide and Proust a common fault: since they place art above life, beauty above Him who created it, their hierarchy of values is lopsided and confused, and this accounts for the artistic as well as the moral defects in their literary production. The tragic conflicts in which Mauriac's characters find themselves entangled illustrate a similar confusion and perversion of the scale of values. His "dark angels" (one of his novels is titled *Les Anges noirs,* 1936) represent the Christian double drama of sinfulness and salvation. They appear at first glance as prisoners, mere puppets of an inexorable fate. However, at the moment of existential crisis, they become dimly aware of a certain freedom of choice: they can either submit to the tyranny of fate or they can revolt and fight against it. Mauriac means to say that as soon as these "dark angels" have the *will to freedom* they *are* free, free to accept unconditionally the grace offered them. Many of his introspective heroes and heroines are spending probably too much of their time with a meticulous scrutiny of their motivations, torturing themselves with an almost clinical observation of their own sufferings. In his novel *Dark Angels* Mauriac himself offers this comment: "Those who seem dedicated to evil may, perhaps, be chosen above their fellows: the very depth of their fall gives a measure of the vocation they have betrayed. None would be blessed had they not been given the power to damn themselves. Perhaps only those are damned who might have been saints."

The novel which perhaps represents the "reconverted" Mauriac in his most seasoned maturity as a writer is probably also his swan song as a novelist. *The Lamb* (*L'Agneau*, Paris: Flammarion, 1954) reminds the reader, in the theological problems it poses and in the manner they are resolved, of the later Mauriac's close affinity with Bernanos.

Some of the characters familiar from the author's earlier novel *Woman of the Pharisees* (*La Pharisienne*, Paris: Flammarion, 1941) are here reintroduced. From a conversation between Jean de Mirbel and Michèle, his unloved wife, the reader learns the story of young Xavier Dartigelongue. On the train that is to take him to the Seminary which he is about to enter as a candidate for the priesthood, Xavier makes the acquaintance of Jean de Mirbel, the corrupt *roué* who suggests to the young man that it is his spiritual vocation as a priest in the making to save Jean Mirbel's soul from virtually certain damnation. He persuades Xavier to return with him to the country estate of the Mirbels. There the youth meets with a weird group of wicked people: Michèle, Jean's coquettish spouse; Brigitte Pian, the mother-in-law (*la pharisienne*); the adopted and abused boy Roland; and Dominique, the young governess, who immediately falls in love with Xavier.

Xavier feels that it is his vocation to embrace with his Christian love all human beings whom God leads into his way, since he knows that he is responsible before his Creator for all of them. It is this absoluteness of the sense of his vocation which makes Xavier subservient to Jean Mirbel's suggestion to bring about a reconcilation between Jean and his wife and thus to show both of them the way to a true Christian marriage. In analyzing the psychological conflicts which torment and divide Xavier's personality and in bringing out symbolically the stark contrasts between the flesh and the spirit, between sexual and "pure" love, Mauriac shows himself once more as the master novelist.

In the end Xavier offers his own life as a sacrificial fulfillment of his "vocation." He is killed by Jean Mirbel's car. And it is no doubt intentionally that the author leaves several questions unanswered. Was Xavier himself responsible for the fatal accident? Did he deliberately throw himself in front of Jean's car? Or was this killing a premeditated act on the part of Jean? Or, finally, did everything happen in accordance with the inscrutable will of God? Mauriac's biographer P. H. Simon speaks of "the dizzying drama of sanctity." Actually the self-sacrificing young Xavier, the candidate for the priesthood, is like a twin brother of Bernanos' poor country priest of Ambricourt. "A saint does not commit suicide," remarks the old village parson, who himself is one of those who have lost (or perhaps have thrown away) their faith. What Mauriac does mean to say and to convey is simply that the "blood of the Lamb" had once again to flow to wash away the sin and guilt of Jean Mirbel and his wife Michèle. Thus the seemingly lost Paradise is regained in the end, and a depraved world is at once illumined by the rays of light which radiate from the sacrificed Lamb. The demons of darkness are dispelled by the gleam of sanctity. Temptation, fall and redemption are modeled in this novel after the eternal paradigm of the sacrificial life and death of the Son of Man.

Vipers' Tangle (*Le Noeud de vipères*) was published in 1930 and thus belongs to a relatively early stage of the second major period in Mauriac's spiritual development. The critics immediately and almost unanimously hailed it as a masterpiece of the theological novel. The work is the minute clinical case history of an obsession neurosis or even, at least in part, of a psychosis. In a sort of foreword the author introduces and simultaneously pleads the case of his protagonist, "this enemy of his own family, this soul eaten up by hatred and avarice"—he merits the reader's pity. What accounts for Louis's predicament is not only his dark passions but even more the kind of "Christianity" that he finds glaringly exhibited in all the members of his family. They, as Mauriac sees it, throw the sinner back upon himself and thus turn him away from the life of truth and reality.

The reader witnesses the development and eventual liberation and salvation of this alienated soul, alienated from others as much as from himself. Concomitantly, there proceeds on the reverse side of the ledger the thickening of a conspiratorial family intrigue. And this dual evolution is revealed, as was the case in the journal of Bernanos' country priest, in the pages of the diary to which Louis, the old miser, the erstwhile respected member of the legal profession, entrusts the secrets of his mind and heart.

Louis, who knows that he is slowly dying of cardial insufficiency, is writing down his reflections primarily to justify himself and his actions, not only before his wife Isa but, above all, before the tribunal of his own conscience. Louis, this "dark angel," possesses two potentially redemptive virtues: a pristine sincerity and a clairvoyant faculty of psychological self-knowledge and self-analysis.

A self-centered and psychologically rather unbalanced young lawyer, Louis married Isa, a young girl who seemed the consoling answer to his profound craving for love. But it needs no more than the casual and inconsiderate remark of his wife concerning an earlier acquaintance with another young man to arouse Louis's jealous suspicion that he is a victim of a deliberate deception. Obviously, he surmises, Isa has really never been in love with him. And so, to all appearances, the flame of his own love is extinguished at that very instant.

What then happens might be described as a collapse of Louis's system of values: the power of love is replaced by the power of money or perhaps simply by what Nietzsche called "the will-to-power," and money seems for Louis the most efficaceous means to feed and exercise this will. Armed with this lethal weapon, he shrewdly and with uncanny logical precision plans his revenge.

First and foremost, he dedicates himself fanatically to his legal career. Then he chooses as his heir the most unlikely person—his illegitimate son Robert, the unsavory fruit of a "love" which he believes he has "bought" with his money. However, this "bastard" is persuaded by some of Louis's closest relatives to sell the secret of his birth to them, in return for the promise of a modest "pension." And where should this shady transaction take place but in the church of Saint-Germain-des-Prés!

With fiendish delight Louis witnesses this performance as an unseen observer. He sees, hidden behind a pillar, how Hubert, his and Isa's son, and Alfred, his brother-in-law, are making a blasphemous travesty of their religion. In the church pew, seated between Hubert and Alfred, he espies Robert, "that poor larva . . . this born slave," as the deal is consummated. Louis "feels like a god, . . . ready to grind these entangled vipers" under his feet. He laughingly tells himself that after watching this grotesque spectacle, there was nothing left that could possibly surprise him. But he is wrong: "While Alfred and Robert proceeded to the door of the church, Hubert reached with his hand into the font with holy water and, turning toward the high altar, he made a large sign of the Cross."

Yet something else occurs at almost the precise time when Louis witnesses this macabre happening in the church: Isa dies. And her death with one stunning blow completely upsets Louis's coldly calculated scheme of revenge. It had never occurred to him that Isa might precede him in death. This sudden shock invades and permeates his entire being, and almost immediately he asks himself whether this entire game has really been worth the candle. What is worst, Isa died without really knowing him, that is, without knowing Louis's real and total self, without even suspecting that there were hidden layers in his psyche, a sort of second nature, which had remained unknown even to Louis himself.

With Isa's death Louis's hatred and bitterness have also died. As he would never see his wife again, as she would never be able to read the pages of his diary, there could never be any explanation of the motivations which prompted his conduct. Nor would she ever see the tears which now furrow his cheeks. What was going to happen? And suddenly Louis realizes with a kind of incredulous amazement that he had suddenly "simply become human."

And what had happened to his idols, money and power? For the first time in his life Louis experiences the meaning of "detachment": what had been his "absolute," his *summum bonum*, simply vanished from his horizon; it no longer interests or concerns him at all. He feels "like a patient, coming out of surgery," a patient who, when he awakens from anaesthesia, can truthfully say that he has felt nothing. That malignant growth, that cancerous tissue, has been removed, and now he feels nothing but a tremendous relief. Obviously, he had always been in error about the real object of his desires. "We do not know what we desire. We do not love what we think we love."

Louis feels that he has escaped from an ugly prison. At age sixty-eight he has awakened from a deep sleep, from a nightmare, born again when he was already on the point of dying! It is this kind of awakening that is described in minute detail by the wise practitioners of Zen Buddhism, that rebirth which they have called *Satori* and which the Greeks had named *kairos*. But it is of course identical with that "being born again" promised by Christ and experienced by practitioners of the Christian faith. Externally, it would seem that nothing at all has changed, and yet everything is totally different. Paradoxically, everything still looks the same, and yet everything is new! Everything, writes Louis, still interests him as it did before, with the only difference that nothing is his any more and that he does not even feel his newly gained "poverty." "Suddenly we find ourselves in the middle of autumn. . . . But for us, perhaps, it is never too late." This last sentence is of pivotal significance. We will have to remember it when we shall hear Albert Camus have his judge-advocate in his novel *The Fall* (*La Chute*) affirm the exact opposite: "It is too late; it will always be too late!" (Chapter V).

The old man's ruminating thoughts center on the nature of the capital *crime* he has committed. This crime was not confined to "that hideous nest of vipers"—the hatred of his children, his desire for revenge, his love of money and of the power it conveys to its possessor. His crime extended beyond all this. Its essence consisted rather in his inability to break through all the surface appearances in order to reach the innermost substance of those people—blood relations as well as strangers—with whom he had associated. Now, when his life is ebbing away, he makes this discovery which he should have made when he was in the prime of his life. For now, "those whom I should have loved are dead, and dead are those who might have loved me." Would there be any time left to put his glorious discovery to the test? It was worth a try. "I would go straight to the hearts of my children. . . . The tangle of vipers was at last cut through."

Where, however, could Louis find the strength needed for this final acid test? Strength, yes. But what kind of strength? One needed not something but *Someone*—"Someone in Whom we are all one . . . , Someone Who would bear witness for me. . . . The world must be touched at its heart." Louis seeks Him Who alone can help him achieve that final breakthrough, that desired victory. He must Himself be "the burning center of all love." Since with the demise of his hatred Louis's attitude toward his children also undergoes a radical change, he makes over his will in their favor. Stripped of all his possessions, Louis remains alone with himself, his memories and reflections.

Among Louis's children and grandchildren it is only Janine who slowly begins to understand her grandfather, and she is also the only one who is privilged to witness his spiritual rebirth. When the long-anticipated hour of death approaches, Louis entrusts his final thought as well as his recent precious discovery to the pages of his diary: "That which stifles me tonight, even as I am writing these lines; that which makes my heart ache as though it were going to burst is that love of which, at long last, I know the name ador—." The word "adorable" remains forever unfinished because it is Death who has the final say and terminates the diary.

This diary is all the "*bien-pensant*" members of Louis's family need to confirm them in their conviction that these pages offer conclusive evidence that this evil old miser was really insane. In addition, he obviously had fallen prey during the last days of his life to a sort of perverted mysticism. Then it is Janine, who was herself "awakened" from her spiritual sleep by a new kind of clairvoyance, who comes to the defense of her grandfather's memory. After the shipwreck of her own marriage she asks Louis whether he thinks she will ever get over the pain of this wound. And he, who is surely no expert in the art of counseling and consoling others, puts his arm around her shoulders and reminds her that not all is lost because she still has her religious faith. Janine looks at her grandfather without understanding, not being aware of any connection between religious faith and the events of daily life. Of course, she admits, she "is religious," that is, she fulfills her religious "duties." She speaks of religious "duties" as others speak of a citizen's duty to pay his income tax. This was precisely what

Louis had always abhorred, "this crude caricature . . . this mean parody" which all these "professed Christians" made of the Christian life. But it is not long before the understanding dawns on Janine. And when it does she hesitates not a moment to express in a letter addressed to her uncle Hubert her conviction that the "Christians" in her family had set a very bad example for this unhappy man. She testifies to the fact that she was the only one who had witnessed her grandfather's spiritual transformation. She asserts that she is not trying to picture him as a saint. In many respects, she agrees, Louis was a dreadful human being, but this "does not change the fact that a great light shone upon him during the last days of his life." It was he, she tells her uncle, who consoled her with his compassion after her own life seemed ruined by her broken marriage. She closes her letter by telling of her recent association with people who have many weaknesses and faults but who have one thing which she has failed to observe in any member of her "Christian" family: "They live according to their faith, and they die in the fullness of grace." What, she asks, was the basic fault of herself and her closest blood relations? "Where our treasure was, there was our heart also. . . . Will you understand me if I tell you that where *his* treasure was, there was *not* his heart also?"

Mauriac sums up his intentions in writing this theological novel in these words: "The book ends after I had succeeded in restoring to my hero, to this son of darkness, his right to light, to love and, in short, to God."

When, in 1940, Mauriac began actively to participate in political controversy, at the time of his country's deepest humiliation following the Nazi invasion, he opened his documentary *Cahier noir* (*Black Book*) with a quotation from Hermann Grimm, the German literary historian (1829–1901): "The cause of the human race is hopeless." But then, as with an afterthought, he continued: "Let us therefore proclaim our faith in this hopeless cause." Shortly afterwards Mauriac was passionately involved in and committed to the French *Résistance*, choosing, as someone remarked, "the most imperiled of all parties, the party of mercy." He wanted to be the advocate of "the cause of humanity." When after the end of World War II Mauriac interceded on behalf of some former collaborators with the German invaders, the communist majority in the French National Committee of Writers (of which he was one of the cofounders) demanded and achieved his expulsion. When, later on, jointly with the Nobel Prize laureate, Roger Martin du Gard, Mauriac placed his signature at the head of an appeal of French intellectuals, demanding a pardon for the convicted Rosenberg "atom spies," he became suspect in the ranks of all the parties of the Right. And when the Holy Office in Rome condemned and decreed the dissolution of the movement of the French "worker priests," Mauriac registered his energetic and uncompromising protest and therewith established once and for all his reputation as a nonconformist in every established camp—religious, social and political.

CHAPTER FIVE

Albert Camus

THE PLAGUE

THE QUESTION might be asked whether Albert Camus, a self-avowed atheist, should have been included in a treatise that deals with the modern "theological" novel. To answer this question and to justify the inclusion of the author of *The Plague,* we refer to a distinction first made by Henri de Lubac, S.J., between *a*-theism, in the strict sense of the word, and *anti*-theism (see *The Drama* of *Atheist Humanism* (New York: Sheed & Ward, 1950, p. 277). Leslie Dewart, in his controversial and provocative book *The Future of Belief: Theism in a World Come of Age* (New York: Herder & Herder, 1966), further amplifies this distinction by comparing the respective atheisms of Sartre and Camus. He says of Sartre that "he takes the trouble to *deny* the existence of God and to attempt to disprove it. And whoever does so, has so much departed from a-theism and entered into anti-theism. The denial of the existence of God as an actuality requires the admission of the existence of God as at least a logical possibility. . . . For the anti-theist God is . . . thinkable. For the a-theist he is not" (p. 53). Of Camus the same author says that he was clearly not an a-theist, but "an anti-Christian anti-theist . . . whose contempt for Christian belief was motivated by a noble and profound devotion to a human truth which, to his mind, Christianity had hopelessly corrupted and totally betrayed" (p. 55). Expressed differently, the distinction made by de Lubac and Dewart is between what the latter calls "absolute" and "relative" atheism. And Dewart quotes Camus as an example of an "absolute" atheist. Whether or not this does justice to the Weltanschauung and the work of Camus, our analysis of *The Plague*, in which Camus's difficult creed has received its densest expression, will have to show.

Camus was born in 1913 at Mondovi in Algeria. He died prematurely in an automobile accident in 1960. Following his death, one of his friends wrote in a letter to the magazine *Venture* (New York, Vol. 3, No. 4, p. 25): "Because of him, so many of us are better than we might have been. Mourning is inevitable, but I say to myself over and over—thank God the man lived."

Camus grew up on the shores of the Mediterranean which he called "that happy sea," and which instilled in him the *pensée solaire*, the "sunny thought" of the southern Hellenic tradition with its cherished values of measure and proportion and its sense of limited horizons. The North, on the other hand, represented for Camus the mentality of lofty as well as nebulous abstractions, of limitless goals and ambitions, of the ever restless Faustian striving. He was the son of a Spanish mother and an Alsatian father, who was killed in the Battle of the Marne when Camus was only a year old. His childhood was clouded by poverty, but he never regarded this as a calamity because, as he wrote in his first book, *L'Envers et l'endroit*, "it was always balanced by the richness of light." He felt that he was placed halfway between misery and the sun. "Misery kept me from believing that all was well under the sun; and the sun taught me that history was not everything" (quoted from Charles Rolo, Albert Camus: A Good Man," *The Atlantic*, May 1958, p. 29).

Camus succeeded in winning a scholarship to a secondary school and subsequently obtained the master's degree at the University of Algiers with a thesis on Hellenism and Christianity. He paid for his education by working at a number of odd jobs. His work for a doctoral degree was cut short by a bout with pulmonary tuberculosis. He became passionately interested in the theater and eventually joined a touring company of actors, traveling with them in Algeria. The repertory consisted mainly of French classical plays. Finally he established his own theater group and adapted for the stage Dostoevky's *The Brothers Karamazov*, a successful venture which he repeated later with a stage adaptation of the same Russian author's novel *The Possessed*. He also translated and adapted works by Calderon, Lope de Vega and William Faulkner and achieved his greatest stage success with Faulkner's *Requiem for a Nun*.

While still a student at the University of Algiers, Camus contracted the already mentioned tuberculosis but regained a reasonably balanced health after an enforced rest. When World War II began, he was working as a journalist in Algiers, supporting the cause of the Arabs. Having moved to Paris in 1940, he began to engage in political activities, and his underground paper, *Combat*, became a rallying point for the anonymous fighters of the French *Résistance*. In 1942 Gallimard in Paris published the two books which established the author's fame in his homeland and abroad, *L'Etranger* (*The Stranger*) and *Le Mythe de Sisyphe* (*The Myth of Sisyphus*). The plays *Caligula* and *Le Malentendu* (*The Misunderstanding*) were published in 1938 and 1942, respectively. The plot of the latter play was based on the melodramatic "fate tragedy" by the German romanticist Zacharias Werner (1768–1823), titled *Der vierundzwanzigste Februar* (*The Twenty-Fourth of February*). Both plays are of great significance in view of Camus's subsequent elaboration of the notion of the Absurd.

The absurdity of existence, according to Camus, reveals itself to man as soon as he asks the question "Why?" Has life any meaning at all? Man finds himself in the universe as an outsider, a stranger, inexplicably cast into a brief intermezzo between the events of birth and death. In the surrounding world, man encounters a prevalence of irrationality, and when he begins to use his reasoning power to obtain satisfactory answers, he fails miserably. It seemed to Camus, especially in the early phase of his thinking and writing, that the human condition is irremediably absurd. Man's desire for immortality and the absolute certainty of death; human misery and man's desire for happiness; isolation, aloneness, and the longing for union with others; the bewildering riddles of life and the rational striving for lucidity—all appear as irreconcilable opposites, and since they are all integral parts of human existence, they amount in their sum total to total absurdity.

What distinguishes Camus's thinking from that of protagonists of metaphysical and moral pessimism, such as Schopenhauer and Sartre, is that he finds in the ultimate absurdity of existence not a cause for despair but rather an incentive for happiness and eventually even a reason for hope. Perhaps the hero of the novel *The Stranger* comes closest to yielding to what Kierkegaard called "silent despair." At least this is what the total indifference of Meursault to anything but his immediate physical sensations suggests. This total alienation from all human and social involvement or commitment is the main reason for the death sentence imposed on him by the court that tries Meursault for the killing of an Arab, notwithstanding the fact that he may have killed in self-defense. "Emptied of hope" but happy and contented nonetheless, Meursault faces his death by the guillotine. *The Stranger* thus wants to convey the message that there are no absolute or inflexible standards of morality; that there is only a "situation ethics" but no "categorical imperative" applicable to all and of timeless validity.

Meursault dies, "emptied of hope." It was not many years later that Camus was to sign as the editor of a collection of books and essays that bore the title *Espoir* (hope). However, before this change of emphasis and perspective occurred, Camus wrote *The Myth of Sisyphus* (1942), the most thorough exploration of the concept of Absurdity. The hero of Greek mythology was condemned by the gods for all eternity to push a heavy rock up to the top of a mountain, whereupon the rock would roll down again, and his purposeless travail had to begin over and over again. Why was Sisyphus so cruelly punished? There are several different versions explaining his guilt, but the most plausible among them relates his punishment to his stealing some of the divine secrets. Camus' Sisyphus faces his fate without despair and without hope but rather with a kind of sober realism. It is this attitude which makes it possible for him to triumph over the obvious absurdity of his condition. He triumphs by virtue of his experienced superiority and his freedom in accepting the inevitable. In struggling toward the mountain heights he overcomes the despondency of the ever recurring "fall."

The message and the somewhat forced elation of Camus's Sisyphus are not quite convincing within the mythical frame which is their setting. The idea the author had in mind becomes clearer in his preface to the American edition of 1955. There he explains that "even within the limits of nihilism it is possible to proceed beyond nihilism." Despair is for Camus what it is for the Christian— one of the greatest, perhaps *the* greatest sin. Despair, "the sickness unto death" (Kierkegaard), can for the Christian be healed by faith. For Camus it can be overcome by rebellion against tyranny and injustice. And in this kind of rebellion all men of good will can and must unite. If they do, they thereby establish a human solidarity that transcends all national, racial and religious boundaries. This thought becomes the main theme of Camus's most mature and best balanced novel, *The Plague* (New York, 1948; *La Peste,* Paris, Gallimard, 1947).

But before turning to a discussion of this "theological" novel, a brief discussion of two later works of Camus seems to be called for: the one is the philosophical-historical study (*The Rebel,* New York, Gallimard, 1956; *L'Homme révolté,* Paris, 1952), the other is Camus's last novel *The Fall,* (New York, Gallimard, 1961; *La Chute,* Paris, 1956).

In *The Rebel* Camus proceeded from the nihilistic revolt of Sisyphus against Absurdity to the concept of an affirmative and creative form of rebellion: in revolting (as the fighters in the French *Résistance* did) against tyranny, a unity of purpose and ends is created which joins the lonely individual to other men of good will and thus overcomes the Absurdity of existence. Man, who is by his very nature a rebel—"the only creature who refuses to be what he is"—achieves his true freedom by metaphysical revolt. While such "idealistic absolutists" as Hegel and Marx perverted the true spirit of revolt by advocating not rebellion but "revolution," the creative rebel does not condone violence and murder under any circumstances. All ideological abstractions are forms of escapism, at their best utopian and at their worst dehumanizing and destructive. They excuse the crimes committed against their contemporaries in the name of idealism by promising a compensatory earthly paradise in the future. The entire argument in *The Rebel* is directed against absolutist extremes of every shade and a defense of the Aristotelian "mean" of limitation, moderation and good common sense.

The Fall appeared nine years after *The Plague*. This novel has been called the most ambiguous of Camus's fictional writings. It is written in the form of a soliloquy, and the scene is laid in Amsterdam, the northern city which, like the North in general, seems to incline its inhabitants to introspection and brooding reflection.

The book contains the confessions of a former Parisian lawyer who tries to unburden his conscience to a listener whom he has met by chance in a tavern and who remains faceless and anonymous throughout.

What is it that tortures the conscience of Jean-Baptiste Clamence, that mysterious man with the symbolic name (this John the Baptist, this *vox clamans in deserto*)? He is no longer the former judge-advocate but has become a "judge-penitent." For Camus he seems to symbolize the tragic hero of today, the man who no longer has a religious faith but who has retained a feeling of guilt. However, the question which can be read between the lines is this: How can there be guilt if there is no judge? To put it differently: how can man "sin" if there is no God? And, furthermore, how can man live a meaningful life in an absurd and meaningless world? The identical problem is implicit in the queries of Nietzsche and Sartre. Their answers suggest that this is possible only if man occupies the place vacated by the "death of God." What is the answer of Camus?

The reader meets once again with the problem that was posed in *The Myth of Sisyphus*. He remembers that Sisyphus was irretrievably tied to the rock—the rock of existence—without being willing to blame the gods for his misfortune. Camus had described Sisyphus as a "happy" man because, instead of cursing the gods in Promethean rebellion, he has succeeded in transforming the fatal rock into a self-chosen "project," and his absurd travail into a self-chosen destiny. The Absurd, Camus meant to say, can maintain its force only when man refuses to accept it. Once Sisyphus is willing to accept and affirm his fate—as the perennial carrier of the rock— he has made a mockery of the divine "decree." Actually, Zeus (that is, God) does not exist unless and until Sisyphus may decide to make the decisive "leap" into faith. And he is determined never to make that leap.

However, does not the Absurd remain by virtue of the fact that the consciousness of guilt persists even though the belief in God has died? *The Fall* is essentially a prolonged meditation on this question. In this novel the last flicker of hope seems to be extinguished. Jean-Baptiste Clamence is existential despair personified. As he tells his melancholy story, the only relief might lie in the remote possibility of an existential communication with this faceless stranger whom he has met while roaming aimlessly through the streets of Amsterdam. But the soliloquy comes to an abrupt halt when the stranger disappears in the fog. Then follow the ominous words: "It is too late; it will always be too late. Fortunately!" Perhaps the author here addresses the reader in the vague expectation that there might be some response to the tragic question concerning the meaning of an existence that is constantly threatened by the specter of the Absurd.

Clamence is an "I" without a "thou." In this he resembles Meursault, the "stranger" in the earlier novel. But while Meursault is "frozen" in the self-sufficiency of his solitary existence, haughtily closing himself to the human emotions of sympathy and love, Clamence shows in the course of his soliloquy more than he cares to admit, an ever-increasing desire for existential communication.

In *The Rebel* Camus quotes a saying of Ivan Karamazov which may help to elucidate the apparent nihilism of Clamence. Ivan expresses the conviction that virtue is impossible without a belief in immortality. It would seem that it is this same vaguely conceived idea which makes it possible for Clamence to continue his meaningless existence. In his monologue he engages in a kind of auto-vivisection, as if trying to find out experimentally how long a human being can continue to live with an idea which, existentially speaking, is completely self-destructive. Thus these confessions of the judge-penitent illustrate not only the difficulty but the impossibility of casting out from the modern mind the spiritual and moral heritage of two millennia of Christianity. Here a moralist speaks in the disguise of a skeptical cynic, a moralist who is condemned to remain a moralist, even though all the traditional tables of values seem to have vanished. Here speaks a lonely individual, longing for perfection despite the fact that, in the midst of an absurd and insane world, he no longer even remembers how to conceive the idea of perfection. Clamence feels *"la vocation des sommets"* (the vocation to live on the summits of existence) but, like Meursault, he has lost the capacity to love. And he is trying desperately to fill this vacuum by the pale substitutes of humanitarian gestures of camaraderie.

In his legal profession, Clamence had frantically tried to persuade himself that he was obligated to aid the poor and oppressed. But, again like Meursault, he remained existentially and emotionally unaffected by the death of relatives and friends. And yet, unlike Meursault, he is tortured by the realization of this moral defect, and he therefore makes an endeavor to create or imitate artificially the emotions of sympathy and love. In this attempt he makes the surprising discovery that "man is capable of love only when he loves, first of all, himself," that is, when he accepts himself or consents to himself. Is it possible, however, to love oneself if such self-love is no longer rooted in a moral principle that both underlies and transcends the individual human being? Camus paradoxically seems to affirm that man remains a moral being even when he no longer acknowledges any kind of universal moral law. This is the bewildering residue that remains unresolved in the negations of nihilism.

What lives on in Clamence, what keeps him alive and alert is the consciousness of guilt, an individual guilt as well as that collective guilt which made Dostoevsky say that everyone is guilty and co-responsible for all the crimes and injustices committed. As to Clamence's personal guilt, he can never forget that dark November night when he was walking across the Pont Royal in Paris and saw the shadowy form of a woman who was staring down into the waters of the river. He remembers that something had struck him at this sight and made him hesitate for a moment, but then he had continued on his way. Shortly thereafter he had heard the noise of a body plunging into the river, a partly stifled outcry, but he had not turned back to save a human life. He had always been averse to becoming "involved."

Nonetheless that incident had continued to haunt him, so much so that in his dejection he had for days not dared to open a news-paper. But he had gone on living as usual, telling himself over and over again that human existence was, after all, a very trivial matter. And yet the feeling of guilt could not be silenced by rationalizations. At times he had even felt a passionate desire to see the same scene reenacted, to see that young girl throwing herself into the river once more, so that this time it might be possible for him to save her and to save himself!

Clamence, the skeptical yet inveterate moralist, refuses to believe that there are any authentic judges authorized to pronounce judgment over their fellowmen. No authentic judges? But what about authentic and real guilt? He knows only too well from experience that guilt is a universal and ineradicable heritage of the human race. "My dear fellow," he addresses his anonymous and soon evanescing partner, "for someone who is all alone, without a God and without a Master, the weight of these days is terrible. So in the end one must go out and seek a Master, since God has become unfashionable." At any rate, one cannot help believing in *sin* even though one may no longer be able to believe in *grace*. Sin and guilt for the despairing nihilist are not unqualified evils but may perhaps be the last remnants of a vanishing morality; they may even make it possible for such a man to reaffirm his humanity in spite of the apparent absurdity of existence.

At the age of forty-six Camus confessed that he was a man without a faith. Yet he had discussed the problem of faith publicly and privately with such eminent writers and men of faith as François Mauriac and Gabriel Marcel. In such discussions Camus always came back to the crucial point, namely, that it was impossible for him to believe either in God or in Christ, or even in the meaningfulness of human existence.

No doubt Camus was speaking the truth. As L. Roynet wrote in the journal of the French Dominicans, *La Vie intellectuelle,* in a world in which everybody swindles, Albert Camus has remained an honest man. In 1946, The Dominicans of the monastery of Latour-Maubourg invited the author to visit their community and, while staying there as a guest, to deliver some lectures and engage in a series of dialogues with prominent French Catholic intellectuals. This invitation appealed to Camus very much, for dialogue was what he wanted and what he thought all men of good will needed.

In these lectures and conversations as well as in many subsequent public addresses and discussions with Christian individuals and groups, Camus always admitted that he realized that being a Christian was neither easy nor comfortable, and that he was far from regarding Christian theology as an "illusion." What he stressed was simply that he saw no compelling reason to accept Christianity. He did not want to tell his audiences to become better Christians, but neither did he want to be "converted."

Moreover, he indicated that he could see a close parallel between Christians and Communists in that both negated many aspects of the present in the name and for the sake of some euphorically anticipated future. While he himself felt profoundly puzzled and disturbed by the *mysterium iniquitatis*, the least he could do was not to add to the immensity of the evil caused by man's inhumanity to man.

Camus called specific attention to the fate which he shared with his entire generation. They were cast into a dissolving and disintegrating civilization, into an age of wars and revolutions on a global scale, an age in which all the time-honored norms and standards of thinking and doing were called in question. He told his audiences that he had begun his way as a man and a writer with two basic experiences—the beauty of the universe and the absolute horror of death. These two experiences are obviously contradictory and mutually exclusive. And what makes human existence absurd is precisely this contradiction between the happiness of fulfilled moments and the ever-present threat of total annihilation by death.

A new dimension was added to Camus's range of experience by World War II, the rape of France and his own activity in the *Résistance*. Face to face now daily with grossest injustice and monstrous cruelty, his spirit rose in revolt against every kind of injustice and every inhuman act. And this greatly heightened sensitivity to evil with a correspondingly intensified determination to rally the men of good will in every camp in the cause of humanity found its literary expression in *The Plague*, especially in the three main characters of the novel, Dr. Rieux, the physician; Tarrou, the journalist—the atheists—and Father Paneloux, the Jesuit priest.

At the height of the disaster which has stricken Oran in North Africa in the form of the bubonic plague, the city is quarantined. Thus isolated from the rest of the world, Oran and its citizens become a sort of magnified cross section of the human race, facing a radical "limit-situation." Gradually, with the rising figure of deaths, social boundaries become blurred and meaningless. The two personalities who stand out while the crisis lasts, first as antagonists and later on as fighters for a common cause, are Dr. Rieux and Father Paneloux. The priest's first sermon runs true to an established theological schema: he takes it for granted that this pestilence is a "divine judgment" passed on the city to shake its inhabitants out of their complacency and tepidity, a castigation of their greed and sensuality.

When the crisis has reached its climax, Father Paneloux preaches a second sermon that reveals a radically changed perspective. He suggests that the moment has arrived when every individual is confronted with the question of either total acceptance or total refusal. This ultimate "either-or" applies especially to those happenings which are the hardest to understand, such as the suffering of the innocent, the suffering of innocent children in particular. This relates to the same kind of mystery which made Ivan Karamazov want to "return his ticket of admission" to a heaven under whose domain such horrors were providentially permitted. Under such circumstances, says Father Paneloux, the resignation demanded of the ordinary Christian, and even a certain heroic humility no longer suffice. When all exits are closed and all evasions have become impossible, the Christian must make his ultimate choice: either total faith or total denial, either the integral love of God or undying hatred. "And who would dare choosing hatred instead of love?"

Dr. Rieux is unwilling to accept this harsh alternative. So is Tarrou, the journalist, and so is the author himself. All three admit that they cannot believe in God, but the implied and yet unarticulated question is: Can they not be saints without having faith in God, saints by virtue of a perfect love of man? Thus, when asked whether he believes in God, Dr. Rieux replies: "No. But what does this mean, after all? I am groping in darkness, but I am trying to see clearly." For Dr. Rieux the question whether God exists is not very pertinent. What tortures him is again the same thing that tortured Ivan Karamazov: "I shall refuse unto death," Rieux says to Father Paneloux, "to love a creation in which children are made to suffer. . . . What I do hate is death and evil, you know that. And whether you want to or not, we two must stand together to suffer both death and evil and to fight against them."

In this novel, then, the thinking of Camus seems to center on the problem of evil as it had become familiar to him in the experiences of the war and its aftermaths. Evil was for him equivalent to the negation of those three basic human values as he had defined them in his discourses in the cloisters of Latour-Maubourg—justice, freedom, sincerity. Evil meant violence, will-to-power, terror, murder. Christians and Marxists alike appeared to him as absolute idealists willing to sacrifice concrete individual man to their respective abstract absolutes. The Christians named their absolute "God"; the Marxists called theirs "historical necessity." However, both Dr. Rieux and Father Paneloux indicate that as far as the justification of resistance to evil and terror is concerned, Camus was willing to ally himself with Christianity. What unites and transcends the individuals who profess different creeds is the community of goodness among all men of good will.

The Plague contains phrases and describes moods which are borrowed from the world of religious faith. The evening, for example, is described as the most suitable time for an examination of conscience. And it is said that suffering gives strength only when it has its roots in sorrow and remorse. Again, however, it is Father Paneloux's second sermon which probes most deeply the darkest depths of reality and thus testifies incidentally to the author's own insights. The priest is convinced now that these dark riddles cannot be explained away by referring to the "inscrutable ways" of divine love or to reward and punishment in a life to come. The Cross of Christ demands that the Christian be capable of facing with courage even the most incomprehensible paradoxes. Only *total faith* can do that, and only this kind of faith can have a positive meaning for contemporary man. There are times, says Father Paneloux, "when Christians are not permitted to place too much hope in Purgatory, times in which one can no longer speak of 'venial' sins, when every sin is a 'mortal' offense and every indifference a crime."

The central theme of this novel—and this is what makes it a "theological" novel *stricto sensu*—is that of the essential community linking those contemporary "good pagans" who accept reality *in toto* without any subterfuge with those Christians whose acceptance of this same reality rests on an unconditional religious faith. The "plague" symbolizes the precarious condition of modern man and modern mankind, a condition in which all share inasmuch as all are equally exposed to the dangerous temptation of harming their fellow humans, thereby threatening with death, destruction and total annihilation the human race and the earth it inhabits. Camus sees in this kind of infectious and highly contagious disease the necessary effect of the conformist egalitarianism of the present age. Thus to live without harming others has become extremely difficult in a world in which all are in constant danger of becoming coresponsible for the suffering of others and thereby guilty in a moral as well as metaphysical sense.

Peace of heart and mind, according to Camus, never derives from purely worldly activities: it has its source in pure unselfish love. It is this insight which makes Tarrou desire to become a saint, if this goal is attainable without a faith in God and thus without grace.

In thus leading the reader, as it were, to the threshold of sanctity, Camus, the self-styled atheist, came actually closer to the Christian concepts of morality and truth than many of the most prominent thinkers and poets of modern times, who by their idolatrous cults of nature and of man falsified and obscured the condition of man and of the world. Camus's sharpened sense of reality revealed to him the aberrations and perversions of man and nature when they are left to their own often abortive devices and efforts.

In his second sermon Father Paneloux tried to describe the way which has led him to total acceptance and unconditional faith.

Two priests in the congregation of listeners comment afterwards that views such as those expressed by Father Paneloux are very "dangerous"; he will probably never obtain the *imprimatur* for the book he is engaged in writing. What Camus means to say is that the kind of Christianity which Father Paneloux preaches in his second sermon differs radically from a habitual "faith" which has never been challenged and tested in the crucible of agonizing doubt. What Father Paneloux calls "the adventure of the soul" is the personal experience of divine love and the total surrender to its call, in the midst of the almost total darkness and apparent meaninglessness of the modern world. The priest calls it *acceptation totale,* that is, a total assent to all that which seems totally unacceptable. And thus Dr. Rieux and Tarrou, the radical "good pagans," and Father Paneloux, the radical Christian, are united in their surrender to a Reality which in its ultimate ground remains the *Deus absconditus,* the unknown "God" cloaked in darkness.

Father Paneloux concluded his second sermon with the observation that the perfect love of God is very hard to realize: "It demands a total surrender of one's self. . . . But this alone can make us accept the suffering and death of a child; this alone can make us see that it was necessary; and since it is impossible to understand it, we can only accept it. . . . That is faith, cruel in the eyes of man, but decisive in the eyes of God." As it did to St. John of the Cross, so the love of God appears to Camus as the summit of a mountain to which man must ascend with painful effort: "On that summit," says the priest, "everything will be reconciled and harmonized, and truth will emerge from the deceptive appearance of injustice." Thus at the peaks of this novel the greatest contrasts and contradictions of the present age are reconciled for a brief moment, "beyond blasphemies and prayers," as Dr. Rieux says at the end of his first conversation with Father Paneloux.

CHAPTER SIX

Graham Greene

Victory in Failure

IN MANY of the modern and contemporary theological novels the exemplary Christian is portrayed as an individual who has suffered shipwreck in one or several limit-situations of existence, one who has been broken by life through his own fault and who, without the unmerited saving grace, would be irretrievably lost. Some critics have spoken in this connection of "a morbid mysticism of sin" which tends to picture the hopelessly stranded sinner as the only true Christian, so that the abnormal deviation becomes the standard and the norm. Other critics have attributed the overemphasis on human weakness and sinful depravity to Gnostic-Manichaean influences, to account for the fact that matter, nature, the flesh are conceived by some of these authors as metaphysically evil and thus essentially perverted and corrupt.

In their defense, writers such as Bloy, Mauriac, and especially Graham Greene might successfully plead their case by pointing out that their novels—as does most of the world's great literature— do not deal with the healthy average personality but rather with the borderline of the "normal," with exceptional rather than socially and morally well-adjusted personalities. This holds true of Antigone as well as Oedipus Rex, of Hamlet and Richard III as much as Werther and Faust. Similarly, the authors of modern theological novels had no intention of writing for the edification of their readers: what they wanted to interpret in terms of an integral realism was simply "the human condition" as they saw it. As John Henry Newman wrote in his essay *On the Paradox of Christianity*, "It is self-contradictory to attempt writing a literature free from sin when we are dealing with sinful human beings." This does not exclude, of course, but rather implies a cultivation of the art of indicating symbolically or metaphorically the feeble traces of a divine guidance in human existence, those "tokens, so faint and broken, of a superintending design" (Newman).

What has been said applies, as has already been indicated, in a heightened degree to the novels of Graham Greene. This author, who more than any other contemporary writer has shocked his readers into a realization of the immensity of evil within man and his world, was himself convinced once and for all of evil's frightening presence when, at the age of fourteen, he read Marjorie Bowen's novel *The Viper of Milan*. Greene said much later that this book had provided him with a leitmotif which was afterwards confirmed by his religious conviction. Goodness, he explained, had entered only once into a human body in a perfect manner, but evil had its abode there at all times. Evil was stalking a world in which perfect goodness would never again become incarnate. And the precise locus where God and His adversary, "the enemy," are always copresent is the human conscience. The one who is most clearly aware of this condition is, according to Charles Péguy's saying, the sinner: he "is in the midst of the heart of Christianity. No one is more at home in the center of Christianity—no one, unless it be the saint." This conviction is more indigenous to Eastern Orthodoxy than to Western Roman Catholic Christianity. It is a thought familiar to Dostoevsky, for whom the sinner and the saint are brothers.

Graham Greene was born at Berkhampstead in Hertfordshire in 1904, and he received his early education at Berkhampstead School of which his father was Headmaster. He then attended Balliol College in Oxford and, in 1926, during an apprenticeship in journalism at Nottingham, he converted from Anglicanism to Roman Catholicism. A grand-nephew of Robert L. Stevenson, Greene's mind was preoccupied with literature at an early age and experienced lasting influences from the works of Henry James, Joseph Conrad, Mauriac and Dostoevsky.

Having moved to London, Greene accepted the position of a subeditor on the staff of the *Times* and subsequently became a film critic for the *Spectator*. He married in 1927, and after a brief period of happiness and the birth of a son and a daughter, the couple separated. Between 1935 and 1939 Greene traveled in Liberia and Mexico and later on (1942–43) for the *Sunday Times* and the British Foreign Office in Kenya and Indochina. From 1941 to 1948 he held a leading position in the publishing firm of Eyre and Spottiswoode.

For his Mexican travel book, *The Lawless Roads* (1939), Greene chose as an epigraph a passage from J. H. Newman's *Apologia pro Vita Sua:* "To consider the world, . . . the greatness and littleness of man, his far-reaching aims, his short duration, the curtain hung over his futurity, the disappointments of life, the defeat of good, the success of evil, physical pain, mental anguish, the prevalence and intensity of sin, the pervading idolatries, the corruptions, the dreary hopeless irreligion, that condition of the whole race, so fearfully yet exactly described in the Apostle's words, 'having no hope, and without God in the world'—all this is a vision to dizzy and appal. . . ." Like Greene, Newman finds human existence "heartpiercing, reason-bewildering." What is the answer? "I can only answer," wrote Newman, "that either there is no Creator, or this living society of men is in a true sense discarded from His presence. . . . If there be a God, since there is a God, the human race is implicated in some terrible aboriginal calamity."

Owing to some partially remembered and partially repressed childhood experiences, the nature of which remains somewhat obscure, these words of Newman accurately describe Greene's own outlook on life, even prior to his conversion. The human situation appeared to him characterized by that radical break or absurd ambivalence which made Jean-Paul Sartre say that "man's hands are always dirty." He thus found it very difficult indeed to discover in this broken human world the traces of any "superintending design." The world and man's "being-in-the-world" were ambiguous and double-faced. While Greene as a writer would never deny the Aristotelian-Scholastic saying that *bonum est quod omnes appetunt* (the good is what all desire), he would immediately qualify this definition by adding that more often than not human beings pursue the good on errant ways and under multiple guises of evil, ugliness and sin. An unequivocal explanation and resolution of the paradoxes and multifaceted events of the actual and historically situated condition of man remains a virtual impossibility. As Greene suggests in the title of one of his many short stories, "the hint of an explanation" is the best and the most we can hope for.

Greene divides his fictional works into "novels" and "entertainments." The latter are, like Chesterton's stories of Father Brown, detective stories, although there is no denying the fact that Greene's novels are always "entertaining" and his detective stories always simultaneously "moralities" in the sense of the medieval "mystery plays." They tell of hunted human beings who in the thickets of existential despair may or may not find an exit by the intervention of a deus ex machina. However, neither in his novels nor in his "entertainments" is Greene ever trying to edify or concerned with apologetics. In both categories his chief concern is with the lonely exposed individual in whose interiority the decisive battles of existence—the struggle between good and evil—are being fought and either won or lost. And yet the moral credo underlying Greene's narratives may be said to be "beyond good and evil" because it is a morality which is thoroughly positive and affirmative, leaving behind the conventional injunctions of a morality of prohibitions.

The year of Green's birth (1904) makes him a member of that "lost" generation to which Gertrude Stein referred as the "hopeless generation." Perhaps this explains in part Greene's fascination with seediness, decay and failure. Seediness attaches to the childhood environment in which Greene's heroes of mediocrity grow up. Seediness characterizes the schools they attend, those antiquated educational institutions of an old but no longer so "merry" England. The travel book titled *Journey Without Maps* (1936), in which Greene tells of his visit to Liberia, contains the revealing phrase: "There seemed to be a seediness about the place you couldn't get to the same extent elsewhere, and seediness had a very deep appeal." The same book contains frequent references to a second preoccupation of the author's mind, the search for the lost paradise of childhood, that search which also permeates much of the work of Marcel Proust. It was in part prompted by the same desire for a return to the primitivity of the "noble savages" which caused Gauguin, the painter, to leave the Paris boulevards and the civilization of Europe for the tropical paradise of Tahiti. Greene, too, wanted to "go deep," to leave behind the melancholy dreariness of decaying political, social and religious structures, in search for the unspoiled youth of man. And what did he find? He tells us that in Duogobmai he found rats, leprosy, yaws and smallpox. So he had travelled to Africa only to find himself in an atmosphere which had been his natural habitat, only this time without the glittering veneer of "culture." As Greene himself had expressed it when he was about to sail for Africa: "I find myself always torn between two beliefs—the belief that life should be better than it is and the belief that when it appears better it is really worse." Thus the journey to the African Negro republic became for Greene a journey into his own deeper self, a psychoanalytic exploratory adventure.

The question for which Greene had sought but not found an answer was this: Is it possible to achieve the catharsis by returning to the very sources from which the human race had sprung, returning to the origins in order to discover or remember the point at which man first went astray? However, the traveller had to come home without having found an entrance to the land of man's childhood: the scenes of the early dawn were overgrown and disfigured by the infectious disease of European "civilization." What then remained as the residue of Greene's dual journey into the past and into his own self? On the one hand, the conviction that the dominion of evil was of overpowering magnitude and, on the other, that there still remained "those tokens, so faint and broken, of a superintending design" (Newman) and of man's original image as a child of God. It was this dual conviction which provided the scaffolding of Greene's future production as an author.

Among those of Greene's novels which may be designated as "theological" in the strict sense of the term, three stand out as masterpieces: *The Power and the Glory* (1940), *The Heart of the Matter* (1948), and *The End of the Affair* (1951). They are preceded, among other narratives with a theological tinge, by *Brighton Rock* (1938) and followed by *A Burnt-Out Case* (1960). The former portrays in the character of Pinkie Brown an extreme case of a "lost soul" which nonetheless cannot in the end escape "The Hound of Heaven" (Francis Thompson)—the grace and mercy of God. The latter tells the story of Querry, the erstwhile famous builder of Catholic churches who, fleeing from civilization as much as from himself, is looking for the remotest place on earth. He finds it in the Congo at a location "where neither the road nor the river goes any further." This dismal place is a leproserie, run by priests and nuns and a physician. This time Dante's "Io non mori, e non rimasi vivo" ("I did not die, yet nothing of life remained") serves as one of two epigraphs. Like the leper who becomes his servant, Querry is a "burnt-out" case. Whether Querry is, as Father Thomas surmises, a potential saint who experiences the dark night of aridity, or a forlorn soul facing nothingness, remains undecided. Both *Brighton Rock* and *A Burnt-Out Case* lack the density of plot, the dramatic suspense, and the spiritual depth of Greene's three great theological novels; nonetheless the milieu as well as the characters point unmistakably to the identity of their creator. A short entry in Querry's diary furnishes a sure clue with its parodistic variation of the Cartesian "cogito, ego sum": "I feel discomfort, therefore I am alive." And Rose, the evil Pinkie's mourning young widow, tells the aged parish priest that she would like very much to hope, but she knows not how.

The protagonists of the three great novels, too, are exceptional individuals in catastrophic limit-situations. Like Dostoevsky's heroes and heroines, they belong to the category of "the humiliated and offended," but the revolutionary social pathos of Dostoevsky is found nowhere in Greene's works. His compassion and pity remain confined to the individual's personal predicaments and sufferings. When asked by the French writer Marcel Moré whether he regarded the present age as particularly prone to excessive and catastrophic personal tragedy, Greene replied in the negative. He said in effect that this was the normal condition of human beings in every age and that only rarely the surface impression of calm prevails. In short, Greene regards man as a creature destined to live in limit-situations and catastrophies.

The Power and the Glory

Traveling in Mexico as a journalist, Greene had collected material on the religious situation as it prevailed in 1938, the year in which the persecution of the Church had reached a climax. What he saw happening in some parts of the country filled him with a massive hatred of the secular authorities, a hate which spilled over into his view of the entire country. Eleven years earlier Padre Michael Pro, S.J., and his brother had been executed by the anti-clerical revolutionaries. Greene was told of a hunted priest—a "whiskey-priest"—in Tabasco, and he was struck by a passage in the priest's surviving letters which spoke of "an awful sense of impotence—to live in constant danger and yet be able to do so little; it hardly seemed worth the horror."

The mood expressed in this letter pervades the entire novel. The theme of a "huge abandonment" provides the tragic suspense in this story of a hunted (nameless) priest in the state of Vera Cruz.

A price has been put on his head. He is pursued by the police and finally captured and executed. Even all the "bystanders" in this tense drama represent various shades and stages of dereliction and alienation.

The priest in *The Power and the Glory* is hunted not only by the police but equally by the consciousness of his own guilt and sin. He had not always been one of the poor, helpless and abandoned, but he came from a well-to-do average middle-class environment. Though by no means an "intellectual," he had been shrewd, practical and ambitious in his parish work, a "loyal" citizen of his country, subservient to the secular authorities until the day when the red flags were raised. This event put an end to his sheltered, comfortable and secure existence.

The opening pages of the novel already hint at the predominant themes—isolation, decay, pain, despair. They show Mr. Tench, the dentist, as he walks in the white heat of a blazing sun to fetch the ether cylinder which he expects in the cargo of the *General Obregon,* a boat that has just arrived from Vera Cruz. Tench is a British citizen, living in self-chosen exile and keeping himself afloat with the repair work done on the decaying teeth of his clients. He typifies the general atmosphere that pervades "this evil land," natives and foreigners alike.

The reader meets the whiskey-priest first in the company of Mr. Tench. The shabby stranger, his hollow face unshaven, has just arrived in a canoe. He carries an attaché case and his breviary, disguised by a flamboyant sexy cover. The man follows the dentist back to his home and into the operating room. One pane of a stained glass window with a Madonna catches the stranger's eye. Mr. Tench says he picked it up when the Redshirts sacked the church, for he thought that at home, in England, a dentist's room without some stained glass would not have been considered quite civilized.

When the stranger makes the remark that Mexico was a happier land before the Redshirts came because then the people still had God, Tench replies that "there is no difference in the teeth" and that "it was always an awful place." He originally thought he would stay five years at the most, but then the peso dropped, and now he is caught in this forsaken place. He knows he will never get out. And the letter to his wife in England, which he has delayed writing for ten years, will never be finished and mailed.

When there is a knock on the door, the stranger hurriedly slips his attaché case under his chair. But at the door is only a child, searching for a doctor who might come to look after his dying mother. Tench is only a dentist, not a doctor and, besides, the child says that their place is six leagues away. If his mother is dying anyway, says the dentist, there is no point in having a doctor see her. But now the stranger rises: as so many times before, he has received an unwelcome summons which he cannot ignore. Before leaving, he asks for and is given the brandy which he seems to crave; then he turns to the child, saying merely "Vamos."

The stranger leaves behind his book, and the dentist is surprised and taken aback when, upon opening the pages, he discovers that the inside does not match the flashy cover: the print is in Latin. Meanwhile the *General Obregon* sounds her siren. The boat is about to cast off, leaving the priest behind, abandoned. He feels "an unwilling hatred of the child ahead of him and of the sick woman— he was unworthy of what he carried." With the smell of the brandy still on his lips, he prays, "Let me be caught soon. . . . Let me be caught." Once more he has tried to escape, and he has failed.

The second chapter of the novel introduces the police lieutenant, the whiskey-priest's chief antagonist. He is described as a man with a sharp crooked nose that juts out of a lean face—the face of a fanatic and, perhaps, also the face of an ascetic. A face, at any rate, in whose features are indelibly engraved the traces of an unhappy childhood, an early acquaintance with suffering and deprivation. It is this very real and yet forcibly repressed acquaintance with suffering that accounts for the fact that there is not only antagonism but also a strange likeness between the lieutenant and the priest.

More light is cast on the hate-love relationship between these two men in the description of several scenes inside the police station. The lieutenant looks at the photograph of a "wanted" American gangster, a "gringo," and he compares it with a photograph that shows the hunted priest in the prime of youth. The lieutenant's sympathies are with the "gringo"; his undying hatred is reserved for the priest and all of his kind. It infuriates him to think that there are still people in the state of Vera Cruz who are so unenlightened as to believe in a loving and merciful God. As for the lieutenant, he feels the passionate desire to destroy everything that has to do with religious faith, everything that reminds him of a past which he wishes to blot out completely.

And yet, paradoxically, as the lieutenant walks home from the police station there is "something of a priest in his intent observant walk—a theologian going back over the errors of the past to destroy them again." As Greene sees him, the lieutenant is a "mystic" of sorts, a mystic who has not an experiential knowledge of God but an equally authentic experience of total vacancy, of nothingness, "of a dying, cooling world, of human beings who had evolved from animals for no purpose at all."

Like many an avowed agnostic or atheistic humanist, the lieutenant never stops to ask himself why, after all, he goes on living and, paradoxically, not only hating but also loving. For the lieutenant really does love the people of his town, his state and his country. But what horrible kind of love is this? A love that has nothing to offer to the beloved except "a vacant universe and a cooling world," and "the right to be happy in any way they choose"? Happy? But how? And to what end? It is at this crucial point that every atheistic man-centered humanism defeats itself.

But what about the priest? Where and how does he differ from the lieutenant? Humanly speaking, the priest is as guilty as the lieutenant. They are also alike in their complete loneliness and isolation. The lieutenant's room "looks like a monastic cell." The lieutenant tries in vain to ingratiate himself with the children of the town, while the priest tries repeatedly and desperately to gain the love of Brigida, his own illegitimate child, conceived in lust rather than in love, in a moment of utter forlornness, in misery and despair and after half a bottle of whiskey. Brigida, this child of sin, is already mature far beyond her tender years, already tainted with the knowledge of sin and corruption. It is this child more than anything else that stands between the priest and God. Although he has gotten over despair, he knows that he is a bad priest, "but every failure dropped out of sight and out of mind: somewhere they accumulated in secret—the rubble of his failures. One day they would choke up . . . altogether the source of grace. Until then he carried on, with spells of fear, weariness, with a shamefaced lightness of heart." He prays for his child's salvation even if this means that he must give up his own hope of eternal life: "O God, give me any kind of death— without contrition, in a state of sin—only save this child." Thus the priest is even more powerless than the ascetic lieutenant to prevail against a massive world of terror and lust.

This is the negative side. On the positive side, both the priest and the lieutenant are committed men, the former committed to a faith he has betrayed and which he yet can never forsake, the latter committed to the idol of a "humanity" which is nothing but an empty abstraction deriving from a false absolutization.

There is a stark contrast, on the other hand, between the whiskey-priest, for whom existential despair was not really a "sickness unto death" because it was eventually healed by the still-flickering flame of faith, and old Padre José, for whom despair becomes the un-forgivable sin, a deadly disease. Padre José has lost not only the moral and theological virtues—all courage, all faith, all hope and all love—but also every trace of self-respect. To save his life, he has allowed himself to be forced by the state authorities into marrying his housekeeper. Every night he has to endure the mocking cries of the neighborhood who, imitating his wife's voice, cry "José, José. Come to bed, José." There is nothing left for Padre José to hold on to, "in his house, in the town, in the whole abandoned star." Still, some people of the town occasionally ask him to perform a burial rite or to say a prayer for a departed loved one, and then he will feel "an enormous temptation . . . to take the risk and say a prayer over the grave." But "fear comes back, like a drug." Hopelessly Padre José begs the townspeople to leave him alone, to take him for what he is, a despicable coward, fat, ugly, old and utterly humiliated—truly a lost soul. The whiskey-priest has never sunk to this depth of degradation. He has sinned grievously again and again, broken his priestly vows, lost his human dignity, but the divine spark in him has never been quite extinguished: he has never really abandoned God and has—contrary to his own opinion—never been abandoned by Him. In all his weakness there has remained a hidden strength, in all his cowardice a potential for suffering and for bearing witness. He prays: "O God, forgive me—I am a proud, lustful, greedy man. I have loved authority too much. These people are martyrs—protecting me with their own lives. They deserve a martyr to care for them—not a fool like me, who loves all the wrong things."

Aside from Brigida, the priest's illegitimate daughter, there are other children who play significant roles in the story. There is Coral, the little daughter of the British Captain Fellows, who offers shelter to the priest on her father's banana plantation. She too is mature beyond her years, but in a more healthy way. She not only hides the priest in a shed but with good-natured sagacity and daring makes plans for his escape.

And then there is Luis, the little son of devout Catholic parents who are trying to bring up their three children in the traditional way. But Luis rebels. He detests the sentimentality in the pages of a biography of a Christian martyr which the mother is reading to the other members of the family. And Luis's father speaks nostalgically of the days "when the Church was here." He counters Luis's objections with the remark that it is not the boy's fault, that they have all been deserted. But the rebellious mood of Luis, too, is actually a healthy reaction against a somewhat moldy kind of piety: the boy in his spiritual ferment is in the end brought back to the Church by the whiskey-priest's partly involuntary but nonetheless genuine martyrdom. Luis is the one who in the night that follows the priest's execution is awakened by a knock on the outer door of their home. A stranger stands in the street, "a tall pale thin man with a rather sour mouth." He carries a small suitcase. With a wild and shy smile the stranger mentions the name of the boy's mother and, lowering his voice, he says that he has a letter of introduction for the Señora and that he is a priest. "My name," he says, "is Father——." "But the boy had already swung the door open . . . before the other could give himself a name." In admitting this other as yet nameless stranger, Luis unknowingly confirms the old saying that martyrdom is the seed of faith. This episode symbolizes in the simplest possible manner the continuity of the Priesthood and the continuity of the Faith. Luis was one of those children whose sympathy had been wooed by the lieutenant. But this child at any rate cast his lot with affirmation rather than denial. And the author argues convincingly that the continuity of faith depends entirely on the free commitment of the individual human being.

Maria, the mother of the priest's child, also gives temporary shelter to the outlaw, albeit reluctantly. She has no respect, only contempt, for the father of her child. The same is true to a lesser degree of the men and women of the village who are present at the priest's secret celebration of Mass on a makeshift packing case altar. The priest realizes that his offer to celebrate Mass among the villagers and for them is a sort of bribe. However, despite their fear and hesitancy, these people do not betray him. They merely ask him at the end of the sermon to go away and never to return. As he leaves behind him this place and a guilty past that can never be erased, riding away on the back of a mule, he carries with him no other link with his past but a tiny scrap of paper. It contains the penciled notes which he once jotted down in preparing a "bromide" after-dinner speech he delivered on the tenth anniversary of his ordination. Soon this shabby relic too will have to be relinquished, as an external sign of the finality of "the surrender of a whole past."

In the next episode of the novel the priest meets with a mestizo (a half-caste) who has recognized the identity of the man in the shabby clothes of a peon from the picture on the public posters and—assuring again and again that he is "a good Catholic"—is hopeful of obtaining the reward placed on the priest's head. From then on the mestizo attaches himself to the priest as his dark shadow. He forces his presence upon his unwilling companion, and the two men spend a night together in a hut. The priest knows that he is "in the presence of Judas."

There follows the priest's grotesque, frantic and desperate hunt for brandy, to satisfy his personal craving for alcohol as well as to serve as a substitute for the unobtainable altar wine. An old beggar shows the priest the way to a seedy "hotel," where in a large bare room he meets—his identity still unrecognized—with the Chief of Police and several other officials of the town. His eyes filled with tears, the priest has to watch helplessly as these guardians of the state's prohibition laws lustily consume the precious altar wine which the priest has finally been able to purchase with his few remaining pesos. Through his tears the priest stammers that the hope of the world is draining away, and these upright citizens boisterously praise him for uttering such sublime wisdom.

In the end the priest manages to escape, carrying with him a small remnant of the brandy that was hidden in the mattress of the bed. However, he is soon arrested by some Redshirts: he has violated the prohibition laws. But he escapes once more and tries to find refuge from persecution in the house of Padre José. There he is witness to the sordid humiliations to which this poor wreck of a priest and a man is constantly being subjected. Padre José threatens to call the police. He does not want martyrs in his house: "Go and die quickly." And then the door of the patio suddenly opens, and the police are there.

The whiskey-priest realizes that this at long last is the beginning of the end. He attempts to say silently an act of contrition, but he fails: "That was the fallacy of deathbed repentance—penitence was the fruit of long training and discipline: fear wasn't enough. He tried to think of his child with shame but he could only think of her with a kind of famished love. . . . And the sin itself was so old that like an ancient picture the deformity had faded and left a kind of grace." They take him away, still unaware of his identity.

The priest spends the night in a crowded and dark cell of the local jail. This horrid place, it seems to him, is very much like a cross section of the world: filled to overflowing with lust and crime and unhappy love. The many figures in the dark bespeak every kind of destitution, degeneracy and despair: an old man tells of how the priests have taken his daughter away because she was a "bastard" child. Two lovers wrest what little sensual pleasure they can out of their shared misery. Others among the many prisoners in the cell recall the memories of religious persecution, or present *tableaux vivants* of treachery, of compassion and pity, of spiritual pride, of the obsessive desire for escape and freedom. The priest decides that one of these wretched creatures might as well earn the reward placed on his head. But a voice out of the dark says: "Nobody here . . . wants their bloody money."

Among the prisoners there is also a "pious" woman, a female of the type of Mademoiselle Planude in Bloy's *The Woman Who Was Poor*, a woman of pharisaical self-righteous "virtue," a type which the Spaniards call a *beata*, the British and Americans a bigot, and the Germans a *Betschwester*. She complains bitterly that her religious "vocation" had not been recognized by the nuns; she is scandalized by the shameless behavior of the two lovers in the prison cell, and she sternly reproves the priest for sympathizing "with these animals." Here a rancid religious sentimentalism masquerades as piety and poses as virtue.

Once more the priest manages to escape, for the last time. Prior to this final leap for freedom he has made a bargain with God: if his identity remains unrecognized by his jailers, it will be a sign that God wants him to leave the dread of capture and execution behind:

he will then try to cross over the border of Vera Cruz into the safety of neighboring Las Casas. Actually, his escape succeeds in a most unexpected way: the lieutenant whom the priest has met once before when the officer of the law was searching the village where Maria and the priest's child live, does not recognize the prisoner and even gives him a modest amount of money before dismissing him with a good-natured warning. "You are a good man," the priest says in a low voice and in happy surprise. And he means it. The lieutenant is surely not one of those who are neither hot nor cold, not one of those whom the Lord will "spit out of His mouth."

After the priest has been released from prison, he goes about fulfilling *his* terms of the bargain he has made with God. His first stop is at the bungalow of the Fellows family because he hopes that Coral will again give him temporary shelter. But he finds the house deserted by everyone except a hungry dog that fights with the priest for a bone with "a lot of meat on it still. . . . Then suddenly he laughed: this was human dignity disputing with a bitch over a bone." In the end the priest captures the bone, and though it seems to him that "no food had ever tasted so good," he immediately begins to feel pity and thinks: "I will eat just so much and she can have the rest." But then he feels real hunger and eats everything but the bone itself. When he finds an abandoned book on the veranda of the house, he suddenly realizes that when at last this long agonizing struggle is over and when he has crossed the mountains and the border, "life might, after all, be enjoyed again." Seated on the steps of the veranda, the priest opens the book at random, and he reads some of the English poetry it contains. This kind of poetry seems strange to him, for the poetry he is familiar with has always dealt with agony, remorse and hope. Then his eyes come to rest on the lines,

> "Come back! Come back!" he cried in grief
>   Across the stormy water,
> "And I'll forgive your Highland chief—
>   My daughter, O my daughter."

In these words the priest feels the ring of genuine passion, and he repeats to himself the last line of the poem—"My daughter, O my daughter." These words seem "to contain all that he felt himself of repentance, longing and unhappy love."

The priest has by now passed into "a region of total abandonment." Life recedes, and nothingness begins to spread. He feels himself wandering "in a kind of limbo," a man not good enough for heaven and, perhaps, not quite bad enough for hell. Though the rain has not arrived yet, it is coming up from Campeche Bay and will soon cover the entire state. And the mountains with the saving state line beyond are still twenty miles away.

Near one of the huts which occasionally appear to leap up in the flashes of lightning, the priest meets an Indian woman "of uncertain age—an old woman's face, but one could never tell with Indians." These creatures "looked as if they had come out of the Stone Age." The woman leads the priest to her hut, where her child lies dying from a gunshot fired by the police in their attempt to capture the fugitive American gangster. The woman and the priest proceed with the body of the dead boy toward the still-distant mountains. The woman wants the priest to lead her to a place near a church where her child can be buried properly. "It was a fantastic notion."

On the second day of their journey, at sunset, they reach a plateau where "an old grove of crosses stood up blackly against the sky"—the first Christian symbols the priest has seen publicly exposed for more than five years. The crosses were made by Indians, and they "had nothing in common with the tidy vestments of the Mass and the elaborately worked out symbols of the liturgy. It was like a shortcut to the dark and magical heart of the faith—to the night when the graves opened and the dead walked."

The woman hopes for a miracle that will restore the life of her child. She carries the dead baby on her back. Near the tallest of the crosses she takes the child down and holds first his face and then his loins against the wood. Why, the priest ponders, should the expected miracle not be granted to her? Are we not told that faith can move mountains? And did not this woman have faith—"faith in the spittle that healed the blind man and the voice that raised the dead?" When no miracle occurs, "it was as if God had missed an opportunity."

Part Three of the novel brings a relaxation of the tension and a final respite prior to the unhappy-happy end. In an idyllic interlude we find the priest in the Lutheran Lehr Mission on the other side of the mountains and on the safe ground of the neighboring state. There is again an almost forgotten orderliness of life and worship. As in the days of old, the priest hears the confessions of the people and celebrates Mass. In three days, he tells himself, he will be in Las Casas; he will have confessed his own moral lapses and will have been absolved. However, he immediately asks himself, how can that be? "The thought of the child [his child] on the rubbish-heap came automatically back to him with painful love. What was the good of confession when you loved the result of your crime?"

In reality, Las Casas is farther away than heaven or hell. As the priest makes ready to mount his mule and to depart, the mestizo reappears. He brings a desperate call from the American gangster who has been caught and lies mortally wounded in the banana plantation of the Fellows family. The half-caste says that he is here "on an errand of mercy." The whiskey-priest is the only priest this side of Las Casas, and the young man wants to confess before he dies. The priest feels "the trap close again, irrevocably." For even more anxiously than for the "gringo," the police are lying in wait for their victim. "But the American was there, dying." The priest knows that his "Judas" has betrayed him for the pieces of silver promised him, but "there was no question at all that he was needed. . . . The oddest thing of all was that he felt quite cheerful: he had never really believed in this peace." Then the priest turns his mule around and starts on his way back to certain capture and death.

The priest meets the dying man, but the outlaw believes himself damned and dies without a confession and with only a "conditional absolution," which the priest gives in case, for one second before his spirit crossed the borderline between life and death, the young man might have felt remorse for his many crimes. The priest prays over the dead body, but without conviction, because "at the best, it was only one criminal trying to aid the escape of another—which-ever way you looked, there wasn't much merit in either of them." Another failure.

The priest and the lieutenant meet for the last time when the lieutenant appears in the door where the "gringo" has died. On the way back to town and to the jail the two men learn to know and even to understand each other in the course of several revealing dialogues. When the journey nears its end, the lieutenant's attitude has undergone a significant change.

For a while the conversation turns on the cruel facts of pain and suffering. The lieutenant accuses the Church for not having done anything to eliminate suffering, especially among the poor. How can anyone say that suffering and pain are something good or salutary? The lieutenant wants to have the money that goes into the building of churches spent for the poor, to give them food, to teach them to read, to give them books. The priest admits that he was never any good at books, that his memory has always been bad. Yet one thing has always puzzled him about people like the lieu-tenant: "you hate the rich and love the poor. . . . We have always said the poor are blessed and the rich are going to find it hard to get into heaven. Why should we make it hard for the poor man too? . . . Why should we give the poor power? It's better to let him die in dirt and wake in heaven—so long as we don't push his face in the dirt."

This, it seems to the lieutenant, is sophistic reasoning, and he does not want to reason. He wants to let his heart speak. "Oh well," says the priest, "perhaps when you're my age you'll know that the heart's an untrustworthy beast. The mind is too, but it doesn't talk about love. Love. And a girl puts her head under water or a child

is strangled, and the heart all the time says love, love." The lieutenant retorts with some irritation that the priest never talks straight.
He says one thing now, but to another man or woman he will say:
"God is love." Why this meaningless juggling of words? "Oh,"
says the priest, "that's another thing altogether—God *is* love. . . .
We wouldn't recognize *that* love. It might even look like hate. It
would be enough to scare us—God's love. It set fire to a bush in
the desert . . . and smashed open graves and set the dead walking
in the dark. Oh, a man like me would run a mile to get away if he
felt that love around."

The lieutenant remarks that evidently the priest has not much
confidence in Him Whom he calls his Lord. "He doesn't seem a
grateful kind of God. If a man served me as well as you've served
Him, well, I'd recommend him for promotion, see he got a good
pension . . . if he was in pain, with cancer, I'd put a bullet through
his head." And the priest replies, now with great earnestness and
sincerity: "I'm not as dishonest as you think I am. Why do you
think I tell people out of the pulpit that they're in danger of
damnation if death catches them unawares? I'm not telling them
fairy stories which I don't believe myself. I don't know how awful
the human heart looks to Him. But I do know this—that if there's
ever been a single man in this state damned, then I'll be damned
too."

The priest also has already told the lieutenant a summary of the
sordid story of his own life: "One thing went after another. I got
careless about my duties. I began to drink." Why did he alone
stay behind when all the other priests left? "It would have been
much better, I think, if I had gone too. Because pride was at work
all the time. Not love of God. . . . I thought I was a fine fellow to
have stayed. . . . And then I thought I was so grand I could make
my own rules. I gave up fasting, daily Mass. I neglected my prayers
—and one day because I was drunk and lonely—well you know
how it was. I got a child." When the lieutenant replies furiously
that, after all, the priest will have the satisfaction of dying as a

martyr, the prisoner replies sadly: "Oh no. Martyrs are not like me. They don't think all the time—if I had drunk more brandy I shouldn't feel so afraid."

In the final moments of his life the priest, his courage artificially propped up by the brandy which the lieutenant has given him, recalls the image of his child and repeats his earlier prayer: "O God, help her. Damn me, I deserve it, but let her live forever." He realizes that

this was the love he should have felt for every soul in the world: all the fear and the wish to save concentrated unjustly on the one child. . . . He thought: this is what I should feel all the time for everyone, and he tried to turn his brain away towards the half-caste, the lieutenant, even the dentist he had once sat with for a few minutes, the child at the banana station, calling up a long succession of faces. . . . For those were all in danger too. He prayed: "God help them," but in the moment of prayer he switched back to his child . . . and he knew that it was only for her that he prayed. Another failure.

On the morning of his death, the priest wakes up, "crouched on the floor with the empty brandy flask in his hand." He tries to remember how to make an act of contrition, but he knows this death

was not the good death for which one always prayed. . . . What an impossible fellow I am, he thought, and how useless. I have done nothing for anybody. I might just as well have never lived. . . . Tears poured down his face: he was not at the moment afraid of damnation—even the fear of pain was in the background. He felt only an immense disappointment because he had to go to God empty-handed. . . . It seemed to him at that moment that it would have been quite easy to have been a saint. It would only have needed a little self-restraint and a little courage. He felt like someone who had missed happiness by seconds at an appointed place. He knew now that at the end there was only one thing that counted—to be a saint.

The priest is shot in the courtyard, and his body crumples against the wall. This can hardly be called the blazing exit of a martyr, but his last reflections prior to his execution call to mind not only Clotilde and the concluding words of Léon Bloy's *The Woman Who Was Poor* but, in their childlike simplicity, they show the nameless whiskey-priest's essential kinship with Bernanos's likewise nameless country priest. They are all paraphrasing the identical theme: man becomes less human and eventually inhuman and even subhuman when he turns away from the simplicity of childhood. And they underscore the rather frightening scriptural saying that unless men become as little children, they cannot enter into the Kingdom of Heaven.

The Heart of the Matter

This second of Greene's major theological novels is a sophisticated and penetrating piece of fiction that exposes, with the author's usual adeptness at creating suspense, the theological, ontological and psychological differences among pity, compassion and love. While love saves and compassion builds bridges and ennobles both the giver and the recipient, pity isolates, humiliates, corrupts and destroys. As Greene sees it, pity is thus not a virtue but a vice. In the words of W. H. Auden, "Behind pity for another lies self-pity, and behind self-pity lies cruelty. To feel compassion for someone is to make oneself their equal; to pity them is to regard oneself as their superior" ("Heresy of Our Time," in *Renascence,* Vol. I, 1949, p. 24). Thus egotism as well as anguished fear may disguise itself as pity.

This thesis is illustrated by the character study of Major Scobie, a mediocre and somewhat pedantic police official in the British colonial service in North Africa. His habitual honesty and sense of justice and eventually the entire scale of his religious and moral values are gradually undermined and corroded by his susceptibility to pity. Scobie, unable to see others suffer without taking upon himself the responsibility for relieving their pain, even though this may make it necessary to lie and to betray, comes to the conviction that "in human relations kindness and lies are worth a thousand truths."

This same problem of the truth that may hurt and the lie that may redeem human pain and suffering had preoccupied Henrik

Ibsen in several of his social-ethical dramas, especially in *The Wild Duck*, in *An Enemy of the People* and in *Ghosts*. A middle-of-the-road maxim of practical wisdom is contained in the old Norwegian proverb: "Never tell a lie, and the truth only when you have to."

Major Scobie's first "life-lie"—to use Ibsen's own term—told in the name and guise of generosity, leads inevitably not only to intensified suffering of the "victims" of his pity but eventually to his own moral disintegration and final self-destruction.

Scobie, a Roman Catholic, feels his love for Louise, his wife, waning as she shows unmistakable signs of aging. But in proportion as his love diminishes, his pity increases. When he meets Helen Rolt, a young woman who is brought to the colonial outpost after a shipwreck, he almost immediately succumbs to a strange infatuation which he at first mistakes for love. But again it is really only pity that her defenseless frailty evokes in him: "He watched her with sadness and affection and enormous pity. . . . He had no sense of responsibility towards the beautiful and the intelligent. They could find their own way. It was the face that would never catch the covert look, the face which would soon be used to rebuff and indifference, that demanded his allegiance. The word 'pity' is used as loosely as the word 'love': the terrible promiscuous passion which so few experience."

Helen knows with the sure instinct of womanhood that it is pity, not love, that motivates Scobie's affection. She tells him in a fierce outburst that what she wants is love, not pity. "But it was not a question of whether she wanted it—she had it. Pity smouldered like decay at the heart."

Can a man so totally deceive himself as to mistake pity for love? Evidently not. For Scobie seems to see clearly "the heart of the matter" before he writes on official stationery the untruthful letter to Helen in which he asserts that he loves her more than himself, more than his wife, more than God. He wants "more than anything in the world" to make her happy.

There are, as Scobie sees it, three alternatives for him. He can abandon Helen and assume again his obligations as a husband. But this means unhappiness and suffering for Helen. Or he can abandon Louise and live in an adulterous relationship with Helen and thus cruelly harm his wife. Or he can escape this unhappy choice between two evils by eliminating himself from the scene, by killing himself. Three possibilities, but from the moral point of view of a Roman Catholic Christian they are all impossibilities. The third is not only the most cowardly "solution" but actually no solution at all. And yet suicide is what Scobie—now in the clutches of existential despair—elects.

Before Scobie chooses this final act of desperation, he considers unburdening his troubled conscience by confession. But, he tells himself, "what would be the use? I know the answers as well as he [the priest] does. One should look after one's own soul at whatever cost to another, and that's what I can't do." Such a reflection shows that either Scobie or Graham Greene or both are bad theologians. For what this sentence seems to recommend and condone is a rather crude kind of spiritual egotism, an attitude which no informed Catholic—theologian or layman—could find acceptable. Such a thesis seems to overlook the fact that "looking after one's own soul" implies looking after all other souls, or that personal salvation without the fulfillment of the first *and* second Commandments— love of God, love of self, *and* love of the neighbor—is a virtual impossibility.

Pity—that sad "parody of love" (W. H. Auden)—has led Scobie first to lying, then to treachery and betrayal, then to loss of faith in himself, and finally to self-destruction. Before taking that fatal last step, Scobie tries again to find release by confessing his sin of adultery. He makes this second abortive attempt when Louise, as a test of her husband's fidelity, insists that they jointly receive Holy Communion. But once in the confessional, Scobie cannot bring himself to lie this time, and thus he fails to obtain absolution. "When he came out of the box it seemed to Scobie that for the first time his footsteps had taken him out of sight of hope. . . . It seemed to him that he had left for his exploration only the territory of despair."

Again it is pity which impels Scobie to go through with his wife's plan, to receive the sacrament of Communion without having been absolved and thus to invite his own eternal damnation.

Once more Greene's theology at this point appears to be somewhat twisted, a fact which may have been the cause of Evelyn Waugh's calling the entire novel a "mad blasphemy."However, it should not be forgotten that a corrective of sorts is offered in two significant passages of *The Heart of the Matter*. The first quotes Scobie's last words, after he has taken the fatal dose of medicine and has made an unsuccessful effort to make an act of contrition: he says aloud, "Dear God, I love. . . ." The question immediately suggests itself: did Scobie mean to say that he loves both Helen and Louise, or did he mean to say that he loves God? The probability is that he meant both, love of the two women and love of God. But the answer is not clear, and there is nothing more than "the hint of an explanation" (the title of one of Greene's short stories). Did the author mean to say that Scobie loved God in His creatures and that this was a redeeming love that saved him from damnation? We do not know the answer.

The second passage occurs in the final pages of the book. The ambiguity remains, but there are again some "hints of an explanation." The book ends with a revealing dialogue between Mrs. Scobie and Father Rank. Louise asks the priest whether he has no comfort to give her. He tells her that Scobie had given her a great deal of comfort while he was alive. But Louise thinks she knows much more about the bad things in her husband's life than the priest. And Father Rank agrees: "You have been his wife . . . for fifteen years," he says. "A priest knows only the unimportant things. . . . I mean the sins. A man doesn't come to us and confess his virtues." Mrs. Scobie insists that her husband was "a bad Catholic." The priest replies that this is the silliest phrase one can use. But what about this horrible end? She says that her husband

must have known that he was damning himself. "Yes," retorts
Father Rank, "he knew that all right. He never had any trust in
mercy—except for other people." When Louise says that it does
not even make sense to pray for her dead husband, the priest says
furiously: "For goodness' sake, Mrs. Scobie, don't imagine you—or
I—know anything about God's mercy." But does not the Church
say that receiving Holy Communion without absolution and perfect
contrition is sacrilegious and that committing suicide is a mortal
sin? "I know what the Church says," answers Father Rank. "The
Church knows all the rules. But it doesn't know what goes on in
a single human heart."

Louise has told the priest that there is no bitterness left in her
heart. Does she really think then, persists the priest, that "God is
likely to be more bitter than a woman?" From what he has seen
of Scobie, Father Rank concludes that her husband really loved
God. "He certainly loved no one else," Louise says in reply. To
which the priest adds these final words: "And you may be in the
right of it there, too."

Although the reader may remain doubtful as to the correctness
of this diagnosis, here is actually more than a mere "hint of an
explanation." Here we are very close to the real "heart of the
matter," namely, the great mystery of the infinite mercy of God!
For Graham Greene, God is truly the *Deus absconditus,* the forever
hidden God of the mystics, the God also of Martin Luther,
Kierkegaard, Newman and Karl Barth, the God Who mysteriously
presides over His creation and over all His creatures. Though the
gates of hell have been conquered, the hell in the human heart
and the human soul endures to the end of time. This is the spiritual
climate of the world of Dante as of the worlds of Marlowe and
Shakespeare and equally of Graham Greene.

The End of the Affair

The publication of *The Heart of the Matter* caused a good deal of
perplexity and even indignation among many Roman Catholics.

This reaction was somewhat puzzling to Graham Greene. He expressed his theological intentions in writing this controversial piece of literature in an interview with a reporter of *Time* magazine: "I wrote a book about a man who goes to hell—*Brighton Rock*— another about a man who goes to heaven—*The Power and the Glory*. Now I've simply written one about a man who goes to purgatory. I don't know what all the fuss is about."

The End of the Affair did not worry Greene's Catholic readers nearly as much as it perturbed those who were either Protestants or nonbelievers. *Time* called the novel "a shocker," and the review's headline read: "Adultery can lead to Sainthood." Had the reviewer been familiar with the "case history" of Mary Magdalene and a host of other Christian converts, he would have known that this theme was not a new one.

The main problem of *The End of the Affair* is that of *pursuit*— pursuit on the human and the suprahuman levels. The former kind of pursuit is represented by Parkis, a detective, and by Maurice Bendrix, a writer; the latter kind, by God, the "Hound of Heaven," to use again the title of Francis Thompson's poem. The entire novel may indeed be called a paraphrase of this poem's five lines:

> All which thy child's mistake
> Fancies as lost, I have stored for thee at home:
> Rise, clasp My hand, and come! . . .
> Ah, fondest, blindest, weakest,
> I am He Whom thou seekest.

Both Sarah Miles, the adulterous heroine, and Maurice Bendrix, her atheistic and libertinistic lover, are unable to escape the relentless pursuit of the divine Hunter. Both are in the end captured by a divine love which redeems and transfigures their illicit human love affair.

A second major theme of the novel is the psychological exploration and presentation of the dialectical ambivalence of both hate and love, and of the problem of "love-hatred" that is familiar from August Strindberg's plays and novels as well as from the same

Swedish author's autobiographical works. Some of the hatred that Bendrix feels for Henry, Sarah's husband, is frustrated love. He stays with Henry after Sarah's death and shows in increasing measure his concern and affection. He goes to look up Henry and finds him asleep. "He was just a man," Maurice Bendrix says to himself, "one of us. He was like the first enemy soldier a man encounters on a battlefield . . . just a human being."

And the same is true of Bendrix's hatred of God, to Whom he has transferred his love-hatred of Sarah, who has been taken from him by God twice: first, when her newly germinating faith makes her renounce Bendrix, and a second time by her death. Bendrix's words of hate are given the lie by his deeds of love.

Briefly told, *The End of the Affair* is the story of the love and hate of Maurice Bendrix for Sarah. This end comes almost at the very beginning of the novel. Bendrix's passionate love for Sarah soons turns into hate. After Sarah has inexplicably terminated her love affair with Maurice, the latter begins to pursue her, following her secretly through the streets of London. In addition, he has—with Henry's consent—had her every step watched by Parkis, a hired private eye, in order to obtain concrete evidence of her suspected love affair with a supposed "third man." But the reason for Sarah's seeming unfaithfulness is a totally different one: she gave up Bendrix in fulfillment of a vow she had made—a vow to a God in Whom she does not even believe as yet.

It happened back in the days of the German Blitz, when Sarah believed Maurice fatally wounded during an air attack. It was then that in utter desperation she vowed to break off her illicit relationship with Maurice if God would bring her lover back to life:

I knelt down on the floor; I was mad to do such a thing; I never even had to do it as a child—my parents never believed in prayer, any more than I do. . . . Maurice was dead. Extinct. There wasn't such a thing as a soul. . . . I knelt and put my head on the bed and wished I could believe. Dear God, I said—why dear, why dear?—make me believe. I can't believe. Make me. I said, I'm a bitch and a fake and I hate myself. I can't do anything of myself. *Make* me believe. ... Let him be alive, and I *will* believe. Give him a chance. Let him have his happiness. Do this, and I'll believe. But that wasn't enough. It doesn't hurt to believe. So I said, I love him and I'll do anything if you'll make him alive; I said very slowly, I'll give him up forever, only let him be alive. ... And then he [Maurice] came in at the door, and he was alive, and I thought now the agony of being without him starts, and I wished he was safely back dead again under that door.

The above quotation is an excerpt from Sarah's diary. And in an earlier passage of the same entry we read: "A vow is not all *that* important—a vow to somebody I've never known, to somebody I don't really believe in. Nobody will know that I've broken a vow, except me and Him—and He doesn't exist, does He? He can't exist. You can't have a merciful God and this despair. . . . But, dear God, what shall I do with this desire to love? Why do I write 'dear God'? He isn't dear—not to me He isn't. *If* He exists, then He put the thought of this vow into my head, and I hate Him for it."

Thus it is only very reluctantly that Sarah fulfills the terms of her bargain with God, and at times she can hardly resist the temptation to renege and break her vow. She is as yet not willing to acknowledge the claims or even the existence of the divine Lover. And Bendrix, in his turn, tries desperately to close himself to the working of grace, even when, after Sarah's death, he is greatly perturbed by several strange occurrences which to all appearances seem to be true "miracles."

The epigraph of *The End of the Affair* is a quotation from Léon Bloy, and it casts light on some of the complexities in the plot of the novel. It states that man "has places in his heart which do not yet exist, and into them enters suffering, in order that they may have existence." In other words, Greene, in this as in his other novels, is very much concerned with the existential meaning of suffering and pain. It is through suffering that both Sarah Miles and Maurice Bendrix enter into new dimensions of existence. "Without suffering there can be no wisdom," wrote Marcel Proust. From the Christian point of view, the positive or negative significance of suffering depends entirely on the spirit with which it is accepted and endured.

We have already seen that Sarah's reaction to suffering is at first negative but in the end wholly positive. It may therefore be more correct to say that in her case not adultery but rather suffering leads her to sanctity. In the case of Maurice Bendrix the reaction is much more ambiguous. Although at first glance the effect of suffering upon him seems to be purely negative and destructive, there are growing indications that—partially owing to Sarah's intercession—grace is beginning to work upon him. When he finally emerges from his initial paranoid hatred, he has indeed grown in wisdom.

Both Sarah and Maurice are—in many errant ways and unknown to themselves—in search of the unknown God. When Maurice observes with silent wonder Sarah's capability of complete self-surrender to the beloved—whether human or divine—he admits candidly to himself that he is adrift in an unknown and unexplored region of his psyche. The fact that one by one all his hitherto accepted values have become questionable causes him a feeling of total insecurity. All of a sudden it seems that everything has become double-faced, dubious, ambiguous, ambivalent. What once had the appearance of loyalty becomes betrayal, and vice versa. Even his literary values undergo a through transvaluation: his belief in "art for art's sake" is shattered and his own literary work acquires new dimensions of ontological and existential significance.

The end of the profane and often seedy love affair becomes for the two lovers the beginning of a movement toward a love that is sacred because it is ennobled by the influx of grace. From a theological point of view, the question may be asked: Is grace conceived by Greene as saving, renovating, and sanctifying grace in the orthodox Catholic sense? The answer will have to be that obviously it is not. Greene's conception of grace here, as in his other novels, has validity only with respect to a forgiving grace which is gratuitously offered by an infinitely merciful God. Nonetheless, the judgment of Jean Guitton and other contributors to the symposium published in the *Partisan Review*, titled "The Intellectual's Return to Religion," seems unnecessarily harsh. Guitton states that Greene, Waugh, Bernanos, Mauriac and others are "portraying characters who do not participate in grace so much as they are knocked over the head by it."

In the character portrayal of Maurice Bendrix, the British author has analytically explored and described a typical state of mind of many contemporary intellectuals in the Western world: a strong desire to believe and a simultaneous almost "constitutional" inability to posit an act of implicit faith. "This struggle," wrote the late German philosopher Peter Wust—the "philosopher of Münster" and Josef Pieper's predecessor in the chair of philosophy—"becomes all the more bitter the stronger the as yet hidden faith stirs underneath the apparent disbelief."

Even the generally biased and hostile critique of John Atkins, in his monograph on Graham Greene, speaks in almost unqualified praise of Greene's masterful handling of the psychology of love: "In the face of such perceptions," Atkins writes, "the serious undergraduate view of love . . . is broken to pieces. . . . We have passed beyond romantic love, undergraduate wisdom, married decency, the Indian Summer, to the final stage in love's scaffolding."*

It is the very intensity of their "human all too human" love which in the end kindles in them the love of God. Sarah's love had grown to such proportions that no merely finite object could any longer satisfy it. And a similar observation may be made in regard to Maurice, with the difference that in his case the movement is much slower and the resistance much stronger. But essentially the two lovers share in the growth to love's maturity pointed out by Atkins. Bendrix says:

It was as if, after all the promiscuous years, I had grown up. . . . I remembered how Sarah had prayed to the God she didn't believe in, and now I spoke to the Sarah I didn't believe in. I said, you sacrificed both of us to

*John Atkins, *Graham Greene* (London: John Calder, 1957), p. 200.

bring me back to life, but what sort of life is it without you? It's all very well for you to love God. You are dead. You have Him. But I'm sick with life, I'm rotten with health . . . one can't love and do nothing. . . . *Loving Him there'd be no pleasure in anything at all with Him away.* I'd even lose my work, I'd cease to be Bendrix, Sarah, I'm afraid.

In the last letter Sarah writes to Maurice before her death, she tells him that actually it was he who in his love and his solicitude for her happiness had cleared away the rubble which had prevented her from finding access to God: "I'm a phony and a fake, but this isn't phony or fake. I used to think I was sure about myself and what was right and wrong, and you taught me not to be sure. You took away all my lies and self-deceptions like they clear a road of rubble for somebody to come along it, somebody of importance, and now He's come, but you cleared the way yourself."

And, at the end of the novel, Maurice looks once more at the last page of Sarah's diary and rereads the words: "You were teaching us to squander . . . so that one day we would have nothing left except this love of You. But You are too good to me. When I ask You for pain, You give me peace. Give it to him too. Give him my peace—he needs it more."

Surely in this last prayer Sarah has failed, Maurice thinks to himself. One of her prayers, after all, has not been answered:

I have no peace and I have no love, except for you. . . . I said to her, I am a man of hate. But I didn't feel much hatred . . . my own words were overcharged. I could detect their insincerity. What I chiefly felt was less hate than fear. For *if* this God exists, I thought, and if even you—with your lusts and your adulteries . . . can change like this, then we could all be saints by leaping as you leapt. . . . But I won't leap. I sat on my bed and said to God, You have taken her but You haven't got me yet. . . . I don't want Your peace and I don't want Your love. . . . I hate You, God, I hate You as though You existed. . . . All right, have it your way, I said to Sarah. I believe that you live and that He exists, but it will take more than your prayers to turn this hatred of Him into love. . . . I wrote at the start [of this autobiographical account] that this was a record of hate, and, walking there [over the Commons] beside Henry . . . I found the one prayer that seemed to serve the winter mood: O God, You've done enough. You've robbed me of enough. I'm too tired and old to learn to love. Leave me alone forever.

Thus this recital of a two-dimensional love affair ends. But the reader suspects that this is really not the ultimate "end of the affair" but rather, in the words of St. Gregory of Nyssa, the Greek Church Father, a progress "from one beginning to a new beginning, to the advent of that beginning that is without end."

CHAPTER SEVEN

Evelyn Waugh
Christian Gentleman

KARL LÖWITH says with good reason that a "Christian gentleman" is a contradiction in terms. Evelyn Waugh (1903—1966) was precisely such a living contradiction. As Nietzsche had stated in his *Antichrist,* there is only one gentleman in the New Testament— the skeptical Pontius Pilate, the Roman Procurator. Clearly, a gentleman is a man of the world, while a Christian is a follower of Christ. A Christian is not overly concerned with good manners, but very much with practicing the Christian theological virtues—faith, hope and love. The Christian ethos does not aspire to the Aristotelian "mean" but is willing to face the extreme "limit-situations" of existence, the dichotomies of life and death, sin and grace, despair and faith, sorrow and joy, weakness and power and, above all, the paradox of the cross.

It is only in the works of his later years that Evelyn Waugh began to show a distinct interest in theological problems. And it seems that what determined him to turn from Anglicanism to Roman Catholicism was the fact that he regarded the Catholic Church as the embodiment of the principle of order in the midst of the chaotic disorder which he discerned in the declining civilization of the West.

Thus, in contradistinction to Graham Greene, who was pre-occupied with the dialectic of good and evil, sin and grace, Waugh was intrigued by the dialectic of order and disorder. In developing this theme in his mature works, he went at times far beyond the confines of mere social satire. The social setting of his novels began to acquire symbolic religious significance when he portrayed some of his protagonists either irrevocably immersed in a chaotic world (such as the tragic hero in *A Handful of Dust,* 1952) or mysteriously emerging into a world of order and enduring values. Waugh saw the world of disorder as an upside-down world in which the hierarchy of values has been irremediably perverted.

In *A Little Learning,* the first volume of an autobiography (the second volume was never written), Waugh tells us: "I was christened Arthur Evelyn St. John: the first name after my father; the second from a whim of my mother's. I have never liked the name. In America it is used only of girls and from time to time in England it has caused confusion as to my sex . . . (Once during the Italian-Abyssinian war I went to a military post many miles from any white woman, preceded by a signal apprising them of the arrival of '*Evelyn Waugh, English writer.*' The entire small corps of officers, shaven and polished, turned out to greet me each bearing a bouquet. I was disconcerted; they were overcome by consternation). St. John was more absurd. I had a High Church godfather who insisted that I must be given the name of a saint. They might have left it plain John, but instead added the prefix of sanctity. . . ." (London: Chapman and Hall, 1964, p. 27).

Evelyn Waugh was born the son of Arthur Waugh, the former head of the British publishing firm of Chapman and Hall. He was educated at Lancing and Oxford. Alec, his elder brother, had become a successful novelist when Evelyn's star had not yet risen Evelyn's early novels—*Decline and Fall* (1929), *Vile Bodies* (1930). *A Handful of Dust* (1934), *Scoop* (1938) and *Put Out More Flags* (1942) were biting social satires dealing with the symptoms of decay characteristic of the social scene between the two world wars. In 1930 Waugh became a Roman Catholic. Speaking of this "conversion," he wrote: "Those who have read my works will perhaps understand the character of the world into which I exuberantly launched myself. Ten years of that world sufficed to show me that life there, or anywhere, was unintelligible and unendurable without God."

To the journeys which Waugh undertook in his early life as a newspaper correspondent we owe a number of noteworthy travel books and also some of his novels. Twice he visited Abyssinia, the first time in 1930. *Remote People* (1931) satirizes the coronation of Haile Selassie as Emperor. *Waugh in Abyssinia* (1936), written after his second trip to Ethiopia, shows Waugh's continued contempt for Haile Selassie and simultaneously his admiration of Mussolini and his invading hordes. Both travel books were followed by a novel—*Black Mischief* (1932) and *Scoop* (1949). The former satirizes the "white man's burden," that is, the compulsive efforts of Europeans to superimpose their "superior culture" on Africans, while the latter deals in a similar vein with the Italian invasion of Ethiopia.

Despite his evident sympathy for certain Fascist dictators, such as Mussolini and Franco, Waugh joined the British armed forces in 1939 when the world and his country were threatened by Hitler's aggression. At the age of thirty-six he accepted a commission in the Royal Marines and, after the battle of Dunkirk, volunteered for work in the British Commandos. In 1942 he transferred to the Royal Horse Guards with the rank of captain. He fought valiantly in the theater of war in North Africa and on Crete and later joined the British military mission to Yugoslavia. The proofs of *Brideshead Revisited* (1946)—his first theological novel in the strict sense of the term—were parachuted to him, and he corrected them while hiding in a cave on Yugoslavian soil.

Brideshead was followed by three major works of fiction—*Men at Arms* (1952), *Officers and Gentlemen* (1955) and *Unconditional Surrender* (1961). They were based on Waugh's wartime experiences, and the author later published what he called a "recension" of the three novels in one volume, titled *Sword of Honor* (1965).

Shorter novelistic works, written after World War II, include *The Loved One* (1948), a hilarious and macabre satire on life and death in Hollywood; *Love among the Ruins* (1953), offering frightening glimpses of the spectre of an anticipated totalitarian future of mankind, and *Helena* (1950), a fictional and partly satirical account of the life of the mother of Emperor Constantine the Great, the legendary discoverer of "the true cross."

The short novel *The Ordeal of Mr. Pinfold* (1952) is of special interest because, being in part autobiographical, it affords an insight into Waugh's state of mind in his later years. Subtitled *A Conversation Piece,* the novel tells of a "brief attack of hallucinations" which the author actually experienced in 1954. A similar and yet in many respects totally different experience was recorded by the Spanish novelist José Maria Gironella, the author of the best-selling *The Cypresses Believe in God,* in *Los Fantasmas de mi cerebro* (1962). In both instances the authors describe in minute detail a terrible period of temporary mental illness; in Waugh's case it was induced by overdoses of sedatives and alcohol.

What is truth and what is fiction in Pinfold-Waugh's partly humorous and partly grotesque self-analysis can best be determined by comparing it with the autobiographical sketch titled "Fan-Fare," published in *Life* magazine in 1945, in which Waugh, "finding his latest book (*Brideshead*) a best-seller, explains himself and his works to his new American admirers." His "answer to the ladies all over the U.S.A. (and to the one man) who have been kind enough to write to Evelyn Waugh about his recent novel" shows that in the decade following this self-portrait nothing seems to have changed except that Waugh's conservatism had hardened and his pessimism regarding "the decline of the West" deepened. And this process went on unchecked to the end of Waugh's life. In *A Little Learning* (1964) one finds the revealing statement: "To have been born into a world of beauty, to die amid ugliness, is the common fate of all us exiles."

Although Waugh believed he had found in the Roman Catholic Church that principle of order which could cope with the chaos of the modern world, he was profoundly shocked by the ecclesiastical reforms in liturgy and doctrine that came in the wake of Vatican Council II. Of Mr. Pinfold, who here obviously is merely a pseudonym for Mr. Waugh, we are told that "he had been received into the Church—'conversion' suggests an event more sudden and emotional than his calm acceptance of the propositions of his faith—in early manhood, at the time when many Englishmen of humane education were falling into communism. . . . And at the very time when the leaders of his Church were exhorting their people to emerge from the catacombs into the forum, to make their influence felt in democratic politics and to regard worship as a corporate rather than a private act, Mr. Pinfold burrowed ever deeper into the rock. Away from the parish he sought the least frequented Mass; at home he held aloof from the multifarious organizations which have sprung into being at the summons of the hierarchy to redeem the times" (*The Ordeal of Mr. Pinfold,* pp. 9 ff.).

In other words, the gentlemanly course of Pinfold-Waugh's life must not be disturbed by matters which are out of the ordinary, by anything that exceeds the measure of established traditions and ingrained habits: Mr. Pinfold "wished no one ill, but he looked at the world *sub specie aeternitatis* and he found it flat as a map; except when, rather often, personal annoyances intruded. Then he would come tumbling from his exalted point of observation. Shocked by a bad bottle of wine, an impertinent stranger, or a fault in syntax, his mind like a cinema camera trucked furiously forward to confront the offending object. . . . He was too old a dog to learn new tricks" (p. 13).

The trilogy of novels which Waugh issued under the title *The Sword of Honor* underscores the convictions expressed in *Helena,* in particular a rejection of the kind of irrationalism and mysticism that he had encountered in Ethiopia when he visited the monastery of Debra Lebanos: He was equally appalled by the Abyssinian ritual with its "secrecy" and "unintelligibility" and by the disorderly life and the ignorance of the monks. Compared with the hidden sanctuaries and the "obfuscations" prevalent in the esoteric

sects of the non-Christian East, the classical Christian basilica and
the open and exposed altar appeared to him as "a triumph of light
over darkness . . . and I saw theology as a science of simplification
by which nebulous and elusive ideas are formalized and made
intelligible and exact. I saw the Church of the first century as a
dark and hidden thing. . . . The priests hid their offices practicing
trades; their identity was known only to initiates. . . . And the pure
nucleus of the truth lay in the minds of the people, encumbered
with superstitions, gross survivals of the paganism in which they had
been brought up; hazy and obscene nonsense seeping from the other
esoteric cults of the Near East, magical infections from the conquered
barbarian. And I began to see how these obscure sanctuaries had
grown, with the clarity of Western reason, into the great open
altars of Catholic Europe, where Mass is said in a flood of light"
(*Remote People,* pp. 88 ff.). This view of primitive Christianity, if
not historically correct, is at least original.

Like Mr. Pinfold, his double, Evelyn Waugh was "affectionate,
high-spirited and busy in childhood; dissipated and often despairing
in youth; sturdy and prosperous in early manhood; he had in middle
age degenerated less than many of his contemporaries. He attributed
this superiority to his long, lonely, tranquil days at Lychpole, a
secluded village some hundred miles from London" (p. 5). Actually,
Waugh lived with his wife and their children in a Gloucestershire
manor named Piers Court. Waugh wrote in that ironic self-appraisal
in *Life* of 1945:

I live in a shabby stone house in the country, where nothing is under a
hundred years old except the plumbing and that does not work. . . . I have
a fast-emptying cellar of wine, and gardens fast reverting to the jungle.
I am very contentedly married. I have numerous children whom I see
once a day for three, I hope, awe-inspiring minutes. . . . It was not always
thus with me. In youth I gadded about, and in those years and in the
preposterous years of the Second World War, I collected enough experience
to last several lifetimes of novel writing. . . . When I gadded, among savages
and people of fashion and politicians and crazy generals, it was because I
enjoyed them. I have settled down now because I have ceased to enjoy them.

Before firing the final salvos at his admiring female correspondents in the United States, Waugh made an attempt to answer some of the questions they had asked him after the publication of *Brideshead*:

A lady in Hempstead, N.Y. asks me whether I consider my characters "typical." No, Mrs. Schultz, I do not. It is horrible of you to ask. A novelist has no business with types; they are the property of economists and politicians and advertisers and the other professional bores of our period. The artist is interested only in individuals. . . . The Common Man does not exist. He is an abstraction invented by bores for bores. Even you, Mrs. Schultz, are an individual.

In the same essay in *Life* Waugh takes issue with one of the more prominent American critics, Edmund Wilson, who after the appearance of *Brideshead* changed his former generous eulogies to outraged condemnation. Why? "He was outraged (quite legitimately by his standards) at finding God intruding into my story. I believe that you can only leave God out by making your characters pure abstractions. . . . So in my future books there will be two things to make them unpopular: a preoccupation with style and the attempt to represent man more fully, which, to me, means only one thing, man in his relation to God." This promise Waugh kept, notwithstanding the fact that soon his seemingly irrepressible irony was to get again the better of him, dimming and blurring at times the theological contours that were so clearly marked in *Brideshead*.

The theological theme is dominant throughout *Brideshead Revisited*. Edmund Wilson called the work "disastrous" because, he argued, Waugh's commitment to Roman Catholicism had completely distorted his view of reality. It would of course be more correct to say that it had utterly distorted Mr. Wilson's perspective as a critic.

The novel is subtitled *The Sacred and Profane Memories of Captain Charles Ryder*. Captain Ryder's return to Brideshead, the stately and somewhat decrepit baroque estate of the Catholic Flyte family is a return both to a beginning and to an end. In a huge panorama the decadence of British upper-class society unfolds in autumnal colors. The book centers on the question: What possibilities remain when man has come to that great impasse which appears to be the end of his life's road?

Ryder, the society painter turned soldier, is both the narrator and one of the main protagonists of the novel. A captain in the British Army during World War II, he is billeted in another camp—the country estate of the Flytes. Ryder is deeply moved by this revival of the memories of his association with several members of the family. Spanning two decades and three continents, the novel recalls through the reflections of Ryder the gay company of the college days in the circle of the Oxford intelligentsia and Ryder's intimate friendship with Lord Sebastian Flyte, an eccentric youth of great physical charm. Sebastian's inseparable companion, he remembers, was a toy teddy bear. It was through Sebastian that Ryder, the agnostic, had come to know the other members of the Catholic Flytes, British noblemen and noblewomen, and all, with the possible exception of Cordelia, the youngest daughter, affected by and infected with the spirit of a decaying class and a dying civilization.

It was Sebastian who had told Ryder about the religious tensions and the moral cracks in his family. "So you see we're a mixed family religiously. Brideshead [Sebastian's elder brother] and Cordelia are both fervent Catholics; he's miserable, she's bird-happy; Julia [Sebastian's sister] and I are half-heathen; I am happy, I rather think Julia isn't; Mummy [Lady Marchmain] is popularly believed to be a saint and Papa [Lord Marchmain] is excommunicated—and I wouldn't know which of them was happy. Anyway, however you look at it, happiness doesn't seem to have much to do with it [that is, with the Catholic religion], and that's all I want. . . . I wish I liked Catholics more" (p. 89).

Book One of the novel bears the title *Et in Arcadia Ego* (I too Lived Once in Arcadia), Book Two the symbolic title *A Twitch upon the Thread*. What happens in the second part shows the strength of the hold which the Church has over all the "mixed-up" members of the Flyte family. When Ryder met beautiful Lady Julia, both had already initiated divorce proceedings, and a passionate love affair developed between them. Old Lord Marchmain was unable to obtain a divorce from his devoutly Catholic wife, but they were separated, and he lived with his mistress in a palace in Venice.

Sebastian grew up to be an alcoholic, and he spent his later years as "a sort of under-porter" in a monastery in Morocco. Cordelia had told Ryder that her brother "conceived the idea of escaping to the savages" and that the Father Superior was going to take charge of him:

There are usually a few odd hangers-on in a religious house, you know; people who can't quite fit in either to the world or the monastic rule. . . . I've seen others like him, and I believe they are very near and dear to God. . . . Everyone will know about his drinking; he'll disappear for two or three days every month or so, and they'll all nod and smile and say in their various accents, "Old Sebastian's on the spree again," and then he'll come back dishevelled and shamefaced and be more devout for a day or two in the chapel. . . . Then one morning, after one of his drinking bouts, he'll be picked up at the gate dying, and show by a mere flicker of the eyelid that he is conscious when they give him the last sacraments. It's not such a bad way of getting through one's life.

Ryder remembers with gentle melancholy the joyful young man with the teddy bear under the flowering chestnuts: "It's not what one would have foretold," he replied. "I suppose he doesn't suffer?" "Oh, yes," Cordelia had said, "I think he does. . . . No one is ever wholly without suffering. . . . I've seen so much suffering in the last few years; there's so much coming for everybody soon. It's the spring of love. . . ."

Thus faith triumphs in the end in all the lordly Flytes although their lives were in no way distinguished from those of non-Catholics, non-Christians and nonbelievers. They, like their non-Catholic fellowmen, show the symptoms of the "human all too human." What good then is their religious upbringing to them? Sebastian, the Roman Catholic, considers himself "far, far worse" than

Charles Ryder, the man without faith. As Ryder himself had said to Lady Julia,

There were four of you. Cara [Lord Marchmain's mistress] didn't know the first thing it [Catholicism] was about, and may or may not have believed it; you knew a bit and didn't believe a word; Cordelia knew about as much and believed it madly; only poor Bridey [Julia's brother] knew and believed, and I thought he made a pretty poor show when it came to explaining. And people go round saying, "At least Catholics know what they believe." We had a fair cross-section to-night—.

However, Charles Ryder's diagnosis was a bit off course. He forgot or was not aware of "the twitch upon the thread." It was Cordelia who had used this phrase in reminding Ryder of one of Chesterton's detective stories in which Father Brown is the sleuth: "I wonder if you remember the story Mummy read us the evening Sebastian first got drunk. . . . Father Brown said something like 'I caught him (the thief) with an unseen hook and an invisible line which is long enough to let him wander to the ends of the world and still to bring him back with a twitch upon the thread' " (p. 220). Thus there is, after all, surface appearances not withstanding, a basic difference between those for whom existence as a whole has a religious accent and meaning and those for whom it has no such meaning. The former can never forget entirely where that home is in which alone they can be truly human. Accordingly, the non-believers in Waugh's novel are solely engaged in money-making or in hunting for political jobs or both. They are oblivious of and insensitive to any ultimate *raison d'être* of human existence. They are, in Lady Julia's words, "not all there" or, in the phrasing of Bernanos, "mere stumps" of men and women. Bridey is a respectable but not a very respected figure: a correct Catholic in terms of the Sunday-School catechism but surely not a model Christian, irreproachable and quite boring in his virtuous puritanism.

The two climactic scenes of the novel are the deathbed conversion of Lord Marchmain and the parting of Lady Julia and Charles Ryder. Contrary to the wishes of the dying Lord Marchmain,

Bridey had called for Father Mackey to administer the sacrament of extreme unction. But, as Cordelia told the story, her father had said to the priest: "Father Mackey, I am afraid you have been brought here under a misapprehension. I am not *in extremis* and I have not been a practicing member of your Church for twenty-five years. Brideshead, show Father Mackey the way out." To this Charles Ryder, who was witnessing the scene, had drily observed: "Mumbo-jumbo is off, the witch-doctor has gone" (p. 327). Ryder had felt triumphant: he had been right all along. But before the day ended he had come to realize that he had underestimated the hidden strength of even a repressed religious commitment.

In an argumentative mood and secretly trembling at the thought that the Catholic religion might intrude also upon his relationship to Julia, Charles Ryder had stubbornly persisted in reasoning things out to their logical conclusions: "Let's get this clear," he had said; "he has to make an act of the will; he has to be contrite and wish to be reconciled; is that right? But only God knows whether he has really made an act of will; the priest can't tell; and if there isn't a priest there, and he makes the act of will alone, that's as good as if there were a priest. And it's quite possible that the will may still be working when a man is too weak to make any outward sign of it; is that right? . . . Well, for heaven's sake, what is the priest for?" All logic obviously was on Ryder's side. The presence of a priest seemed quite superfluous. Yet in the silence Cara had said, "All I know is that I shall take very good care to have a priest." And later Julia had told Charles not to start these religious arguments, especially since he cannot convince anyone, not even himself. But Ryder had retorted that he only wanted to know what these people believed (pp. 329 ff.).

For Lord Marchmain, however, the time was not yet. The weeks passed, and in June Lady Julia's divorce would become final, and Ryder's divorced wife was about to get married again. Julia would be free to marry Charles in September. Then in July, Lord Marchmain's condition had worsened. When Julia had told Ryder that she was going to get Father Mackey, he had not been surprised because he had read the resolution in her mind all during the summer. When, after Julia had left, he had asked the doctor to put "a stop to this nonsense," the physician had replied: "My business is with the body. It's not my business to argue whether people are better alive or dead, or what happens to them after death. I only try to keep them alive" (p. 335). Ryder had tried every trick in the book to keep the priest away from the deathbed, but in half an hour Julia had returned with Father Mackey. "Father Mackey," Ryder had said to the priest, "you know how Lord Marchmain greeted you last time you came; do you think it possible he can have changed now?" "Thank God," the priest had replied, "by His grace it is possible. . . . I have seen so many men and women die; I never knew them sorry to have me there at the end" (p. 336). That was different, Ryder had objected: they were Catholics, whereas Lord Marchmain had ceased practicing his religion decades ago. The shock of the solemn liturgical ceremony might even kill the old man. "Christ came to call, not the righteous, but sinners to repentance," was the priest's rejoinder.

By this time Ryder had run out of arguments, and it was the priest's turn to take over: "Do you know what I want to do? It is something so small, no show about it. . . . I just want to ask him if he is sorry for his sins. I want him to make some little sign of assent . . . then I want to give him God's pardon. Then, though that's not necessary, I want to anoint him" (p. 337).

Suddenly it had seemed that there was "a wall of fire between Charles and Julia. Lord Marchmain was lying in his bed, his eyes closed, his hands above the bed-clothes." The priest had bent over Lord Marchmain and had blessed him. He had asked the dying man to make that little sign of recognition and assent. But there had been no sign. Now, the priest had said, "I am going to give you absolution. While I am giving it tell God you are sorry you have offended Him." Ryder had seen the priest making the sign of the cross. Then, strangely enough, Ryder had knelt down with all the others, and he, the nonbeliever, had prayed: "O God, if there is a God, forgive him his sins, if there is such a thing as sin," and then

the man on the bed opened his eyes and gave a sigh, the sort of sigh I had imagined people make at the moment of death, but his eyes moved so that we knew there was still life in him. I suddenly felt the longing for a sign, if only of courtesy, if only for the sake of the woman I loved, who knelt in front of me, praying, I knew, for a sign. . . . Suddenly Lord Marchmain moved his hand to his forehead; I thought he had felt the touch of the chrism [oil used for the anointing] and was wiping it away. "O God," I prayed, "don't let him do that." But . . . the hand moved slowly down his breast, then to his shoulder, and Lord Marchmain made the sign of the cross. Then I knew that the sign I had asked for was not a little thing, not a passing nod of recognition, and a phrase came back to me from my childhood of the veil of the temple being rent from top to bottom. It was over (p. 338).

The parting of Julia and Charles Ryder was heart-rending and soul-piercing, but it had become inevitable. Even Charles had known that this dark hour had to come: "since this morning; since before this morning; all this year." "Oh, my dear," Julia said, "if you could only understand. Then I could bear to part, or bear it better. I should say my heart was breaking, if I believed in broken hearts. I can't marry you, Charles; I can't be with you ever again." He answered that he knew that, and he asked Julia what would become of her: "What will you do?" She replied:

Just go on—alone. How can I tell what I shall do? You know the whole of me. . . . I've always been bad. Probably I will be bad again, punished again. But the worse I am, the more I need God. I can't shut myself out from His mercy. That is what it would mean; starting a life with you, without Him. . . . I saw to-day there was one thing unforgivable . . . to set up a rival good to God's. Why should I be allowed to understand that, and not you, Charles . . . it may be a private bargain between me and God, that if I give up this one thing I want so much, however bad I am, He won't despair of me in the end. Now we shall both be alone, and I shall have no way of making you understand.

"I don't want to make it easier for you," Charles answered. "I hope your heart may break; but I do understand" (pp. 340 ff.).

This "end of the affair" in some respects closely resembles the break between Sarah Miles and Maurice Bendrix in Greene's novel. However, Waugh's characters are more convincing because they live their lives, as it were, autonomously; they stand on their own feet once they have been called into life by the author. In this regard Waugh's creative psychological dexterity is superior to Greene's often overheated and overstated polemical intent. The temperate climate of *Brideshead* therefore not only rivals but surpasses the artistry of Graham Greene. It was Waugh's greatest achievement as a novelist. He never reached this height again.

CHAPTER EIGHT

Gertrud von Le Fort

THE SONG AT THE SCAFFOLD

THE AGE of the Lutheran Reformation and of the Catholic Restoration or Counter-Reformation was, to use a Biblical term, the period of the "unsealed abyss" (Apoc. 6). The centuries of the waning Middle Ages and the incipient modern age were character-ized by vast devastations caused by wars, famines, earthquakes, the trials for witchcraft and violent death in many other forms. Man believed that the world in which he lived was tortured and victimized by demoniac possession, and in his attempt to fight against it he became himself the prey of anguished and cruel obsessions.

However, almost abruptly the age of demoniac possession gave way to the age of Enlightenment. Deism, that is the religion and philosophy of a disappearing God and His replacement by an abstract conceptualization of a Deity no longer concerned with the destiny of the creatures of His creative fiat, became the creed of the centuries following the rebirth of ancient thought in the intellectual climate of Renaissance and Humanism. Nature, reason, natural religion and natural morality supplanted the intricately interwoven medieval system of nature and supernature, of reason and faith, of ethics and moral theology, until the French Revolution (1789) proclaimed solemnly the freedom, equality and fraternity of a Western mankind "emancipated" from the shackles of a super-natural tutelage. Thus modern man tried to fashion a new heaven and a new earth, to be founded on the utopian notion of an "earthly paradise."

Then another radical change occurred in the early decades of the twentieth century. The first traces of a new age of the "unsealed abyss" became gradually distinguishable, and psychoanalysis or depth psychology emerged as an ingenious attempt to control and master those revived neurotic and psychotic individual and collective obsessions which the age of Enlightenment, Rationalism and Natural Religion had in vain hoped to have exorcized once and for all.

From Luther's certitude of "salvation by faith alone" to Descartes' rational demonstration of the certitude of the individual self, man's desperate attempts to master the demoniac possessions and obsessions of Western civilization had been repeated over and over again. Western man had almost learned by his historical-social experience to live with his recurring seizures with "fear and trembling" and with that tormenting anguish that had afflicted the age of the Reformation and Counter-Reformation.

This attempt to cope with and eventually conquer man's meta-physical-theological anxiety appeared in its secularized form most powerfully in the philosophies of Kierkegaard, Nietzsche, Unamuno, Heidegger and Sartre. As first diagnosed by Kierkegaard, *Angst* (anguish) was now seen as being constitutionally ingrained in the very nature and heart of being and of human existence, because man's "being-in-the-world" was—as it had always been asserted by Christianity—leaning hard on nothingness. This is why Sartre could declare emphatically that the naught was lodged in all being and existence "like a worm."

At the opposite end of what might be called a natural meta-physics of anguish is situated, however, the supernatural mysticism of anguish of Blanche de la Force in Gertrud von Le Fort's *Song at the Scaffold*. But before entering into a discussion of the problems underlying the Le Fort novel, it is necessary to examine in some detail the life, the mentality and the work of its author.

The Le Fort family was of French origin. The French religious wars of the sixteenth century compelled the French Calvinists (the Huguenots) to choose between loyalty to their convictions and the love of their homeland. As did many other French Huguenot families, the ancestors of Gertrud von Le Fort chose emigration. They went to Geneva. Two hundred years later, one branch of the family settled in Prussia.

Gertrud von Le Fort was born in 1876 at Minden in Westphalia, where her parents used to spend their summer vacations. The young girl studied Protestant theology at the universities of Berlin and Heidelberg. Among her teachers, she admired especially Ernst Troeltsch (1865–1923), one of the most prominent modern Protestant theologians and sociologists, the author of, among many other works, the two volumes titled *Die Soziallehren der christlichen Kirchen und Gruppen* (1912; translated as *Social Teaching of the Christian Churches,* 1931) and of the earlier and equally influential treatise on *Die Bedeutung des Protestantismus für die Entstehung der modernen Welt* (1906; translated as *Protestantism and Progress,* 1912).

After Troeltsch's death, Gertrud von Le Fort edited some of her revered teacher's unpublished manuscripts. During a stay in Rome, in 1925, she embraced Roman Catholicism. However, her conversion did not signify for her a break with the Protestant tradition of her family. As she wrote in 1937 (in the liberal Catholic Journal *Hochland*),

A convert is not, as is sometimes erroneously assumed, a person who stresses the painful denominational divisions [of the Christian Church] but, on the contrary, one who has overcome these divisions. A convert's essential experience is not that of a different faith but rather . . . that of the unity and continuity of faith. . . . A conversion may be likened to the experience of a child who becomes conscious of the fact that his very personal religious possession—the central Christian *depositum* of the Protestant faith—as it derives originally from his Mother, the Church, is also preserved and endures in the shelter of that Mother. His experience is thus that of a luminous discovery: the schism in the Church is not so much a cleavage in *faith* as it is a cleavage in *love,* and the division in faith cannot be overcome unless the division in love has first been overcome.

It is this truly ecumenical spirit which makes Gertrud von Le Fort anticipate many of the ideas that were later enunciated and articulated by the decrees and injunctions of the Second Vatican Council that was convoked by Pope John XXIII.

What Gertrud von Le Fort presents in her works issues from the very core of Christianity and for this reason is addressed to Protestants and Catholics alike. In the "Prologue" of her *Hymns to the Church* (1923) she describes with great poetic power and profound insight the situation of contemporary man. His soul harbors a dream of God, but the dream cannot become a reality because the doors of the soul are locked: it is imprisoned in a total aloneness, and the images of the spirit have become mere shadows. However, the diagnosis of this disease is already the faint beginning of a cure: God stands at the door and is ready to enter as soon as the soul is willing to open.

These hymns are variations on the theme of the healing of the modern soul by divine grace mediated by the Church. Thus the Church is for the poet the power which is capable of saving man by keeping him from handing himself over to some self-created idol, the power which constantly reminds him that he was created in the image and likeness of God. The Church thus symbolizes for Gertrud von Le Fort the presence of Christ and the biographical history of Christ from antiquity to the present.

What the *Hymns to the Church* celebrate in lyrical free rhythms, the partly autobiographical novels *The Veil of Veronica* (1927) and *The Angels' Wreath* (1946) describe in a prose of lapidary simplicity—the way homeward to the Church. What is at stake is the fate of the individual human being in the modern age and his personal response to challenges which he cannot escape. What is at stake is existence as such, an existence which is endangered on all sides. The author may have remembered the words of her teacher, Ernst Troeltsch: "What Christ and the Bible, what modern life and thought have to offer us acquires vital religious significance only by means of personal appropriation."

In the story of the girl Veronica the alternative is not Protestantism or Catholicism but paganism or Christianity. Modern paganism is embodied in the young poet Enzio and in the imposing figure of the grandmother—both headstrong individuals who are a law unto themselves. They know of neither hope nor dread. They acknowledge no reality which transcends their finite selves. But while these "good pagans" lack the dimension of the supernatural, they possess one thing which imparts meaning to their lives—reverence. "Human life," says the grandmother, "might be lived without any abstract theory, but it can never be lived without boundless reverence." And the following words in the novel no doubt express the author's own conviction: "Every human being has a destiny of his life and a history of his soul but, transcending these, there is also a history that has as its content the relationship of his soul with God. And this history is . . . in the last analysis quite straight and simple. For the fact is that we do not fight our way through to God but rather that God fights His way through to reach *us*, and ultimately almost everything happens despite ourselves."

Enzio, the poet, represents contemporary man in all his concreteness, formed by the history of the West. While the events of the novel take place in the period preceding and following World War I, they are intimately related to the problems with which contemporary man is confronted today and also to those which will confront him in the foreseeable future.

The novel (*The Angels' Wreath*), written after World War II, shows in the further character development of Enzio the rise and decline of an idealistically conceived but wholly man-centered humanism. When man has resolutely divorced himself from religion and from metaphysics, he experiences sooner or later the predicaments of his radical finitude. And nihilism, referred to by Nietzsche as "the uncanniest of all guests," stands then no longer merely "at the door" but is already inside the house, in our midst. "What must be done henceforth," says Enzio, "will be without love, for otherwise the goal remains unattainable." What goal?

One must henceforth live "heroically and dangerously." To what end? There remains "the wild loyalty to that which has no meaning." As Nietzsche, that uncanny prophet, had predicted: in the desert of his newly acquired total freedom—acquired after the "death of God"—"man prefers even to will the Naught to not-willing at all." Thus the proclaimed pure immanence of man-centered "humanism" terminates in nihilism.

In her third major theological novel, *The Pope from the Ghetto* (1929), Gertrud von Le Fort offers a theology of suffering, centered in the problem of the meaning of Christ and His Cross. This is, however, both a historical and a theological narrative, having as its background the historical event of the schism of the Western Church in the twelfth century, which began with the election of Anacletus II (Pier Leonis), the antipope, in 1130. The schism ended with the death of Pier Leonis in 1138 and the return to Rome of the legitimate Pope, Innocent II.

The "Pope from the Ghetto" is, as the title of the novel implies, a baptized Jew. His great-grandfather was Chanoch ben Esra who, when Rome was shaken by an earthquake and the frightened and superstitious Roman populace blamed the disaster on the Jews, barely escaped the fate of being stoned by the frenzied mob. He was saved by the protecting mantle of the Pope, who was just then leading a procession through the streets of the Eternal City. In his mortal terror Pier Leonis recited the beginning of the Credo, "I believe in God the Almighty Father, the Maker of heaven and earth." But when the Pope continued, "and in Jesus Christ . . . ," the young Pier Leonis remained silent, refusing to acknowledge the incarnate Christ.

Even after becoming a priest, a cardinal and eventually Pope, Anacletus II proclaims the "justice" of the Old Covenant and shows himself averse to the "love" taught and lived by Christ and preached by the Church of the New Covenant. He disdains the folly of the Cross, which is the folly of love.

However, Pier Leonis is tortured by a strange existential anguish which he learns to control and master only gradually as his native reasoning power develops and turns into an enjoyment of dialectic and sophistic argument. But there was more truth in the *Angst* of the small boy than there is in the security of the mature man. When he proclaims as his life's aim to do away with all "injustice" on earth, his former teacher warns: "Take care you do not also abolish the Cross." In the words of the Cardinal-Bishop Petrus of Portus, "The world has not been redeemed by those who fight for the innocent (although we ought to fight for the innocent) but rather by the bitter suffering of the innocent."

The reader learns that shortly after his birth Pier Leonis was taken by force from his mother, Mirjam, by Frangipane, a Roman nobleman, after Mirjam's refusal to be baptized like her husband. It may be surmised that somehow this traumatic childhood experience lingers on subconsciously and accounts for the early anxieties of the future antipope.

A disputation between the reigning Pontiff and Pier Leonis concludes with the Pope's admonition, "My son, there is justice only in hell; there is grace in heaven, and on earth there is the Cross." This the young cardinal does not understand. In inner revolt and as if shaken by some indescribable pain, he asks: "The Cross of Christ—is that our reward?"

At his father's deathbed the young cardinal realizes the evanescent nature of all earthly power and wealth. In the face of death he seems to be offered a last chance to renounce his worldly ambitions and to accept the Cross of Christ, to choose "love" rather than "justice." However, his very act of humility turns out to be his greatest temptation. Will the people not say that his humility is a mere cloak of spiritual pride? And so the seemingly inevitable happens: with shouts of "justice and happiness" Pier Leonis is proclaimed antipope and assumes the name of Anacletus II.

The tragic destiny of Pier Leonis is inseparably interwoven with the lives of his mother and his sister, Trophaea. As the old Rabbi had foretold after the birth of the two children, "Mirjam, daughter of Nathan ben Jechiel, rejoice, for your son who was taken from you by Edom [Esau], will split the kingdom of Edom that calls itself Christianity, from top to bottom. . . . But it has been decreed that your second child, your weak child, will guide the strong one: the blind one [Trophaea was born blind] will guide the one who can see, and the sister will bring back her brother."

Mirjam voluntarily takes upon herself the cross of the Jewish people, and she hopefully expects the prophesied return of her estranged son, her "messiah." And the "messiah" comes, but not in the manner she had expected: her son, the antipope, approaches amidst pomp and worldly glory. "Listen to me," exclaims Mirjam, "this one is not the right Pope. This one is not even a Christian—he is my own son, who has come back . . . to tear apart Christianity." In the depth of her sorrow—after Trophaea's death—and at the verge of insanity, Mirjam praises her suffering and that of her people: "Oh, you all-powerful suffering . . . oh, you ever blessed suffering . . . oh, you ever victorious suffering." She dies, like her daughter, "pierced by the sword of sorrow."

The novel concludes in the style of the historical chronicle:

From the annals of our golden City of Rome: What shall we say to these events? Has the blind Jewess been granted the miracle of divine illumination? Has she . . . suffered martyrdom and thus . . . received the baptism of blood? Or does what has happened here testify that since the coming of Our Lord in the flesh even those who do not yet know Him, are moved by Him if they are men of good will and if love abides in their hearts? Suffice it for us to say that this Jewess, her heart transfixed by the sword, has brought back to us the sacred Christ-Child.

When Trophaea's body is carried into the palace of the antipope, Pier Leonis, seized now by silent despair, the "sickness unto death," and "ashen-grey in his face," cries out to the servants that he does not wish to see the dead bodies of the innocent. For the sake of "justice alone" he definitively rejects the Cross of Christ.

The crucial key question in this novel is this: What do you think about Christ? This question is made the ultimate criterion of judgment. It is addressed equally to the Roman nobility and the

Roman people. If man wants to evade the Cross, he becomes all the more the prey of death, because it is precisely the Cross of Christ that alone has overcome death: "The Cross appeared overshadowing the cradle of the [Western] nations when they were born into their historical life; it accompanies them throughout their history . . . it has formed their spirit but, above all, it has formed their hearts." Christian suffering, as seen by Gertrud von Le Fort, is the suffering of the innocent, willingly accepted in the following of Christ. And "the Church is not victorious with the sword in her hand but rather with a sword in her heart."

At the opposite end of metaphysical anguish, as we have said above, is situated the supernatural mysticism of the *Angst* of Blanche de la Force, the unheroic "heroine" of *The Song at the Scaffold*. Anguish, in other words, is essentially ambivalent: it is, on the one hand, the mode and manner by which man becomes aware of the all-pervasive efficacy of God when, following St. Paul's injunction, he works for his salvation "in fear and trembling." For, according to St. Paul, it is God who works in man both the willing and the achievement, according to His pleasure. In such anguish man learns to know the real presence of the sovereign Lord. In this sense anguish is equivalent to that "fear of the Lord" which, as the Psalmist says, "is the beginning of wisdom."

The ambivalence of anguish becomes strikingly evident when we consider that anguish may be the starting point of a movement toward God or, contrariwise, of a movement *away from* God. The paradigm or prototype of the latter movement is Lucifer, the fallen angel, the demon, who desires to be like God in order to be safe and secure from God's claim on His creature, and who therefore hurls at the Deity his defiant *non serviam*. For "the devils [too] believe, and they tremble" (James 2:19). The prototype of the second movement is Christ in the Garden of Gethsemani, Christ in His agony. He also trembled in anguish: "He began to feel sorrowful and anguished . . . and then He said: 'Father, if it is your

will, take this chalice from me, but not *my* will, *your* will be done!' "
(Matt. 25:37–40).

The Song at the Scaffold is the story of the martyrdom of the sixteen
Carmelite nuns of the Carmelite convent of Compiègne who were
guillotined at the Place de la Concorde on July 17, 1794. They were
beatified by the Church on May 27, 1906. Georges Bernanos
recognized in Gertrud von Le Fort's narrative of the anguish,
agony and martyrdom of Blanche de la Force a close kinship with
one of the main themes of his own spiritual life and, at the threshold
of his own imminent death, he wrote with his last remaining strength
his scenario titled *Dialogues des Carmelites* (1949), based on the Le
Fort Novel. More recently, Francis Poulenc used the Bernanos
version as the libretto for his opera *Les Carmelites*.

Gertrud von Le Fort tells us that what interested her in the
historical event and what prompted her to write her novel "was
not primarily the fate of the sixteen Carmelite nuns of Compiègne
but the character of little Blanche. As a historical figure she never
existed; she owes the breath of her fragile existence exclusively to
my own inner life. . . ." Gertrud von Le Fort goes on:

Born of the horrors of an age which in Germany was overshadowed by
the presentiment of coming fateful events, this figure arose before my
mind's eye as an embodiment of the death-agony of an entire epoch that
was nearing its end. . . . This young girl who enters a convent because of
her constitutional fear of the world (*Weltangst*) and who attempts to form
her religious life by a mystical union with the agony of Christ, was already
alive in my poetic imagination prior to my embedding her fate in that of
the sixteen Carmelites of Compiègne. I became acquainted with these
historical events by accident, when I found in a footnote of a book dealing
with the history of Catholic religious orders a reference to those Carmelite
nuns who approached the guillotine singing and chanting, and this
discovery made me transpose little Blanche from the present age to the
age of the French Revolution. . . . In the meagre historical sources I found
a certain factual guideline for the formation of my story only in the
character of Sister Marie de l'Incarnation who in all probability was of
royal blood. The individual nuns too, as they appear in the novel, are
creatures of my poetic fancy.

The reader should keep in mind that the stress placed on the motif of anguish by both Gertrud von Le Fort and Bernanos is not quite warranted by the historical records nor by the nature of the Carmelite form of religious devotion. Historical as well as phenomenological accuracy would rather have to emphasize the voluntary self-sacrifice of the sixteen nuns in offering their lives, in a desire to expiate for the crimes of the revolutionary régime of terror. This is borne out by the frequent blood testimony that occurs in the history of the Carmelite Order and in the biographies of the great personalities and the saints which it produced, men and women alike. This is true as much of St. Teresa of Avila and St. John of the Cross in the Spanish *siglo de oro* in the sixteenth century as of St. Thérèse of Lisieux in the nineteenth and of Edith Stein (Sister Teresia Benedicta a Cruce) in the twentieth. The latter was a German Jewess and a pupil of Edmund Husserl, the founder of Phenomenology. After her conversion to Roman Catholicism she entered the Carmelite Order in the Carmelite convent at Cologne. Having been transferred by her superiors to the Dutch convent of Echt, she was finally hunted down by the German Secret Police and ended her life in the gas chambers of the notorious Auschwitz concentration camp in Silesia. She voluntarily and serenely practiced what she called "the science of the Cross," a science which she says she had learned from her "spiritual father," St. John of the Cross.

According to the theologians of the Carmelite Order, the life of a Carmelite is one prolonged preparation for this kind of self-immolation. Their dedication to the following of Christ, in trying "to gain their lives by losing them," teaches them that the higher they rise in the intensity of the love of God and of their neighbor, the more they are readying themselves for the crucial test of martyrdom, thus bearing witness to the truth of St. Paul's oft-quoted saying, "and though I deliver my body to be burned and I have not love, it avails me nothing" (I Cor. 13:3).

In this frame of mind, physical death assumes the signification of a deliverance, of the liberation of the spirit of love. In the words of St. Teresa, "The mere thought of such deliverance causes me such pain that I die because I cannot die." And in another passage, addressing the nuns of her convent, she says: "When a person begins to serve God in real earnestness, the least he can offer Him is his life." These words were echoed by St. John of the Cross when he said that if the Lord would not grant him to become a martyr by shedding his blood, he would strive to become a martyr by means of his works of love. And Thérèse of Lisieux, the "saint of the small way," wrote: "Martyrdom, that was the dream of my youth, and this dream has come to fruition in the cloisters of Carmel."

The main theme or leitmotif of Gertrud von Le Fort's novel, on the other hand, is the anguish of the totally exposed and defenseless human existence. This anguish is here supernaturalized and eventually assuaged by the blood of the martyrs. However, beyond the pressing immediacy of this theme, the phenomenon of *Angst* is here explored as a basic theological problem. It is shown that though man's entire being may be immersed in extreme *Todesangst* (agonized fear of death), divine grace can nonetheless make its call heard and can find its way into the mind and heart of the frail and anguished creature. In her very weakness Blanche de la Force will then witness to the power of grace (as was the case also with the unheroic "heroes" and "heroines" of Graham Greene's novels, such as the whiskey priest, Scobie, and Sarah Miles) because this anguish fuses with the anguish, the abandonment and the agony of Christ.

Blanche de la Force is the very opposite of what her surname implies: she is "a poor, frightened child." But as Kierkegaard had affirmed many times, human weakness which stands on God's side is stronger than any power that can come to the aid of the purely natural man. Blanche was, as it were, predestined for *Angst:* prematurely born, owing to a traumatic experience of her mother during the last stages of her pregnancy, Blanche had so to speak a hereditary disposition for *Angst.*

It is Blanche's great antagonist, Marie de l'Incarnation, for whom —prior to the cruel experiences of the trial, condemnation and execution of her Carmelite sisters—any kind of anxiety appeared as lamentable weakness and cowardice, who eloquently defends those who are afflicted with "fear and trembling." She asks:

Is there not a possibility that fear and horror may be something much more profound than courage, something which corresponds much more to the reality of things, that is, to the reality of the terrors of this world and the reality of our own weakness. . . . Fear is an important chapter [in human life]: we all have not nearly feared enough. A society, a state should know fear, every government should fear and tremble. For . . . the things we have witnessed have not only happened once: they will happen again and again.

The fictitious narrator of the story is a Monsieur de Villeroi. He addresses his report, dated 1794, on the revolutionary turmoil in Paris to a woman who is a French emigrant and a devotee of Rousseau. He says in his letter to her that he is full of admiration for the serenity of her mind which permits her to retain her faith in the indestructible nobility of human nature, even in the midst of the disastrous ruptures in the thin veneer of an "enlightened" humanity. "However, my friend, remember that chaos too is part of nature, and so are the executioners of the heroines of whom you speak in your letter. The beast in man also is part of nature, and so are fear and dreadful horror." Monsieur de Villeroi, who himself has been a witness to the execution of the Carmelite nuns, confesses in his letter that he, the free-thinking agnostic, joined in their prayers: "Yes, dear friend, in that hour I dropped once again, as I did in my childhood, through all the layers of being, to the ultimate ground of things, an eternal ground because it is a divine ground. They expected the victory of a heroine, and what they saw was the miracle enshrined in human weakness. But is not this precisely a reason for infinite hope? For the merely human is not enough."

There is symbolic significance in the fact that Blanche, upon entering the novitiate, receives the name Sister Marie de Jésus au Jardin de l'Agonie. This occurs in the year 1789. The National Assembly at Versailles is about to take action to bring about the secularization of church property, to relieve the financial depression in France. All religious orders are threatened with eventual suppression, and the law that will prohibit the admission of new members of religious communities is pending. The Superior of the Carmelite Order, hoping that those who are already members may be allowed to stay until their natural death, advises the immediate investiture of postulants. The Superior's letter concludes with these words: "Christ may be said to be in the Garden of Gethsemani. I therefore recommend the name of Jésus au Jardin de l'Agonie for the postulants since under the conditions prevailing today no more suitable name could be found." To this the narrator adds: "You know, my friend, that in Carmelite convents they believe that the religious name which the individual Sister receives at her investiture gives her special access to the mystery expressed by that name."

Of Blanche it is said that "it seemed as if this pitiable small life was in a state of constant anticipation of some dreadful event . . . as if the frightened look of her childlike face were penetrating the firm structure of a sheltered existence, down to the depths of a terrible fragility." Unlike Blanche, Sister Marie de l'Incarnation, the Mistress of Novices, is capable of mastering all her fear of the coming catastrophes. It is this heroic nun who inspires the members of her convent to vow the sacrificial offering of their lives. She desires martyrdom because she sees in it the only means that can save the soul of France. Fearlessly she meets the Commissar of the revolutionary tribunal: "Imagine this tall distinguished woman of noble birth face to face with those proletarians! Picture to yourself this nun, filled with her mystic mission of atonement, confronting those dry officials: a clash was unavoidable." Instead of intimidating her with their demand to leave "this [monastic] hotbed of superstition," they kindle the fervor of Marie de l'Incarnation and the other nuns. "For, my friend, Christianity thrives on persecution, and this is why all brutality, crude or subtle, directed against it, is merely stupid."

It is totally different with Blanche. Her entire life is, as it were, a perpetual flight; at first a flight into the shelter and security of the convent, into the protecting omnipotence of God. When the news of the incipient revolution reaches her behind the convent walls, she exclaims gratefully and almost joyfully, "Here we are safe from all this." Thus religion and the convent represent for Blanche a world from which the "real world" is excluded and where she is surrounded by the "friendly phantom of heaven." Marie de l'Incarnation is quite correct when she remarks that "this poor child . . . is hiding behind the walls of Carmel as a feeble young bird is hiding in its nest."

However, the time had come when all "earthly guarantees" failed and when not even the flight into the shelter of religious life could save from the Cross. On the contrary, in this time of the ulti-mate test this kind of flight was bound to lead straight into the ordeal of the Cross. Religion was no longer offering any kind of "insurance," any kind of protection from suffering and death. And so Blanche is rudely aroused from her artificial and somewhat unreal security. This happens when Madame Croissy, her first Prioress, dies: "This was a very difficult and agonized death. One could hear the moaning of the dying woman for many hours. . . . . Blanche remarked with some consternation how it was possible that God allowed such a saintly woman to suffer so grievously." She suddenly begins to realize that God does not "spare" those whom He loves, and this realization causes a renewed and aggra-vated seizure with *Angst*.

As happened before her birth, there is again a deeply shocking traumatic experience that triggers the acute outbreak of anxiety. A commission appointed by the revolutionaries visits the convent, and its members arrogantly and irreverently examine the cells of the nuns. One of the intruders goes from door to door to lead the way: "At the moment when this short and rather absurd looking fellow opened the door of Blanche's cell and peeked through the opening with a grin, she uttered a heart-piercing scream. . . . At the same time she retreated toward the rear wall of her cell with outstretched hands and then remained motionless as if she were awaiting death."

Yet it is precisely at this point that Blanche enters into a new phase of her religious life. She shows an increasing willingness to embrace the "folly of the Cross" which in her case has assumed the form of anguish and, by accepting this self-annihilation, she achieves in the end total victory over her anxiety and over *Angst* in general. While in the severe trials that follow, and especially after her flight from the convent, she appears to her fellow Carmelites as a coward, only Madame Lidoine, the new Prioress, seems to understand what is going on in Blanche's soul: "I have told the poor child," she says, "that she should seek refuge and tranquility in her anguish since God evidently for the time being does not intend to take it from her. . . . There suddenly emerged before her mind's eye a series of disconnected images: little dying birds—wounded warriors on a field of battle—criminals at the foot of the gallows. She believed to behold not only Blanche's anguish but every kind of anguish."

To the bitter end Blanche remains loyal to her newly found vocation, a vocation which she herself now links with the "mystery" of her name—Sister Marie de Jésus au Jardin de l'Agonie. She thus attains to the peak of that perfection which is demanded by the spirit of Carmel, a state of mind and soul in which neither joy nor suffering, neither honor no dishonor, neither riches nor poverty, neither health nor sickness can separate the individual from God.

When, upon the urgent request of Sister Marie de l'Incarnation, the nuns take a solemn vow to offer their lives in expiation for the crimes committed by the revolutionaries, Blanche in her agonized anguish flees from the chapel during the ceremony. No one but Madame Lidoine can understand what was going on in her soul.

"Poor child," she comments later, "she alone wanted to stay with our Saviour in His agony, and when her strength failed her she ran, as it were, straight into this agony." And she alone empties the chalice to its bitter dregs: in the prison yard she stands near the body of her slain father, and a nasty little fellow with a red cap, holding a cup in his hand, commands her to drink of her father's blood: "Take communion, Citizenness," he screams and forces the cup to her lips while the mob crazily shrieks, "*Vive la nation!*" "Here was nothing but meaningless naked brutality. Or was there some meaning in this scene after all? Was this girl at this moment the tortured French nation itself, a nation that was being forced to drink the blood of its own children?"

It is this grotesque and blasphemous "communion" which gives Blanche the strength to remain loyal to her Carmelite vocation at the decisive moment when such loyalty really counts. After her flight from the convent Blanche is caught in the revolutionary masses and is being dragged along on the way to the Place de la Révolution to witness the execution of her Carmelite sisters. And then the miraculous happens: while Sister Marie de l'Incarnation escapes the guillotine and the wished-for martyrdom, owing to the intervention of the Public Defender of the nuns, Blanche is found worthy of the supreme sacrifice. As the nuns approach singing the *Salve Regina* and the *Veni Creator Spiritus,* and as their voices are silenced one by one by the guillotine, the thin voice of Blanche responds, finishing the interrupted hymn. "At that moment," writes the narrator, "the crowded lines were swayed by a violent upheaval. . . . I saw Blanche de la Force in the seething mass of those dreadful women: her small, pale, pinched face stood out from its surroundings. . . . I recognized this face in every feature and yet I did not recognize it. It was completely without fear! She was singing . . . without any tremor, yes, joyously as a bird. She was singing all alone across the huge, bloody, terrible Place de la Révolution, singing the *Veni Creator* of her Sisters to the very end." The singer is immediately seized and killed by the bestialized women, but with the martyrdom of the young Marquise de la Force the Revolution has run its course. Actually, the régime of terror collapsed ten days later.

In Gertrude von Le Fort's novel the history of the French Revolution is seen theologically and eschatologically *sub specie aeternitatis:* the threatening "chaos of liberty" (that is, the chaos of license) is thus converted into its very opposite, the "freedom of the children of God," a conversion which at any historical juncture and in every concrete existential situation can and should be realized and repeated by every Christian.

Conclusion

THE PRECEDING bird's-eye view of theological novels of modern Europe presents of necessity a foreshortened picture. Since the material discussed in the eight chapters of this book is in the main based on a lecture course offered at Stanford University, neither all the authors whose works fall into the same category nor all the theological novels of the strictly limited number of authors could be included. The intent was to offer a cross section which would be truly representative of the major problems with which the modern theological novel from Dostoevsky to Gertrud von Le Fort has concerned itself. To make the presentation more complete, the names of Leo Tolstoy, Selma Lagerloef, Sigrid Undset, J. Anker Larsen, Francis Jammes, Julien Green, G. K. Chesterton, Ina Seidel, Franz Werfel, Elisabeth Langgässer, Stefan Andres, Edzard Schaper, and several others would have to be included. This, however, would have far exceeded the intended scope of this book.

It might seem at first glance that a major gap separates the Slavophile Dostoevsky from the French, British and German authors whose works are inconceivable without the background of their Western European Judaeo-Christian heritage. In a sense this is true, especially if we consider what for Dostoevsky was represented by that "ideal society" of which he speaks in his *Notebooks*, in *The Diary of a Writer* and also in his novels. This ideal society has no room for the individual human being as seen through Western eyes.

The basis of Dostoevsky's Slavophilism is the society projected by the Russian Orthodox Church as human brotherhood in the free love of God. It was his firm conviction that to Russia Providence had assigned the mission of bringing about the "genuine unification of mankind as a whole in a new, brotherly, universal union whose inception is derived from the Slavic genius, pre-eminently from the spirit of the great Russian people who have suffered so long. . ." (*The Diary of a Writer*, trans. by Boris Brasol. New York: 1954, p. 780).

What then was the function of the individual in this kind of society? Dostoevsky answers that the individual is the carrier of universal human brotherhood (*sobornost*). He says:

The highest use a man can make of his individuality, of the completed development of his *I*, would be to destroy this *I*, to return it entirely to all. . . . And this is the greatest happiness. In this way the law of *I* merges with the law of humanity and both are one, and *I* and all (which appear to be two opposed extremes) are both mutually destroyed, while at the same time they attain the higher goal of their own individual development. . . . This is the paradise of Christ. All history . . . is only the growth, the struggle, the yearning for, and the attainment of this goal (*Notebooks*, April 16, 1864, trans. by Jesse Zeldin).

On the other hand, however, the novel *The Possessed* shows clearly that there is much that ties Dostoevsky to the West. The alternative, pregnant with the most far-reaching consequences, of either "God-Man" or "man-god," as it was strikingly exemplified in the raving madness of Kirillov, was first posed by Dostoevsky before it began to haunt and intoxicate the Western mind in the philosophies and "negative" theologies of Nietzsche and Sartre and the "death of God" theologians.

The common theme and common bond of Eastern and Western theological thinking as mirrored in theological novels is the conviction that man owes all he knows of transcendent reality to a self-revelation of this highest supraphysical and supranatural reality: God goes out, as it were, to find man or, as it has been expressed in theological language, man would never have found God if God had not first found man. Man thus knows by a direct call or address *that* God is and *what* the created contingent world and what his own contingent self are. In other words, God's being present in the world and to the world makes it possible for human beings to live in the light of revealed truth. The entire Judaeo-Christian tradition affirms that each individual human being stands in a direct and primary relationship to God: not coordinated to the horizontal dimension of the zeitgeist but drawn vertically into the dimension of grace. History remains for Western man unfulfilled as long as man remains unrelated to a trans-historical realm of being.

Since the beginning of the nineteenth century and the European romantic movements in literature, painting and culture, it is the converts to Roman Catholicism who are most articulate in proclaiming the meaninglessness of a world without God and the experience of personal forlornness in such a world. They assert again and again that what has drawn them to the Church is "the principle of incarnation" (Friedrich von Hügel), that is, the penetration of the worldly with the sacred, the consecration of the entire creation by the Incarnation or "God-Manhood" (Vladimir Solovyov) of Christ.

Do these considerations apply to the theological novels of modern Europe? Do they cast additional light on the motivations and intentions of their authors? The answer to both questions must be affirmative. All the authors discussed and all the works analyzed testify to the true vocation of the poet and the writer—to portray reality in toto, that is, to portray life with that integral natural-supranatural realism which François Mauriac had demanded. This vocation might—in an age of faith—have coincided with the spirit of the age. In an age of skepticism, nonbelief, cynicism and despair it is all the more incumbent upon the writer to remain loyal to his vocation, taking, if necessary, his stand resolutely against the spirit of the age, without flinching and without compromise.

Bibliography

INTRODUCTION

ARANGUREN, JOSÉ LUIS L. *Catolicismo y Protestantismo como formas de existencia*. Madrid: Revista de Occidente, 1952.

BARRETT, WILLIAM. *Irrational Man*. New York: Doubleday, 1958.

BARTH, KARL. *Epistle to the Romans*. Translated by Edwyn C. Hockins. New York: Oxford University Press, 1933.

———. *Kirchliche Dogmatik*, Vol. IV. Munich: Christian Kaiser, 1957.

———. *Church Dogmatics*, Vol. IV (*The Doctrine of Reconciliation*), Part I. Edinburgh: T. & T. Clark, 1956.

BOEKRAAD, A. J. *The Personal Conquest of Truth According to J. H. Newman*. Louvain: Nauwelaerts, 1955.

BONHOEFFER, DIETRICH. *Ethics*, ed. Eberhard Bethge. New York: Macmillan, 1955.

———. *The Cost of Discipleship*. Translated by R. H. Fuller. London: SCM Press, 1959.

———. *Christ the Center*. Translated by John Bowden. New York: Harper and Row, 1966.

———. *Letters and Papers from Prison*, ed. Eberhard Bethge. New York: Macmillan, 1967.

BOSSUET, JACQUES BÉNIGNE. *Histoire des variations des églises protestantes*. 2 vols., 1688.

———. *Oeuvres*. Textes établis et annotés par l'Abbé Velat et Yvonne Champailler. Paris: Gallimard, 1961.

BOUYER, LOUIS. *Newman: His Life and Spirituality*. Translated by J. L. May. New York: Kenedy, 1958.

BREMOND, HENRI. *Histoire du sentiment religieux en France*. 11 vols. Paris: Bloud et Gay, 1916–1933.

BUBER, MARTIN. *Eclipse of God*. London: Gollancz, 1953.

BULTMANN, RUDOLF. *History and Eschatology*. Edinburgh: University Press, 1957.

———. *Existence and Faith*. Translated by Schubert M. Ogden. New York: Meridian Books, 1960.

———. *The History of the Synoptic Tradition*. Translated by John Marsh. Oxford: Blackwell, 1963.

CALVIN, JOHN. *Institutes of the Christian Religion*, ed. John T. McNeill. Translated by Ford Lewis Battles. London: S.C.M. Press, 1960.

CUSANUS, NICHOLAS. *Of Learned Ignorance*. Translated by G. Heron, O.F.M. New Haven: Yale University Press, 1949.

DANIÉLOU, JEAN. *Dieu et nous*. Paris: Bernard Grasset, 1956.

DEWART, LESLIE. *The Future of Belief*. Theism in a World Come of Age. New York: Herder and Herder, 1966.

ESCLASANS, AGUSTÍN. *Miguel de Unamuno*. Buenos Aires: Editorial Juventud, 1947.

FEUERBACH, LUDWIG. *The Essence of Christianity*. Translated by George Eliot. New York: Harper Torch Books, 1957.

GARCIA, JOSÉ PERDOMO. *La Teoría del Conocimiento en Pascal. Filosofía crítica Pascaliana*. Madrid: Instituto Luis Vives de Filosofía, 1956.

GUARDINI, ROMANO. *Religiöse Gestalten in Dostojevskijs Werk*. Munich: Kösel Verlag, 1951.

HEER, FRIEDRICH. *Die dritte Kraft*. Frankfurt a.M.: S. Fischer, 1959.

HELLERSBERG-WENDRINER, ANNA. *Mystik der Gottesferne. Eine Interpretation Thomas Manns*. Bern and Munich: Francke, 1960.

JAEGER, WERNER. *The Theology of the Early Greek Philosophers*. Oxford: Clarendon Press, 1948.

JOHN OF THE CROSS, SAINT. *The Dark Night of the Soul*. Translated, and edited with an Introduction by Kurt F. Reinhardt. New York: Frederick Ungar, 1957.

KIERKEGAARD, SÖREN. *Two Minor Ethico-Religious Treatises*, in *The Present Age*. Translated by Alexander Dru and Walter Lowrie. London and New York: Oxford University Press, 1940.

―――. *Stages on Life's Way*. Translated by Walter Lowrie. Princeton: Princeton University Press, 1945.

―――. *Philosophical Fragments*. Translated by D. F. Swenson. Princeton: Princeton University Press, 1936.

―――. *Concluding Unscientific Postscript*. Translated by D. F. Swenson and Walter Lowrie. Princeton: Princeton University Press, 1941.

―――. *The Concept of Dread*. Translated and with an Introduction by Walter Lowrie. Princeton: Princeton University Press, 1957.

KÜNG, HANS. *The Council, Reform and Reunion*. Translated by Cecily Hastings. New York: Sheed & Ward, 1961.

―――. *Justification. The Doctrine of Karl Barth and a Catholic Reflection*. With a letter by Karl Barth. Translated by Thomas Collins, Edmund E. Tolk and David Grauskou. London and New York: Thomas Nelson & Sons, 1964.

LEFEVRE, PERRY D. *The Prayers of Kierkegaard*. With a New Interpretation of his Life and Thought. Chicago: University of Chicago Press, 1956.

LEPP, IGNACE. *Atheism in Our Time*. Translated by Bernard Murchland, C.S.C. New York: Macmillan, 1963.

LUBAC, HENRI DE, S. J. *The Drama of Atheist Humanism*. Translated by E. M. Riley. New York: Sheed & Ward, 1950.

LUTHER, MARTIN. *Works*, ed. Eyster Jacobs. 6 vols. Philadelphia: United Lutheran Publishers, 1915–1932.

MACQUARRIE, JOHN. *An Existentialist Theology*. With a Foreword by Rudolf Bultmann. New York and Evanston: Harper Torchbooks, 1965.

MARCEL, GABRIEL. *Etre et Avoir*. Paris: Aubier, 1935.

NEWMAN, JOHN HENRY. *Apologia pro Vita Sua*. New ed. with Introduction by Charles F. Harrold. New York: Longmans, Green, 1947.

———. *An Essay in Aid of a Grammar of Assent*. Introduction by Charles Harrold. New York: Longmans, Green, 1947.

———. *An Essay in the Development of Christian Doctrine*. New ed. by Charles F. Harrold. New York: Longmans, Green, 1949.

NOGAR, RAYMOND J., O.P. *The Lord of the Absurd*. New York: Herder and Herder, 1966.

PASCAL, BLAISE. *Pensées*. Bilingual ed., with English translation by H. F. Stewart. London: Routledge and Kegan Paul, 1950.

PATRICK, D. *Pascal and Kierkegaard*. 2 vols. London and Redhill: Lutterworth Press, 1947.

TEILHARD DE CHARDIN, PIERRE, S.J. *The Phenomenon of Man*. Introduction by Sir Julian Huxley. Translated by Bernard Wall. New York: Harper, 1959.

———. *The Divine Milieu. An Essay on the Interior Life*. New York: Harper Torch Books, 1960.

TERESA DE JESÚS, SANTA. *Obras*. Edición y notas del P. Silverio de Santa Teresa. Burgos, Spain: El Monte Carmelo, 1929.

THOMAS AQUINAS. *Basic Writings of St. Thomas Aquinas*, ed. Anton C. Pegis. 2 vols. New York: Random House, 1945.

TILLICH, PAUL. *Systematic Theology*. 2 vols. Chicago: University of Chicago Press, 1951–1957.

———. *The Courage to Be*. New Haven: Yale University Press, 1952.

———. *A Handbook of Christian Theology*. New York: Meridian Books, 1958.

TROELTSCH, ERNST. *Christian Thought, Its History and Application*, ed. Baron Friedrich von Hügel. New York: Doran, 1923.

———. *Protestantism and Progress*. Translated by W. Montgomery. New York: Putnam, 1912.

———. *Social Teaching of the Christian Churches*. Translated by Olive Wyon. 2 vols. London and New York: Macmillan, 1931.

UNAMUNO Y JUGO, MIGUEL DE. *Del sentimiento trágico de la Vida en los Hombres y en los Pueblos*. Buenos Aires and Mexico: Collección Austral, Espasa-Calpe, 1943.

———. *The Agony of Christianity*. Translated and with an Introduction by Kurt F. Reinhardt. New York: Frederick Ungar, 1960.

———. *Obras completas*. Prólogo, edición y notas de Manuel García Blanco. Madrid: A. Aguado, 1958.

———. *The Tragic Sense of Life in Men and in Peoples*. Translated by J. E. Crawford Flitch. With an introductory Essay by Salvador Madariaga. London: Macmillan, 1921.

WEBER, MAX. *The Protestant Ethic and the Spirit of Capitalism*. Translated by Talcott Parsons. New York: Charles Scribner's Sons, 1930.
WEIL, SIMONE. *Gravity and Grace*. Introduction by Gustave Thibon. Translated by Arthur Wills. New York: Putnam, 1952.
————. *The Need for Roots*. Translated by Arthur Wills. New York: Putnam, 1952.
————. *Waiting for God*. Introduction by Leslie Fiedler. Translated by Emma Craufurd. New York: Putnam, 1951.
————. *Cahiers*. 3 vols. Paris: Plon, 1951–1956.

CHAPTER ONE: DOSTOEVSKY

DOSTOEVSKY, FYODOR. *The Possessed*. Translated by Constance Garnett. New York: The Modern Library, 1936. (This edition contains the important and long-suppressed chapter "At Tihon's.") *Note:* Almost all of Dostoevsky's works are available in English, many in both paperback and hard-cover editions.

BERDYAEV, NICHOLAS. *Dostoevsky*. Translated by Donald Attwater. New York: Living Age. Meridian Books, 1957.
FÜLÖP-MILLER, RENÉ. *Fyodor Dostoevsky. Insight, Faith, and Prophecy*. Translated by Richard and Clara Winston. New York: Scribner's, 1950.
MOCHULSKY, KONSTANTIN. *Dostoevsky. His Life and Work*. Translated by Michael A. Minihan. Princeton: Princeton University Press, 1967.
STEINBERG, A. *Dostoevsky*. New York: Hillary House Publishers, 1966.
YARMOLINKSY, A. *Dostoevsky. His Life and Art*. New Jersey: S. G. Phillips, 1965.
ZANDER, LEON A. *Dostoevsky*. Translated from the Russian by Natalie Duddington. London: S.C.M. Press, 1948.

CHAPTER TWO: LÉON BLOY

BLOY, LÉON. *The Woman Who Was Poor*. Translated by I. J. Collins. London and New York: Sheed & Ward, 1947.

BLOY, LÉON. *Oeuvres*, ed. Joseph Bollery and Jacques Petit. Paris: Mercure de France, 1964–1966.
————. *Journal*. Présentation et notes de Joseph Bollery. Paris: Mercure de France, 1956.
————. *Pilgrim of the Absolute*. Selection by Raïssa Maritain. Introduction by Jacques Maritain. Translated by John Coleman and Harry Lorin Binsse. New York: Pantheon Books, 1947.
BÉGUIN, ALBERT. *Léon Bloy. A Study in Impatience*. Translated by Edith M. Riley. London: Sheed & Ward, 1947.
HEPPENSTALL, RAYNER. *Léon Bloy* (Studies in Modern European Literature and Thought). Cambridge: Bowes & Bowes, 1953.

CHAPTER THREE: GEORGES BERNANOS

BERNANOS, GEORGES. *The Diary of a Country Priest*. Translated by Pamela Morris. New York: Macmillan, 1948; and Imago Books, 1962 (paperback).

BERNANOS, GEORGES. *Oeuvres*. 6 vols. Paris: Plon, 1947.
————. *Bernanos par lui-même*. Images et textes inédits présentés par Albert Béguin. Paris: Editions du Seuil, 1954.
————. *The Carmelites*. Translated by Gerard Hopkins. Introduction by Robert Speaight. London: Collins, 1961.
————. *A Diary of My Times*. Translated by Pamela Morris. New York: Macmillan, 1938. (This is a translation of *Les Grands cimetières sous la lune*.)
————. *Last Essays*. Translated by Joan and Barry Ulanov. Chicago: Regnery, 1955.
————. *Mouchette*. Translated by J. C. Whitehouse. New York: Rinehart & Winston, 1966.
————. *Plea for Liberty. Letters to the English, the Americans, the Europeans*. New York: Pantheon Books, 1944.
————. *Under the Sun of Satan*. Translated by Harry Lorin Binsse. New York: Pantheon, 1949.
BALTHASAR, HANS URS VON. *Bernanos*. Cologne and Olten: Jakob Hegner, 1954.
MOLNAR, THOMAS STEVEN. *Bernanos: His Political Thought and Prophecy*. New York: Sheed & Ward, 1960.

CHAPTER FOUR: FRANÇOIS MAURIAC

MAURIAC, FRANÇOIS. *Vipers' Tangle*. Translated by Warren B. Wells. New York: Sheed & Ward, 1953.

MAURIAC, FRANÇOIS. *That Which Was Lost*. Translated by J. H. F. McEwen. *The Dark Angels*. Translated by Gerard Hopkins. London: Eyre & Spottiswoode, 1951.
————. *The Desert of Love*. Translated by Gerard Hopkins. New York: Pellegrini and Cudahy, 1951.
————. *Flesh and Blood*. Translated by Gerard Hopkins. London: Eyre & Spottiswoode, 1954.
————. *God and Mammon*. London: Sheed & Ward, 1946.
————. *The Lamb*. Translated by Gerard Hopkins. New York: Farrar, Straus & Cudahy, 1955.
————. *Letters on Art and Literature*. Translated by Mario A. Pei. New York: Philosophical Library, 1953.
————. *Mauriac par lui-même*. Images et textes présentés par Pierre Henri Simon, avec des annotations de François Mauriac. Paris: Editions du Seuil, 1953.

————. *Mémoires intérieurs*. Translated by Gerard Hopkins. London: Eyre & Spottiswoode, 1960.

————. *What I Believe*. Translated and with an Introduction by Wallace Fowlie. New York: Farrar, Straus & Co., 1963.

————. *Woman of the Pharisees*. Translated by Gerard Hopkins. New York: H. Holt and Co., 1946.

————. *Young Man in Chains*. Translated by Gerard Hopkins. New York: Farrar, Straus and Cudahy, 1965.

JARRETT-KERR, MARTIN. *François Mauriac*. (Studies in Modern European Literature and Thought). New Haven: Yale University Press, 1954.

CHAPTER FIVE: ALBERT CAMUS

CAMUS, ALBERT. *The Plague*. Translated by Stuart Gilbert. New York: Knopf, 1948.

CAMUS, ALBERT. *The Collected Fiction*. Translated by Stuart Gilbert and Justin O'Brien. London: H. Hamilton, 1960.

————. *Oeuvres*. Préface par Jean Frenier. Textes établis et annotés par Roger Quilliot. Paris: Gallimard, 1962.

————. *The Fall*. Translated by Justin O'Brien. New York: Knopf, 1957.

————. *The Myth of Sisyphus*. Translated by Justin O'Brien. London: H. Hamilton, 1955.

————. *Notebooks*. Translated and with a Preface and Notes by Philip Thody. New York: Knopf, 1963.

————. *The Possessed*. Translated by Justin O'Brien. New York: 1960.

————. *The Rebel*. With a Foreword by Sir Herbert Read. Translated by Anthony Bower. New York: Knopf, 1954; and New York: Vintage Books, 1956 (paperback).

————. *Resistance, Rebellion, and Death*. Translated and with an Introduction by Justin O'Brien. New York: Knopf, 1961.

————. *The Stranger*. Translated by Stuart Gilbert. New York: Vintage Books, 1954.

BREE, GERMAINE. *Camus*. New Brunswick, N.J.: Rutgers University Press, 1959.

CRUICKSHANK, JOHN. *Albert Camus and the Literature of Revolt*. London and New York: Oxford University Press, 1959.

DENTON, DAVID E. *The Philosophy of Albert Camus*. Boston: Prime Publishers, 1967.

KING, ADELE. *Camus*. New York: Barnes & Noble, 1965.

ROLO, CHARLES. "Albert Camus: A Good Man," in *The Atlantic* (May, 1958), pp. 27–33. "Camus at Stockholm: The Acceptance of the Nobel Prize" in *The Atlantic* (May 1958), pp. 33–34. Translated by Justin O'Brien.

SCOTT, NATHAN ALEXANDER. *Albert Camus* (Studies in Modern European Literature and Thought). London: Bowes & Bowes, 1962.

THODY, PHILIP. *Albert Camus*. London: H. Hamilton, 1961.

CHAPTER SIX: GRAHAM GREENE

GREENE, GRAHAM. *Brighton Rock*. London: Heinemann, 1938.
————. *The Power and the Glory*. New York: Bantam Books, 1954.
————. *The Heart of the Matter*. New York: Bantam Books, 1956.
————. *The End of the Affair*. New York: Bantam Books, 1955.
————. *A Burnt-Out Case*. New York: The Viking Press, 1961.

ALLOTT, KENNETH and MIRIAM FARRIS. *The Art of Graham Greene*. London: Hamish Hamilton, 1951.
ATKINS, JOHN. *Graham Greene: A Biographical and Literary Study*. London: John Calder, 1957.
MATTHEWS, RONALD. *Mon Ami Graham Greene*. Paris: Brouwer, 1957.

CHAPTER SEVEN: EVELYN WAUGH

WAUGH, EVELYN. *Brideshead Revisited*. Boston: Little, Brown, 1945; and New York: Dell, 1945 (paperback).
————. *Brideshead Revisited*. Revised ed. London: Chapman Hall, 1960.

WAUGH, EVELYN. *Black Mischief*. Boston: Little, Brown, 1946.
————. "Fan-Fare," *Life* (April 8, 1946), pp. 53–60.
————. *A Handful of Dust*. Boston: Little, Brown, 1952.
————. *The Loved One*. London: Chapman Hall, 1948.
————. *The Ordeal of Mr. Pinfold*. London: Chapman Hall, 1957.
————. *Helena*. London: Chapman Hall, 1950; and New York: Image Books, 1957 (paperback).
————. *A Little Learning: The First Volume of an Autobiography*. London: Chapman Hall, 1964.
————. *Waugh in Abyssinia*. London: Longmans, Green & Co., 1936.
————. *Sword of Honor*. A Final Version of the Novels *Men at Arms* (1952), *Officers and Gentlemen* (1955), and *Unconditional Surrender* (1961). London: Chapman Hall, 1965.

BRADBURY, MALCOLM. *Evelyn Waugh*. Edinburgh & London: Oliver & Boyd, 1964.
DEVITIS, A. A. *Roman Holiday: The Catholic Novels of Evelyn Waugh*. New York: Bookman Associates, 1956.
HOLLIS, CHRISTOPHER. *Evelyn Waugh*. London: Longmans, Green & Co., 1954.
STOPP, FREDERICK J. *Evelyn Waugh: Portrait of an Artist*. London: Chapman Hall, 1958.

CHAPTER EIGHT: GERTRUD VON LE FORT

Le Fort, Gertrud von. *The Song at the Scaffold*. Translated by Olga Marx. New York: Sheed & Ward, 1933; and New York: Image Books, 1961.

Le Fort, Gertrud von. *The Veil of Veronica*. Translated by Conrad M. Bonacina. London: Sheed & Ward, 1932.

————. *The Pope from the Ghetto*. Translated by Conrad M. Bonacina. London: Sheed & Ward, 1934.

————. *Hymns to the Church*. Translated by Margaret Chanler. New York: Sheed & Ward, 1953.

————. *Aufzeichnungen und Erinnerungen*. Einsiedeln: Benziger, 1951.

————. *Unser Weg durch die Nacht: Worte an meine Schweizer Freunde*. Munich: Ehrenwirth, 1962.

Focke, Alfred. *Gertrud von Le Fort. Gesamtschau und Grundlagen ihrer Dichtung*. Graz: Styria, 1960.

Heinen, Nicolas. *Gertrud von Le Fort. Eine Einführung in Werk und Persönlichkeit*. Luxemburg: Editions du centre, 1955.

O'Boyle, Ita. *Gertrud von Le Fort*. An Introduction to the Prose Work. New York: Fordham University Press, 1964.

Index

Individualism, 41, 51, 91
Infinity, 22
Innocent II, Pope, 222
Institutes of the Christian Religion, The
    (Calvin), 7
Irrationalism, 207
Italy, 17

J

James, Henry, 172
Jansenism, 112, 131–132, 136, 142–
    143
    Pascal and, 16–22
Jansenius, Cornelius, 16, 143
Jaspers, Karl, 27, 29, 61, 145
Jesuits, 17–18, 93
Jews, 222–224, 227
Joergensen, Johannes, 78, 87
    quoted, 92
John XXIII, Pope, 134, 220
Journey Without Maps (Greene), 174
Joy, 16
Joy (Bernanos), 97, 99
Judaeo-Christian heritage, 235, 237
Judaism, 5
Judgment, 43

K

Kafka, Franz, 1, 33
Kant, 20, 26
Kierkegaard, 3, 6, 9–10, 15–19, 22,
    25–30, 73, 120, 133, 158–159,
    218, 228
    quoted, 34, 90
Knowledge, 3

L

Lacordaire, 145
Lafont, Jeanne, 138
Lamb, The (Mauriac), 146
Lawless Roads, The (Greene), 172
Le Fort, Gertrud von, 102, 217–222,
    225–226, 228, 234
Letter Addressed to the British (Ber-
    nanos), 101
Liberia, 172, 174
Life, 3–4, 35–36, 44, 106, 110, 117,
    221
    Christian, 144–145
    inner, 140
    meaning of, 157–158
Life magazine, 206, 208–209
Lima, Jorge de, 112
Listening, 2
Literature, 36, 112
Little Learning, A (Waugh), 204
Liturgy, 134
Loneliness, 132, 140
Love, 44, 67, 106, 130, 138–139,
    142, 147, 149–153, 162, 168,
    179, 188–189, 191–194, 196–
    202, 221–222
    divine, 6
    God as, 12–14, 22
    of God, 129, 144–145, 169, 189,
        193–194, 236
    of mankind, 128–129, 145
    psychology of, 200
    universal, 47
Love among the Ruins (Waugh), 206
Loved One, The (Waugh), 205–206
Löwith, Karl, 203
Lubac, Henri de, 54, 155
Lucifer, 225